NOTTINGHAMSHIRE

THE KING'S ENGLAND

Edited by Arthur Mee

in 41 Volumes

ENCHANTED LAND (INTRODUCTORY VOLUME)

Bedfordshire and
  Huntingdonshire
Berkshire
Buckinghamshire
Cambridgeshire
Cheshire
Cornwall
Derbyshire
Devon
Dorset
Durham
Essex
Gloucestershire
Hampshire with the Isle of
  Wight
Herefordshire
Hertfordshire
Kent
Lake Counties
Lancashire
Leicestershire and Rutland

Lincolnshire
London
Middlesex
Monmouthshire
Norfolk
Northamptonshire
Northumberland
Nottinghamshire
Oxfordshire
Shropshire
Somerset
Staffordshire
Suffolk
Surrey
Sussex
Warwickshire
Wiltshire
Worcestershire
Yorkshire—East Riding
Yorkshire—North Riding
Yorkshire—West Riding

THE KING'S ENGLAND

NOTTINGHAMSHIRE

By
ARTHUR MEE

fully revised and edited by
GUY DENISON

Illustrated with new photographs by
A. F. KERSTING

HODDER AND STOUGHTON

Printed in Great Britain
for Hodder and Stoughton Limited,
St. Paul's House, Warwick Lane, London, E.C.4,
by Richard Clay (The Chaucer Press), Ltd.,
Bungay, Suffolk

INTRODUCTION TO REVISED EDITION

IN preparing the new edition of THE KING'S ENGLAND care has been taken to bring the books up to date as far as possible within the changes which have taken place since the series was originally planned. In addition the editor has made his revisions both in text and illustrations with a view to keeping the price of the books within reasonable limits, in spite of greatly increased production costs. But throughout the book, it has been the editor's special care to preserve Mr Arthur Mee's original intention of providing something more than just another guide book giving archaelogical, ecclesiastical, and topographical information.

In the case of every town and village mentioned in the King's England Series, it has been the intention not only to indicate its position on the map, but to convey something of its atmosphere. And the biographical selections about people who are ever associated with that part of the country in which they lived, or who are commemorated in the parish church—which was such a popular feature of the former edition—have been retained and in some cases supplemented.

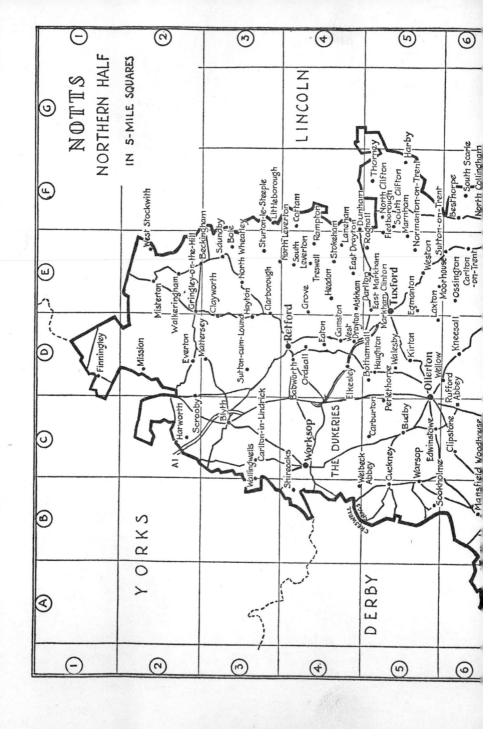

NOTTS

NORTHERN HALF

IN 5-MILE SQUARES

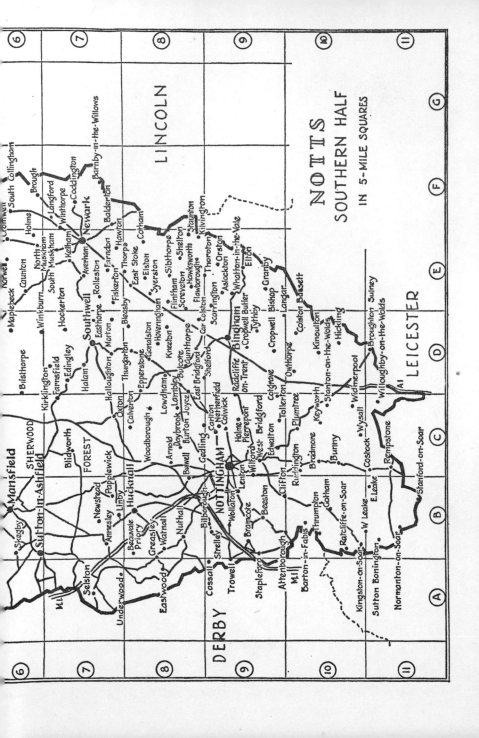

NOTTS
SOUTHERN HALF
IN 5-MILE SQUARES

ILLUSTRATIONS

NOTTINGHAMSHIRE

INTRODUCTION

NOTTINGHAMSHIRE is one of the north midland counties of England, and its shape is in the form of an irregular oval, about 51 miles in length from north to south, and about 27 miles from east to west at its greatest width. It is bounded by Yorkshire, Lincolnshire, Leicestershire, and Derbyshire.

The half-million acres of this midland county, the home of nearly a million people, are mainly divided by the River Trent, running across them from south-west to north-east, and it may be said roughly that the south and east are agricultural and the west industrial. The southern part of Notts continues the Leicestershire Wolds, country well known to the hunting world; on the south-west is the River Soar with its fertile pastures, and on the south-east the Wolds fall away into the fine farming region of the Vale of Belvoir. Even in this hilly part of Notts there is farming as good as can be found in England, and the farm lands continue along the course of the Trent to Newark, which for ages has been a market town. Beyond Newark the land northwards sinks gradually into a dead flat, and the Trent becomes a Lincolnshire river running through the Fen country.

Towards the north of the county the land rises in some places into low ranges of hills, which attain their greatest altitude in the Robin Hood Hills, near Sutton-in-Ashfield, the highest point of which is 650 feet above sea level. Of lesser height are the hills north of Blidworth (500 feet), and Cockpit Hill, near Arnold (508 feet), the Wolds in the extreme south of the county, and the Mapperley Hills in the immediate neighbourhood of Nottingham, which later rise to a height of 470 feet at Dorket Head.

It is the central position of Notts that has made it an average kind of country and given it its striking place in history. In Roman days it was well served by the Fosse Way running from Exeter to Lincoln. When the Vikings came, by way of the Humber, Nottingham could be reached by river, and its commanding site was seized upon as a national stronghold. It was one of the most formidable of the Northmen's citadels, and became the central point of the Danish defence against Saxon invaders from the south. All through our country's history this doorstep of the north has been a busy place; it was the same motive that led the Viking to set up his standard here and Charles I to unfurl his flag here when inviting his Parliament to war.

In the days when man sought security in castles, two of the strongest were built here. There was a castle on the highest point of Nottingham for more than 1000 years, and at Newark the great castle was long regarded as the Key of the North. Even today it is a stirring experience to visit this castle where King John died, and a man shudders as he stands in its dungeon cell. The history of the castle on the rock at Nottingham is one of the most remarkable examples of the way in which the Civil War cut through the life of England like a knife. Here was a peaceful and prosperous countryside, most of it owned by families widely respected. Colonel Hutchinson defended the castle for Parliament, and it happened that his village of Owthorpe was the neighbouring village to Colston Bassett, where the Royalist Sir Francis Golding lived. Six miles away was Shelford manor house, the home of the famous Stanhope family. The Stanhopes fortified their manor house, and, when the war was lost at Naseby, replied to Colonel Hutchinson's offer of peace by threatening to lay Nottingham Castle as flat as a pancake, whereupon the colonel stormed Shelford and burnt it to the ground, and the sender of the boastful message died of wounds. When the Stuarts came back, nine years later, Sir Francis Golding started proceedings against the colonel, who was flung into prison, where he perished from ill treatment. Such things did war with otherwise friendly neighbours. Those were the days of castle strongholds.

The old castle at Nottingham is no more, but nothing can remove the rock on which it stood. The stronghold was centuries older than the Conqueror, whose men rebuilt it so that it stood repeated sieges. It was the scene of the seizure of Mortimer and Queen Isabella, mother of Edward III, and after its long history it passed into the hands of the Duke of Newcastle, who replaced it with a noble house, which was burned down by the mob when the Reform Bill was defeated in 1831. It is now rebuilt, and used by Nottingham as its Art

Gallery and Museum, standing superbly on its wonderful rock. Below the castle on its western side was the ducal deer park, now a residential quarter of the city. Looking across the castle from another height is St Mary's Church, the oldest great structure in Nottingham, and midway between the castle and the church is the fine open space in which the Council House rises, the central building of this central city.

The churches of the county are a wonderful group; we find Roman, Saxon, and Norman work in them. Quite a hundred of them have Saxon or Norman craftsmanship, and about 20 have both. Among those with Saxon masonry are Carlton-in-Lindrick, East Bridgford, Plumtree, and Sutton-on-Trent. Fine fragments of Saxon crosses or carved stones are at Costock, East Bridgford, Kneesall, Rolleston, Shelford, and Shelton. Rampton has a massive pillar and a crude piscina which may be Saxon, and Thoroton has a tiny Saxon window admitting the dawn. Southwell has a Saxon tympanum. A Saxon tomb-cover in Hickling church is one of the finest in the land, and Stapleford has in its churchyard one of the oldest crosses.

The grandest of the many churches we may visit for their Norman work are Blyth, the incomparable Southwell Minster, and Worksop which is a splendid witness to the later Norman days. Littleborough and Sookholme are tiny and modest examples. Halam has what is believed to be a Norman bell. Notable among forty Norman doorways are those at Balderton, Carlton-in-Lindrick, Cuckney, Finningley, Haughton Chapel, Laneham (framing a Norman door), South Leverton, Winkburn, and Woodborough. Fine tympana are at Carlton-in-Lindrick, Everton, Hawksworth, Hoveringham, and Kirklington. South Scarle has one of the best examples of enriched Norman arcading, and Halam and Harworth have fine Norman arches. Annesley, Bole, Markham Clinton, Screveton, and Woodborough have some of the best of about 30 Norman fonts, among which that of Lenton is supreme; it is one of the finest in the country.

Harworth, Hayton, and North Leverton have lovely doorways built when the Norman style was passing. Attenborough, Marnham, Misterton, Rolleston, and South Leverton have some of the beautiful

3

13th century work to be found at its best in Southwell choir and in Thurgarton's western doorway. Half a dozen churches have splendid chancels bearing witness to the 14th century masons whose work is outstanding in Notts, their genius unsurpassed in the chapter house at Southwell. Some of the striking monuments in stone and alabaster for which the county is famed are to be seen at Averham, Clifton, Holme Pierrepont, Hoveringham, Langar, Laxton, Ratcliffe-on-Soar, Sibthorpe, Strelley, Whatton-in-the-Vale, Willoughby-on-the-Wolds, and Wollaton. Wall monuments with the kneeling figures typical of Elizabethan and Stuart days are at Gotham, Laneham, Newark, and Normanton-on-Soar.

The traveller who would run through Notts for historic and picturesque places will have many calls to make. Apart from such famous sights as the Dukeries, with a beauty it would be difficult to surpass, and such prehistoric places as Creswell Crags (which it shares with Derbyshire), or Southwell with its wonderful surprise, there are scores of villages that must be seen by those who know how captivating the county can be.

Worksop, the northern gateway of the Dukeries, has a stately fragment of the early 12th century priory, a charming gatehouse, and a glorious nave. Newark has one of the finest parish churches in the land and the impressive ruin of a castle on the waterside. The two Retfords have fine churches, one with a splendid array of carving outside and in, another noted for its lovely tower and spire. Hawton has in its chancel carving almost without compare in any parish church. Hucknall has the tomb of Lord Byron, Newstead has his home.

Littleborough has Roman tiles in its church walls and the memory of a dramatic peep of a young Roman lady who vanished from sight when her coffin was opened. Clifton is one of our most characteristic English villages, with a dovecot, the maypole on the green, the famous grove the poet Kirke White loved, and a church with a marvellous array of monuments in brass and stone. At Hickling we can open one of the loveliest 14th century doors in England, with its original ironwork. Thrumpton is an oldworld village with a striking War memorial and Radcliffe has a lovely memorial garden high above the River Trent. Attenborough has, near its beautiful church, the home of General Ireton, which Charles I may have passed on his last ride as a free man, and East Bridgford has the home of the Hackers, one of whom led the king to the scaffold. Owthorpe is a modest village with the grave of Colonel Hutchinson. Perlethorpe has a lovely modern church in the loveliest of churchyards, a delightful setting by Thoresby Park. Clipstone has the ruins of King John's palace. Averham has a beautiful church in a delightful setting. Shelford is a typical and pleasant village in the landscape seen from Malkin Hills. Wysall has the oldest wooden pulpit in the county, Laxton the only wooden figure, and Kingston-on-Soar has a pillared canopy with sculptures of 200 babes in tuns. Gedling has a renowned spire and Gotham's spire is unique.

Laxton is famous for a unique survival of the old system of open-field cultivation in strips, quite general in England in mediaeval and Saxon days, but seen nowhere else in these islands. In all our countryside there is no more interesting old custom still prevailing. Wollaton was the home of the Willoughbys for six centuries, and their wonderful house may be seen by all. In Wollaton church is what is thought to be the figure of Hugh Willoughby who was frozen to death in his ship, and at Willoughby-on-the-Wolds is the figure of Richard Willoughby, the judge who was captured by outlaws and held to ransom.

At Widmerpool is some of the most charming scenery out of doors, and indoors a beautiful lady sleeping in white marble, exquisitely carved on a tomb. At Kelham is a new chapel like no other in the county and in it sculpture like no other—a marvellous green bronze Crucifixion scene by Charles Sargeant Jagger, whose masterpiece is at Hyde Park Corner, and whose death robbed English sculpture of one of its most brilliant figures. How few see the mark of his genius in this village: how many pass it in the midst of the busiest throng of traffic in the kingdom! At Shelford lies the Earl of Chesterfield who wrote the famous letters, and Eakring has the grave of one of the most pathetic heroes in the history of our countryside, William Mompesson. Scrooby, with its lovely tower, is the home of William Brewster and the cradle of the Pilgrim Fathers. Harby is the place

where Queen Eleanor died. At Screveton was born Robert Thoroton, the historian of Notts.

Of Southwell, which still has the room from which Charles I set
out to deliver himself up to captivity and death, it is enough to say
that it has perhaps as great a surprise as any village holds for an
English traveller, for here is the least known of our cathedrals, with
a doorway that John Ruskin never forgot and a chapter house with
carving that no one ever forgets.

Sherwood Forest, the most remarkable natural area of the county,
is the most impressive remnant surviving of the vast forests which
once clothed the low-lying parts of England. It is famous over the
world, for it is the home of Robin Hood. It is said that in the old
days it covered nearly a fifth of the county, a tract of dense forest,
heath, and woodland, about 25 miles long and 10 miles broad in
parts, stretching from Nottingham to Worksop. Belonging originally
to the Crown, the right of hunting in it was reserved for the king,
and cruel were the Forest Laws guarding this right. Its great oaks
were felled for the navy in the Commonwealth, and it is believed
that some of the beams in St Paul's are made from them. So it was
for centuries till the great landowners began to enclose their parks.
In 1683 the Earl of Kingston formed Thoresby Park with 2000 acres
of forest land; a little later Clumber took half as much again; and
with the Enclosure Acts of the 18th century came the disappearance
of much more.

The chief remnant of the old Forest is the area known as the
Dukeries, comprising the three great estates of Welbeck, Clumber,
and Thoresby.

Of the old forest there is nothing grander than the two magnificent stretches of Birklands and Bilhagh, side by side; of the later
trees there is nothing finer than the famous Duke's Drive, an avenue
of lime trees with a double row on each side, making a crescent three
miles long on its way through Clumber Park.

Those who would see the forest at its best should do so from
Edwinstowe and Ollerton, on the edge of the Dukeries; they should
leave the roads and seek the paths.

Man or myth, Robin Hood is forever linked with Sherwood

Forest. Such a forest demanded a romantic outlaw chief, and traditions in fable, legend, ballad, and plays furnish ideal heroes in Robin Hood with his Little John, Will Scarlet, Friar Tuck, and the rest of the Merry Men of the Greenwood. We have a Robin Hood literature which makes him a veritable King Arthur of the woodland bandits, who was ever chivalrous to women, who did no wrong to field or fold, who opposed oppression and the terrible Forest Laws, and robbed the unworthy rich to give to the deserving poor.

James Prior Kirk wrote delightfully of the manners and customs of the old forest in his Forest Folk, and Washington Irving as he wandered through the forest lived again in the days of Robin and his merry band, writing of them:

He clothed himself in scarlet then,
His men were all in green;
A finer show in all the world
In no place could be seen.

Good Lord! it was a gallant sight,
To see them in a row;
With every man a good broadsword
And eke a good yew bow.

And whether or not we believe the story of Robin's death at Kirklees, through the treachery of the prioress of the nunnery there, we like to remember his last words to Little John:

Lay me a green sod under my head,
And another at my feet:
And lay my bent bow by my side,
Which was my music sweet;
And make my grave of gravel and green
Which is most right and meet.

Let me have length and breadth enough
With a green sod at my head,
That they may say when I am dead,
Here lies bold Robin Hood.

Historians are not agreed as to the origin of Robin. Some see in him a myth surviving on the shores of memory from the time of our pagan ancestors. Modern research would have it that Robin was some benevolent wood sprite, deriving his name from the hood such little people wore. It is known that his Maid Marian springs from French gallantry, for French literature has a Robin, too. Another authority holds that there have been real Robin Hoods, whose actual achievements give a foundation of reality to many of the stories. That is to say, a Robin Hood has succeeded a Robin Hood, inheriting name and fame, traditions and domain, as oak succeeds oak for a thousand years. Blidworth claims many associations and Edwinstowe his marriage to Maid Marian.

The country abounds with suggestions of Robin Hood, far beyond the confines of Sherwood Forest; but the favourite story brings Robin into prominence in the reign of King Richard the Lion Heart, the period which Scott has turned to such magnificent purpose in Ivanhoe. In Scott, Robin is a figure of dignity as well as of valour and well-doing, but Scott, alas, denies him his Maid Marian, and pays tribute to the Yorkshire ambition to have the hero as a native of Loxley.

Whatever the foundation for the story, Robin stood to England for centuries as the embodiment of the resentment of the poor against the Forest Laws, the breaking of which involved loss of eyes and limbs. In his pillaging Robin is vindicating democratic right against tyrannous Authority. Patriotism, too, this woodland hero typifies, his superb feats of archery reflecting the national pride in the English bowman who has conquered France and is the finest soldier in the world.

Late Plantagenet or early Tudor, he held the imagination of poet, playwright, and broadsheet-writer for century after century. Games and festivals were organised all over the country in his honour, and so prevalent and absorbing were these games that Hugh Latimer raged, in a sermon he preached to Edward VI, over an experience he had had in a village to which he had sent notice overnight that he would preach there in the morning, the occasion being a holiday. The church stood in his way, he said, and he took his horse and went thither, but found the church door locked. At last the key was found, and one of the parish came to him and said, "Sir, this is a busy day with us; we cannot hear you. It is Robin Hood's day. The parish are gone to gather for Robin Hood; I pray you hinder them not."

Robin Hood and his Merry Men have peopled the woods and the pages of our literature for some 700 years, and as long as children love a greenwood tale they will not let him die. He is one with this famous county, woven into the spirit of the greenwood near the very heart of England.

Annesley. There is old and new Annesley, but it is the old that is of historic interest, for here with the ruined church is Annesley Hall, home of Mary Chaworth. It stands in a park with a lake, and has been the home of the Chaworth-Musters family since Byron's first love brought together the two families by her marriage. The Chaworths have lived in Notts since the Conquest, their chief homes being at Wiverton and Annesley.

The beautiful Mary was the last of her house, and the romance of Byron's boyhood love for the "bright morning star of Annesley" must always cling to this place. In the park is Diadem Hill, 578 feet above the sea and seen for miles round. It was here that Byron and Mary often met, and here they parted, after which Annesley lost its enchantment for the poet:

> *Hills of Annesley, bleak and barren,*
> *Where my thoughtless childhood strayed,*
> *How the northern tempests, warring,*
> *Howl above thy tufted shade.*

> *Now no more, the hours beguiling,*
> *Former favourite haunts I see,*
> *Now no more my Mary smiling*
> *Makes ye seem a heaven to me.*

He was genuinely in love with her, but she did not return his love, and before he went to Cambridge she had married John Musters, the sporting squire of Colwick Hall. She died in 1832 as a result of exposure during an attack on the hall by Reform Bill rioters.

Mary was the heiress of William Chaworth who was killed in a duel with his cousin, the 5th Lord Byron, great uncle of the poet. The dual arose from an after-dinner quarrel at an inn in Pall Mall, Chaworth and Byron settling the dispute by fighting in a room lit only by a candle and a dying fire. Lord Byron was tried by the peers and found guilty of manslaughter, but the verdict brought only nominal punishment. Chaworth lies in the ruined old church.

Though the old church is unsafe now even for visiting, there is enough of it left to tell of its beauty. The 14th century tower still has its belfry windows, and the south aisle has a lovely east window and fine sedilia. This aisle was added in the 14th century as a chantry, and was known as Felley Chapel after a small priory founded two miles away in the 12th century.

Two treasures from the old church are in the new one, dedicated to All Saints, which was built in 1874 and stands high on a hilltop, its tower and spire a landmark. One of the old treasures is a splendid Norman font like a tub, carved with lattice pattern and a band of stars. Another is the alabaster figure of a man wearing a round embroidered cap with scalloped edge, a sheet draped over him.

Arnold is an Urban District of 4505 acres whose southern boundary borders Nottingham. It appears in the Domesday Book as Ernehale, but in all probability was pronounced Arnehale. This name is generally accepted as meaning a place frequented by eagles, and an eagle is included in the Council's Coat of Arms, which was granted in 1948. Arnold's civic motto is "Alta Sententia" which translated means "with high purpose".

The parish church of St Mary is situated on Church Lane and dates from the late 12th century. The nave and chancel are of the 14th century, while the pinnacled tower was built in the 15th century. In 1958 the Coal Board carried out mining beneath the church, which was put on a concrete raft to prevent damage by subsidence. A new roof was also constructed and the church was reconsecrated in March 1959.

In a large three-storeyed house in the High Street on October 25, 1802, Richard Parkes Bonington was born. His boyhood was spent in Nottingham at houses in St James's Street, Park Row, and Park Street. At the age of 15 he accompanied his parents to France, and was already showing an aptitude for drawing. He became a pupil of Louis Francia and later went to Paris and attended the school of Baron Gros. In 1822 he exhibited works at the Paris Salon, and in 1826 made a tour of Italy. The same year saw his first exhibition at the Royal Academy, London. For some years Bonington had been in ill-health and returned to London for medical treatment, but to no avail. He died on September 23, 1828, within a month of his 26th birthday. Paintings by this great artist are to be seen in the Castle Museum and Art Gallery in Nottingham, in the Wallace Collection in London, and the Louvre in Paris.

Another great man, this time an engineer, was Thomas Hawksley, who was born in Arnold on July 12, 1807. He became a great civil engineer and carried out about 150 schemes for the supply of water to many cities and towns. He died on September 23, 1893, aged 86.

In the field of sport, the Oscroft family consisting of grandfather, six sons, and two grandsons, were all top in their profession as cricketers. One of the grandsons, William, was the last captain of the all-professional All England XI, and led the batting averages in Australia in 1873 and Canada in 1879.

Today Arnold is changing rapidly, and a large new shopping centre is emerging in the place of old buildings which have now been demolished. Among its other amenities is Arnot Hill Park, which covers some 13 acres, and also a modern indoor swimming bath.

Adjoining Arnold to the south is the residential suburb of Wood-thorpe. The railings of the park that takes its name mark the boundary line between Nottingham and the County. The church of St Mark's was consecrated on June 23, 1962. Its magnificent coffered ceiling is decorated in blue, magnolia brown, and green to give colour to the building and emphasise the contemporary char-acter of the interior. At the east end the free-standing altar is sur-mounted by a cross which hangs in front of a silk dossal, the whole being framed by two Norman style arches at the entrance to the chancel and sanctuary. The side chapel, dedicated to St Mark, is separated from the main part of the church by a glass and wood screen. The tower of the church is a familiar landmark and is topped by a cross which is floodlit at night.

Askham is an attractive little village close to East Retford. The church of St Nicholas has a 15th century tower and 13th century chancel and 14th century east window with some very fine tracery.

There is an old priest's doorway now blocked up, while the spiral altar rails are 17th century. On one side of the churchyard are three small almshouses rebuilt last century from a foundation of 1658 by one of the Elwes family who lived here. A Gervase Elwes, who was one time lieutenant of the Tower of London, was hanged on Tower Hill for his part in the murder of Sir Thomas Overbury.

Aslockton is a quiet village and is perhaps best known for having been the birthplace of Thomas Cranmer. He lived here for 14 years after which he went to Cambridge, where he was a student of Luther. It was Cranmer who suggested that Henry, when deeply engaged with his efforts to divorce Catherine, should ignore Rome and have the legality of his marriage decided by English divines from the Scriptures themselves. Henry was delighted, ordered him to write a book on his idea, appointed him one of his chaplains, and sent him to Rome and Germany to expound it. While in Germany Cranmer married a second time. Returning to England, he was consecrated Archbishop, and a few weeks later declared the king's marriage invalid.

His first great act as Primate was, within a week, to marry publicly Henry to Anne Boleyn, having already been present (it is believed) at their private bigamous marriage four months before. Three years later Cranmer declared this bigamous marriage null and void, and in 1540 he presided over the convocation which annulled Henry's marriage to Anne of Cleves.

The die having been cast, Cranmer strove his utmost for the Reformation; he placed an English Bible within all men's reach: he urged Henry to dissolve the monasteries, with a view to devoting their revenues to religion and learning; and he denounced the distribution of lands and abbeys among Henry's friends.

Thrust against his will into statecraft, Cranmer was at heart a scholar-recluse, and was happiest when engaged in literary pursuits. His melodious English lives in the Prayer Book, of which the Litany, the Articles, and most of the Collects are probably his work.

The conspiracy which induced Edward VI to change the order of the succession once more betrayed Cranmer into weakness, and at the same time doomed him, for at Mary's accession he was arrested, with Latimer and Ridley. Sentence was passed, and there followed the melancholy spectacle of Cranmer's six abject recantations; and then, at the last minute, his declaration that he had abjured only to save his life, and that he died a Protestant.

The old manor house of the Cranmers has disappeared; it was probably in a field where the path called Cranmer's Walk set off to Orston. Near this path, just beyond the modern church, is a moated mound which may be part of an ancient earthwork. It is known as Cranmer's Mound, for it is said that as a boy the archbishop loved to sit here and look round the countryside as he listened to the bells of Whatton church ringing across the River Smite.

The present church, dedicated to St Thomas, was built in 1891 and consecrated on July 21, 1892. It is built in the Early English style, to the design of Sir Arthur Blomfield, of Ancaster stone faced internally with red brick, and consists of nave, south aisle, south porch, and chancel with vestries on the north side and organ chamber on the south. There is a bellcote with single bell at the west end.

Attenborough, five miles south-west of Nottingham, lies between the busy bypass and the river. Although much development has taken place in recent years, the road that leads to river and church retains much of its former charm.

In the shadow of the church tower, its garden adjoining the churchyard, is a farmhouse which has still traces of the old home of the Iretons, and here were born two famous brothers, John who became Lord Mayor of London, and Henry who married Cromwell's daughter Bridget. Henry's baptism in 1611 and John's in 1615 are both in the register.

Henry studied law, and at the outbreak of the Civil War, when he was living here, offered his services to Parliament. He fought at Edgehill and Marston Moor, and was one of Cromwell's right-hand men. He signed the death-warrant of the King, died of plague, and was buried in the Abbey; and at the Restoration was taken from his grave, dragged to Tyburn, and hanged from sunrise to sunset. His

15

brother John was thrown into prison and transported to the Scilly Islands.

The church of St Mary, so well known to those two brothers, in the nave of which Cromwell is said to have stabled his horses, is beautiful without and within; and, though its atmosphere is eloquent with the story of the years, it has been so cared for that it might have been built yesterday. It is a charming blending of stone and woodwork old and new, with lovely mediaeval windows.

The 500-year-old tower has a lofty spire and traceried windows. The rebuilt porch shelters a 14th century doorway and three gravestones carved in the 12th, 13th, and 15th centuries. Its great treasure is the door itself, with three iron hinges of simple scrolls, which may have belonged to the doorway now blocked in the north wall. If so it must be one of the oldest doors in the land, for the doorway comes from the age when the Norman style was passing.

The lofty nave has a 15th century clerestory with a window over the chancel arch, and two 700-year-old arcades which each lost half an arch when the tower was built. The hoods of the pointed arches have bold carving ending in fine corbels of heads and a grotesque. The striking carving of the capitals crowning the round pillars is a feature of the church, those on the south side being a little later and more grotesque than the others. Twelve extraordinary figures on the three south capitals, one at every corner, are all grotesque except for a bishop's mitred head, most of them heads with wings or limbs and no bodies. In company with the bishop is a pig-faced grotesque, a hooded man, and a jester with a wide grin on his contorted face. Others are a pig with cloven feet and a creature with a tiny head, features of a bird, a round body with wings, and huge hands or claws.

The east window, which has at each side an old bracket carved with a winged figure, sheds a golden light with its picture of two angels and the three Marys looking up at Our Lord risen from the tomb. Lovely glass in the north aisle shows Joseph in red and gold with a lantern and staff, and Mary in red and blue with the Holy Child. The peace window has St Nicholas, St George, and an angel with a crown, and three small scenes from the front. There are fragments of old glass.

Beautiful oak lines the chancel walls, adorns the organ, and makes the pulpit lovely with panels of intricate tracery. Four Jacobean panels, set in the splendid modern choir stalls, are carved with a mermaid, a merman with his tail in the mouth of a sea monster, and a dragon which seems to be charmed by a small figure blowing a horn. The old chancel screen has gone, but two splendid 15th century stall-ends over six feet high are by the priest's doorway. The nave and chancel have fine flat roofs, that of the nave keeping some of its old moulded beams. The massive altar-table is Elizabethan, the font is 600 years old, and the rood stairs and doorway are in the south aisle which is strengthened by two flying buttresses inside the church.

In 1954 extensions were carried out. A collar of two vestries and a central entrance was built round the tower, and a bellringers' gallery has been added. At one time there was a minstrels' gallery, the old entrance to which has been re-opened.

In the churchyard there are a number of graves of those who lost their lives in the Chilwell munition factory explosion in the First World War.

Nottinghamshire's first Nature Reserve at Attenborough Gravel Pits was opened on April 30, 1966. It covers about 200 acres, of which 120 acres are open water and there are some 40 small islands.

Averham, pronounced "Airam", has a fine little church standing high on a bank of the Trent with a wealth of trees in the churchyard, and a magnificent cedar in the lovely garden of the rectory lifting its branches above the tower.

Herringbone masonry in the walls of the church takes its story back to early Norman or even Saxon days, and the rest of it is mainly 14th and 15th century. The tower comes from both these times, the 15th century storey crowned with rich battlements and pinnacles and adorned with quaint gargoyles. The nave and the porch, with the initials of its builder (Sir Thomas Sutton), are also 15th century.

The 600-year-old chancel, which has no arch, has a splendid east window, a priest's doorway, some fine old glass pieced together from fragments found at Kelham Hall, and a plain oak screen mostly 500 years old. There is a Jacobean altar table. Fine oak panelling and seating of this century are in memory of Joseph Walker, who was rector here for 51 years, as Richard Sutton had been before him till 1785.

There are many memorials of the Suttons, and the village is proud of its connection with this old family which has now become Manners-Sutton. They lived here and at Kelham, but only a few mounds are left to mark the site of their Averham house, which Cromwell's soldiers destroyed. Robert de Sutton had the estate in the 13th century after the death of his uncle, Henry de Lexington, the last of three famous brothers of Laxton whose name gave the Suttons the title of their peerage in the 17th century. Charles Manners-Sutton followed Richard as rector in 1785, and became Archbishop of Canterbury; his son became Speaker of the House of Commons, and his brother Lord Chancellor of Ireland.

On a great tomb with painted decoration lies Sir William Sutton in armour, a courtier of the time of Elizabeth. He is with his lady, and part of the inscription runs,

> *Thrice nine years lived he with his lady faire,*
> *A lovely, noble, and like vertuous pair.*

On the opposite wall of the chancel is a memorial to their son Robert who was MP for Notts, served Charles I in the garrison at Newark till its surrender, and was created Baron Lexington for his help in raising money. His son Robert, who was born at Averham in 1661 and became 2nd Lord Lexington, was a great diplomatist, and lost his only son at Madrid while he was Ambassador there. The body was sent home in a bale of cloth, and both parents and son sleep at Kelham, in a great tomb.

Among the trees at Averham Rectory is a unique theatre, the product of the Rev Joseph Cyril Walker who was rector of Averham from 1907 until his death in 1942. Before 1913 he had been producing musicals in the village schoolroom, but he had great ambitions, and in 1912 with the help of Mr Robert Lee, the village carpenter, he commenced the building of this theatre. People came to see it from miles around, and the rector would time his productions to take place when there was a full moon to light the villagers' way to the theatre. It was to flourish for nearly 40 years until in 1950 new fire regulations caused it to close. In 1961 the conditions which caused it to close were met, and the restored theatre was opened on July 1, 1961, by Bishop Mark Way.

Babworth is a singularly charming spot, among gently swelling hills and lovely trees, quiet and secluded, though the stir of Retford is only a mile away.

The little church of All Saints is encircled by mighty horse-chestnuts, sycamores, yews, cedars, and beeches in the grounds of Babworth Hall, a Georgian house. It is adorned with battlements and pinnacles, and has a low 15th century tower. The ancient porch has a stone roof with four ribs ending in tiny corbel heads worth finding, among them being a dainty human face and a grotesque animal. Inside the porch is a plaque saying that Elder William Brewster and William Bradford were worshippers here before they sailed in the *Mayflower* to Plymouth, New England. This plaque also records the date of the sailing of the second *Mayflower* in 1955.

The nave and chancel are all in one, and an old arcade divides the nave from a wide aisle, one of its arches resting on a huge grotesque. The font cover is made from the old Devon cider vat which was cut up to make the wooden pins which fastened the timbers of *Mayflower II*. Of the many memorials there are those to the Simpsons who lived at the hall. On a wall beneath a painting of the return of the *Mayflower* is a small glass case in which there is a Breeches Bible.

Balderton is now almost a suburb of Newark. The village was named after or in honour of one of the Saxon deities, the White God, Baldyr or Balder. Lady Godiva of Coventry fame, the wife of Earl Leofric, had a manor here, and Balderton, along with neighbouring Farndon, was given to the Norman Bishop of Lincoln, Remigius. He removed the See from Dorchester to Lincoln and started building the Minster.

19

The church of St Giles celebrated its 800th anniversary with a three-day flower festival in September 1966. Beneath its graceful crocketed spire is a glorious Norman porch. The church boasts, too, some exquisite 14th century woodwork, early 15th century glass and the work of contemporary masons and craftsmen. The altar has been redesigned and a new screen has been added to the west end. Two new bells have also been hung, making eight in all.

It was here at Balderton that Sir Donald Wolfit, the actor manager, was born in 1902. He became a great Shakespearian actor and toured with his own company. In addition he appeared in films and on television. In 1950 he was created a CBE for his services to the English stage. He died in February, 1968.

Barnby-in-the-Willows. A bright little village on the Witham, it is tucked away in a tranquil countryside, with a tower or spire adding to the friendliness of the scene on almost every hand. It has a fine old round dovecot with a red roof, a house with a quaint porch fashioned from a yew tree, a big house in a park a mile away, and a charming mediaeval church to which we come between deep yew hedges. Over the willow-lined stream bounding the church-yard we step into Lincolnshire.

The two-storeyed tower of All Saints is over 500 years old, the 14th century south porch is much restored, and the splendid 15th century north porch has a niche on each side of its wide entrance arch. A lovely 500-year-old door opens to the charming interior, which has many old benches with a few modern ones, looking like a garden of wooden flowers, their traceried ends crowned with poppy-heads. Some of these are carved with faces and figures. One has a smiling face very like Mr Punch, the head of a grinning youth with his tongue out is between the heads of two women, an old man with staring eyes has a grotesque for a companion; one has two dogs and another two girls with curly locks.

The chancel of about 1300 is notable for the singular treatment of its window tracery. A stringcourse round the walls forms a transom across the side windows, and sometimes the tracery is below this as well as above. Between three lancets in the east wall are strange little openings. Both sides of the chancel are alike, and each has an unusual recessed window shaped like a diamond and filled with quatrefoil tracery.

The font and the nave arcades are 14th century, the altar table and the panelling in the sanctuary are 17th, and the parish chest is over 400 years old.

Barton-in-Fabis (or we may call it Barton in the Beans) nestles under hills by lovely Trent meadows, a quiet gathering of old houses, thatched cottages and farms, a fine old church surrounded by limes and chestnuts, and the old rectory close by.

Brent's Hill was the site of extensive British and Roman fortifications. Many coins have been found there, and at Glebe Farm there could be seen until recent years the remains of a tessellated pavement of small coloured cubes which may have been part of a Roman villa.

For 200 years Barton was the home of the great Derbyshire family of Sacheverells. Their manor house is gone, but the wall that surrounded it and the old brick dovecote are still here, and their memorials are in the church. Henry of 1598 and Rafe of 1605 have inscriptions, and the name Sacheverell is on a marble tomb. William Sacheverell of 1616 and his wife lie side by side in alabaster, their hands and feet gone, both in ruffs, and Tabitha in a pretty headdress and a long gown with rucked sleeves.

Most of the church of St George comes from the close of the 14th century, but the clerestory and the fine flat roof of the nave are of the time of Henry VII. The tower has buttresses and a stair turret climbing to the top, and a fine spire with a tier of windows. Two of the bells are 1617, and four ring out in memory of the men who died for peace three centuries later.

Entered by a porch of 1693, the church is full of light, the stone walls attractive with the lines of their irregular coursing. The splendid nave arcade has four lofty bays; the chancel has three sedilia, a piscina niche with tiny recesses, a priest's doorway, and a canopied niche by the east window. The font is as old as the church. There is a Jacobean table, and the Jacobean pulpit has new panels.

C   21

An old door in the nave has still its old bar fastening, and across the lofty narrow chancel arch is the fine old oak screen with gates.

Beauvale Priory, which is now a ruin, stands in the charming seclusion of green fields and woodland between Underwood and Moor Green. It was founded in 1343 by Nicholas de Cantelupe, a great soldier and friend of Edward III, whose castle was at Greasley a mile away.

It was the last priory to be founded in this county, and the first to be touched with the tragedy of the scaffold in Henry VIII's war on the monasteries. For nearly 200 years it was the home of Carthusian monks, who lived in seclusion from the world and gave themselves to hard work and great privation. Life in the Beautiful Vale perhaps consoled them for the austerity of their daily routine, and these great gardeners, whose beds were of straw and their raiment of hair cloth, made this lovely place blossom as the rose.

Tragedy came upon it in 1535, when Prior Robert Laurence and Prior Houghton went with Prior Webster of Axholme to put forward petitions concerning the king's attitude to the monasteries. When questioned by Thomas Cromwell they acknowledged their loyalty to the king but refused to regard him as head of the church, and they were condemned and hanged at Tyburn. From his prison window Sir Thomas More, who was to follow them in a few weeks, saw them led out to execution, and said to his daughter, "Dost thou not see that these blessed fathers be now as cheerfully going to their death as bridegrooms to their marriage?"

Today a farmhouse stands where the priory stood, and among the ruins seen in the outbuildings is part of the prior's house. Part of the remains have been roofed to house the cattle which come and go by the old doorways, and close by are great ivied walls with traces of a fine window.

In the woods behind the priory is a charming spot known as Robin Hood's Well.

Beckingham is big and pleasant with trees, and lies a mile and a half from the Trent and Lincolnshire.

The beautiful old church of All Saints comes chiefly from the three mediaeval centuries, but has a plain tub font taking its story back to Norman days. The lower part of the lofty tower is 600 years old, but its buttresses and the top storey are a century younger. There are windows of both these times, and the clerestory is 15th century. The two fine nave arcades with nail-head on the capitals are 13th and 14th century, and between the chancel and its chapel are two 15th century bays. The chancel, though much rebuilt, keeps three 13th century seats for priests, with richly moulded arches and detached shafts with capitals of natural foliage. The piscina is 700 years old.

A lovely mediaeval relic is part of the oak chancel screen, now across the tower arch and much restored. There is an ancient image bracket in the south aisle, carved with the strange figure of a little man armed with a sword, his crowned head stuck on to his body at a right angle. Four curious gargoyle heads outside the north aisle have staring eyes and bulging cheeks.

On the wall near the tower is a brass plate engraved with a sinking ship and three or four boats taking women and children from the wreck. Lined up on deck are the heroes who wait for death rather than crowd the boats, and others are clinging to the rigging. It is in memory of Marion Parkinson, one of the survivors of the troopship *Birkenhead* which was wrecked off the Cape in 1852; she was the daughter of the drum major. One of about 190 who were saved, she saw 500 soldiers and sailors stand in line to go down with the sinking ship. She lies in the cemetery near the church.

Beeston is about 4 miles south-west of Nottingham, and is perhaps most widely known for its large factories turning out pharmaceutical products. The man behind this great industry was Jesse Boot, who in 1863 at the age of 13 left school to help his mother behind the counter of their herbalist shop in Goose Gate, Nottingham. Looking out from the lovely boulevard between Lenton and Beeston (now known as University Boulevard) is the bronze bust of this great man, and the inscription beneath it reads: "Our great citizen, Jesse Boot, Lord Trent. Before him lies a monument to his industry: behind him an everlasting monument to his benevolence."

His bust is at the entrance gates of Nottingham University which (with the whole of the Highfields estate now turned into playing fields, lovely gardens, boating lake, open air swimming pool and boulevard) he gave to Nottingham, his birthplace. The building, which he provided, is known as Trent Building, and was opened by His Majesty, King George V, on July 10, 1928, in the presence of Sir Jesse.

The parish church of Beeston is that of St John the Baptist, which was restored just over a century ago by Sir Gilbert Scott. This made it new except for a chancel which, though modernised, has its 14th century sedilia and piscina, and an old image niche by the east window. The font bowl is 12th century, a pillar almsbox is 1684, and the altar table in the north aisle is Elizabethan.

Besthorpe is near the Lincolnshire border, and from here can be seen the spire of Carlton-on-Trent's church. It is a delightful spot, for here the little River Fleet, running in an old channel of the Trent, widens out to a great sheet of water like a lake. It was here that the devastating flood of 1875 reached its height.

Bilsthorpe. It lies on the border of Sherwood Forest, and the new Bilsthorpe which has grown up round the colliery has left the old village in its seclusion, with the church set high on a little hill.

There are shapely old yews and two splendid beeches among the fine trees in the churchyard. Part of the old Hall survives in the farmhouse facing the church, and it still has a cupboard in which Charles I is believed to have hid during the Civil War. Traces of the moat which once surrounded the church and the hall can still be seen.

The tower of the tiny church of St Margaret was refashioned in the 17th century. The nave is partly 14th century, and the chancel a little later. The Norman font is set on a low base which may be part of a Saxon cross. Covered with glass on a wall of the tower is a tapering stone, crudely carved with a cross, which may also be Saxon. A floorstone in the nave, with a Calvary of unusual design, is perhaps 600 years old. Three solid oak benches, perhaps older than the Reformation, were used as penance seats. The fine old pulpit has panels of linenfold.

The Saviles, who have held the manor from the 16th century, have a modern chapel with four wooden angels on the ends of its oak roof beams. A fine stone tomb, carved with arcading, has a brass inscription to Henry Savile of Rufford Abbey, who died in 1881.

Bingham is a busy market town east of Nottingham in the Vale of Belvoir.

The church is dedicated to St Mary and All Saints, and has a square, embattled, and highly enriched 13th century tower with a short and handsome spire 120 feet high of a later date. The tower is Early English (1225) built of skerry from St James's Church and originally from the Roman rampart encircling Margidunum, by the first Rector, Robert Bingham. One of the charming things inside the church is the sight of its west lancet, curiously set in a buttress, lighting up a deep splay of wall eight feet thick.

Among the interesting capitals of the 600-year-old arcades is one with curious masks said to represent the Deadly Sins, one having foliage realistically carved as if blown by the wind from the doorway, and another, a fine example of undercutting, showing small animal heads eating the leaves. The sedilia and piscina and many windows are as old as the arcades; the east window is 15th century.

A cross-legged knight of 600 years ago, with praying hands, a shield on his arm and a lion at his feet, may be Richard de Bingham, son of the Nottingham wool merchant Ralph Bugge, who founded the Willoughby family. The fragments of another figure are 15th century. A worn floorstone in the chancel has something left of the engraved portraits of one of Nottinghamshire's most famous warriors and his wife. He was Thomas de Rempstone, who helped to put Henry IV on the throne and was one of the band who set out with Henry from Brittany and landed with him at Ravenspur. The story of this adventure lives in Shakespeare's Richard II, where Sir Thomas's name is altered to John, perhaps for the sake of metre.

For his services Sir Thomas was made Constable of the Tower, Admiral of the Fleet, and Knight of the Garter, and he was brought here for burial after being drowned in the Thames. His son Thomas, who fought with Henry V at Agincourt, was taken prisoner and ransomed for an enormous sum; like his father, he is buried in this church, but his memorial has disappeared.

The Norman font, restored by children in 1922, was dedicated by the Lord Bishop of Derby in 1926, with later panelling and the figure of St Christopher; the Canon Hutt memorial screens and the Elizabeth Wright memorial furnishings, complete and beautify the baptistery. The great oak reredos, carved and gilded, is a study of beautiful craftsmanship and its story symbolises the history and industry of Bingham.

There are beautifully carved oak choir-stalls, and every choirboy on each front row sits under a canopy.

There is a statuette, 18 inches high, of a saintly woman, one Ann Harrison, who was born in 1829 and who attended this church throughout her long life. She used to go about the town with a bag collecting odds and ends, and all the money this devout and gener-ous woman made was put into one of the church collections as soon as it amounted to two half-crowns. She died in 1928, and to honour her memory the church used some of this money to purchase a book of remembrance, in which her photograph is to be seen on the first page.

In the Market Place is the picturesque Butter Cross. It was at Bingham that the author James Prior Kirk spent his last years. He was born in 1851 at a house in Mapperley Road, Nottingham, and married his cousin, Lily Kirk, in 1886. *Forest Folk* is perhaps the best known of his works, but others include *A Walking Gentleman* and *Fortuna Chance*. He moved to Bingham in 1891 and died there after a short illness in 1922.

Bleasby is a small village close to the Trent. It is quiet and charming, with its church, an inn with white walls and red roof, and a hall about 400 years old.

The church of St Mary has in its churchyard a fine old cedar as high as its sturdy embattled tower. The church has lost most of its original work, and has nothing older than the 13th century arcade, with round pillars and capitals. There is an Elizabethan chalice. Bright inside when the sun shines, and filled with mellow light from tinted glass when the day is dull, it has lovely glass in a south window glowing red and blue and purple, with a charming group of the Madonna and Child and a minstrel angel at each side. It is one of the fine windows from the workshops of Christopher Whall whose glass we so often come upon with pleasure in our churches.

The Old House at the south-east end of the village is mainly 16th century, and was carefully restored early in 1967.

Blidworth is in the heart of Sherwood Forest, and has many associations with the outlaw Robin Hood.

The church of St Mary crowns the hilltop. Except for its plain 15th century tower, it is mainly in the classical style of the 18th and 19th centuries, but the lofty south arcade of round arches and pillars is said to have been the work of a pupil of Christopher Wren. The 15th century font has a bowl on which is carved the head of a child, and its modern oak cover was made by the village carpenter.

On the wall above the font hangs what is called the Register of Rockings, a reminder of an old custom revived here in our time after a lapse of a century. Once a year, on the first Sunday in February, the last baby boy to have been baptised is dedicated at the altar and rocked in a cradle in the sanctuary. In olden days the Rocking was observed as a simple miracle play, representing the taking of Jesus to the Temple.

Built up in the churchyard are fragments of the mediaeval church which collapsed two centuries ago, including many old coffin stones, a doorway, a window, and a piscina niche. In the outside wall of the church is a tiny tapering coffin stone, and a 15th century floorstone in the nave has a hammer and a carpenter's square.

The oak panelling in the chancel, with a few richly carved panels, came from Southwell Minster. So, too, did the unusual oak pulpit adorned with 18th century plasterwork showing 31 tiny heads and a panel of the Madonna and Child. One very odd possession the church has, for the spring which carries the pendulum of the clock in the tower is made from a sword carried at Waterloo.

A slate tablet on the wall has a rhyming epitaph telling how Thomas Leake fell in single combat near the end of the 16th century. He was a Ranger of the Forest, and carved in the alabaster frame of his memorial are hunting trophies of horns, knives, long-bows, and cross-bows, and hounds, one hound chasing a deer. The massive stone cross in the churchyard was brought here from the spot in the woods where he fell.

The churchyard has extensive views, and on a clear day can be seen Newark spire, the towers of Lincoln, and the walls of Belvoir Castle. It is said that Robin Hood's Will Scarlet lies here, and that Maid Marian, who lived at Blidworth, was married in this church.

Across the road from the church are the remains of an old windmill, but away from the village the rural scene has been spoilt by mining developments and a large estate.

Blyth. It is old and lovely, one of the most gracious villages in Notts. It has a road where the Danes came over a thousand years ago, a noble church with rare Norman remains, and a school with a doorway over 700 years old.

On the old highway from London to York, it was of great importance in early days, when it had a market and fairs, and was close to one of only five tournament grounds in England licensed by Richard I. Now the wide road through the heart of the village is lined with trim houses, some of them clothed with creeper, some red-walled, others painted white, cream, and gold, and all red-roofed. On the long green island down the middle of the road is an elm plantation and a building with a roof resting on ancient beams, with mullioned windows in stone walls, and a beautiful 700-year-old doorway through which the children of Blyth once went to school. The building is said to have belonged to a Hospital of St John, founded for lepers in the 12th century; a farmhouse stands on the site of the hospital at the southern end of the village, and not far away is a row of six almshouses reminding us of the old charity.

The church of St Mary and St Martin is all that is left of the priory here in 1088 by Roger de Busli, as a cell of the Abbey of St Catherine at Rouen, but the strength and grandeur of what remains is eloquent of its magnificence. At the Reformation all the monastic part of the church was destroyed, as were the domestic buildings on the site where the hall now stands. The preservation of what is left is due to the fact that the nave and aisles served as the parish church, and it is in these that we see what is said to be the oldest example of Norman architecture in England in its style, though perhaps not actually in date. It is thought either that the plans used in the building of the Abbey of Jumièges in Normandy were borrowed for Blyth Priory, or that builders came over here for its construction. The abbey was built about forty years before the priory.

The pure work of very early Norman days, severe but majestic in its simple strength, is seen in the nave (with a splendid 13th century vaulted roof), the two arcades, the clerestory, the triforium on the south side, and the north aisle with its original vaulted roof. When this roof was moved to a lower level, the triforium openings on the north side had to be filled up, and 15th century windows were inserted under the round arches.

The arcades are of five bays with round arches on lofty pillars, and a sixth bay projects into the hall grounds. Among the heads enriching the capitals are two close together, perhaps representing Roger de Busli and his wife Muriel, who may be buried under two recesses in the outside north wall. The south aisle was enlarged to its present size in 1290, whence come its five windows, and seven gargoyles of ugly winged animals and a bird. The fine porch is also of this time.

The beautiful west tower, 100 feet high and a landmark, comes from the close of the 14th century. Eight pinnacles crown its charming parapet of open arcading; it has buttresses of seven stages, a canopied doorway, a west window with a niche on each side and another above it, and a great arch reaching to the nave roof.

The 17th century font has a bowl with cherubs, a base which may be Norman, and a Jacobean cover. The round bowl of a Norman font lies on the floor. The oak pulpit and a table are 17th century, an old almsbox is heavily banded with iron, and two quaint collecting boxes of 1661 are still used. The oak panelling on a wall of the chancel is part of the 17th century box-pews, as are the backs and ends of some benches. On the east wall are faint traces of 15th century paintings of Time, Judgment, and Eternity.

The east end of the south aisle forms the chancel, and has a beautiful 15th century oak screen with tracery and a vaulted loft. Six of the old paintings on the base panels are still clear, showing Stephen with stones, a woman slain with a sword, St Edmund crowned, St Helena, St Barbara with a lamp and a palm leaf, and St Ursula with eleven maidens. With the old work still left in the screen across the nave are eleven paintings of saints.

Lovely modern glass has a share in the glory of Blyth. In the five windows on the south side of the church are about 150 figures in Bible scenes. We see Samuel being taken to Eli, Moses found in the bulrushes, Joseph cast into the well, Abraham with Isaac carrying wood to the altar, the anointing of David, and scenes telling the story of Jesus. The beautiful west window of this aisle frames ten splendid figures.

Three ancient floorstones are carved with crosses. The battered knight wearing armour with a great shield and an unusual square-topped helmet was perhaps a Fitzwilliam of the time of Richard I. On the projecting tomb of a big monument with a long inscription reclines the short, stout, cross-legged figure of Edward Mellish, who died in 1703.

The Angel Inn dates back to 1274, and is one of the oldest in this part of Nottinghamshire. In recent years the custom of hanging the ale-garland has been revived, and takes place each Christmas.

Hodsock Priory (which never was a priory) is situated at the end of a beautiful shaded lane two miles from Blyth. It stands in lovely gardens, on the site of the old home of the Cressys and the Cliftons. The moat is here still, its water crossed by a small stone bridge in front of the lovely Tudor gateway, which has 15th century windows and an embattled turret on each side of the archway.

Bole lies at the end of the road, with the Trent a mile away dividing the county from Lincolnshire.

The church of St Martin with its snow-white walls shelters two treasures worth finding. One is a massive Norman font with double arcading round the eight sides of its bowl; the other is the pulpit, which contains four interesting carved panels of the story of Haman, with ladies and gentlemen in Elizabethan ruffs and tall crowned hats. The panels are Flemish work and were given by the late Sir Charles Anderson, of Lea, a parish on the other side of the Trent. The tower, crowned by eight pinnacles, is 14th and 15th century, and a few old windows remain.

At each side of a brass on a window-sill, with an inscription to John Danby who died in 1400, is a tiny brass engraved with an angel and a bull. On the front of a pew near the pulpit is an old oak panel carved with the letter B and a tun, the rebus of the Bartons, who lived at Holme in the 15th century.

The royal arms are a curious amalgamation of those of Queen Anne and George I, the king's white horse painted over the middle to save expense. The rose and thistle badge of Queen Anne remains, though she was the last sovereign to have a personal badge, and it should have been painted out.

Bothamsall lies north-east from Ollerton and overlooks the valley of the rivers Meden and Maun.

The 19th century church of St Peter and Mary looks at its best outside with battlements and buttresses and a tower. Among the few relics of the old church are two floorstones with crosses in the chancel, a fine 600-year-old font, and an old pewter flagon. In the vestry is the tomb of Henry Walters, who gave the church its silver paten of 1698. A floorstone marks the resting-place of Sir Charles Gregan-Craufurd who died in 1821 after a notable military career, and a brass plate with arms has an inscription to him and his wife.

Just outside the village is a fine green mound by the wayside, known as Castle Hill. A dry moat runs all round it, splendid sycamores, beeches, oaks, and elms grow all over it, and a grand old oak rises from its hollowed crown. The site of an ancient camp or a fortified place, it looks out on a great panorama of fields, patches of woodland, and stretches of forest.

In the vicinity is Bevercotes Colliery, the world's first push-button pit and the most modern. It began production in January, 1967.

Bradmore is a small village six miles south of Nottingham on the road to Loughborough. Its church was destroyed by fire some 200 years ago and only the tower and spire remain. A small mission room built on to it in 1880 is used for services. It has recently acquired a bell which came from Bunny Church of England School, and formerly hung in St Mary's Church, Bunny.

Bramcote lies some four and a half miles south-west of Nottingham.

The tower of the old church is a well-known landmark and stands at the top of Town Street. Popularly known as the sunken church, it dates from the 13th century. The churchyard surrounding it is planted with flowering shrubs, and has been maintained for many years now as a memorial garden.

The present church of St Michael and All Angels is a handsome Victorian building dating from 1861. There are a number of memorial tablets and furnishings that were transferred from the old church. These include the font, the bells that were re-cast in 1862, and the Hanley monument dating from 1650. The church register dates from 1652. There are a number of memorials to local families; four windows on the north side refer to the Pearson family, while in the south aisle there is a window in memory of F. C. Smith, the Nottingham banker formerly of Bramcote Hall. The carved alabaster reredos and panelling in the sanctuary were the gift of the late Lt.-Col. N. G. Pearson.

Among the amenities of this pleasant residential area is the Bramcote Hills Park of 80 acres, to which has recently been added a magnificent indoor swimming pool.

Brough, which is believed to have been the Roman station of Crocolana, is now a hamlet on the Fosse Way, two miles from the Collinghams. Here have been found many Roman coins (called Brough pennies here) and remains of Roman dwellings with stone foundations and timber walls.

The tiny church dedicated to St Stephen dates from 1885. It is neat and trim and surprisingly pleasing, just a chancel and nave divided by an ironwork screen. There are a number of windows dedicated to the saints, among them Catherine with her wheel, Agnes with a lamb and Margaret on a dragon. Very charming is the Christopher Whall glass in two lancets, showing the Madonna and Child in blue and white looking at St Hugh in mitre and rich green robes; a great swan at his side is trying to reach the golden chalice the saint holds. An angel at prayer crowns the cover of the font.

A bronze plaque by Sir George Frampton has figures of Fortitude in armour and Sympathy with a wreath, and an inscription to Thomas Smith Woolley telling us that he served this hamlet for 38 years and built the church and school.

Broughton Sulney, also known as Upper Broughton, is attractively set above the Vale of Belvoir in the very south of Nottinghamshire. It is well-known for its spring waters, which are supposed to cure all ills, and the well here was once known as Would Heal. Standing on a grassy slope in the heart of the village is the pillar of an old cross, which was erected as a thankoffering for deliverance from the Black Death. In front of a house near the cross is a late 18th century lead cistern beautifully carved with the signs of the Zodiac.

The church of St Oswald is of the late 13th century, but with numerous later additions. The porch by which we enter was made new in 1733 and given a classical entrance, but it keeps fragments of the old work, and has in its east wall crudely carved stonework which may have belonged to a tomb of 400 years ago. The low tower with quatrefoil moulding under its battlements is 13th and 14th century, and a mediaeval arcade leads to the north aisle, which, like the chancel, was made new last century. The oldest part of the church (now built into the south wall) is a fragment of an arcade set up when the Norman style was passing; it led to an aisle which was pulled down probably when the porch was made new. The traceried bowl of the font is from the end of the 14th century.

Budby was built as a model village by the first Earl Manvers in 1807. Great stretches of forest and the parklands of ducal homes

surround this beauty spot where the little River Meden runs by
the road under a bank of trees, making a sharp bend at the
old stone bridge under which it flows to Thoresby Park. A few
hundred yards through the park it runs through the arch of another
picturesque bridge to fill a lake a mile long and girt with trees. We
pass a grand old oak on the way to the lake, and catch a glimpse of
Castle William on the hill, a grey house with battlements and
turrets.

Bulcote is a small and picturesque village situated between
Burton Joyce and Lowdham. The church of Holy Trinity stands
high on a wooded slope, overlooking the main road that separates
it from the village. This church was built in 1862 in the Norman
style and replaced an ancient edifice said to date from Saxon times.

Bunny, a village that owes much of its beauty and interest to the
Parkyns, is some six and a half miles south of Nottingham. Sir
Thomas Parkyns, the second baronet of a family honoured by
Charles II for their service in the Civil War, was known as the
wrestling baronet. Born in 1663, and educated at Westminster
School and Trinity College, Cambridge, he was a lover of Latin,
had a knowledge of mechanics, mathematics, and architecture. He
lived at Bunny Hall, a strange mixture of architecture, standing in
a park with a wall three miles long. He also built the village school,
which is to be seen outside the church gates, and bears the date of
1700. He had many eccentricities, among them a fondness for dis-
playing Latin quotations about his estate, while another was his
habit of collecting stone coffins which he gave to anyone who wanted
one. But his fame lay in his love of wrestling. He established an
annual wrestling match in the village for which the prize was a gold
laced hat, and the practice was kept up for nearly 100 years after his
death.

The church is dedicated to St Mary, and is mostly 14th century.
There are many monuments to the Parkyns family, including one
of Dame Ann Parkyns, who was the mother of the wrestling baronet,
and who died in 1725. But the monument that draws all eyes is that
of her son, who stands ready for a wrestling bout, a lifesize figure,

while at the side we see his tiny figure stretched out on the floor, defeated at last by Time. Part of his epitaph runs:

> *That Time at length did throw him it is plain,*
> *Who lived in hope that he should rise again.*

It is said that Sir Thomas had the monument made before his death and set up in the chancel; now it is in the north aisle. He lies in the vault he built, in one of the stone coffins he used to collect.

The north wall of the church and its foundations were thoroughly strengthened, and its buttresses rebuilt in 1965.

Burton Joyce is approached from Nottingham by the busy A612 road. The village itself is reached by a side road which turns off the main road rather abruptly. This has enabled Burton Joyce, despite progress, to retain much of its old world charm.

The main road divides the village from the church, which is surrounded by many beautiful trees and shrubs. The church is dedicated to St Helen—Helena, the mother of the Emperor Constantine —who was once thought to have been British-born. For a time round about the 14th century the church was known as St Michael and All Angels. The low spire, with two tiers of windows, was struck by lightning half a century ago, and eight feet of the top was taken down and built into a pyramid near the porch.

As old as any part of the building is the beautiful east window of the north aisle, coming from the time of Edward I. The bowl of the font and the middle pillar on which it rests are 13th century; so is a floorstone carved with a cross in the north aisle. Leaning against the wall of this aisle is the massive stone altar with two consecration crosses found when the church was restored. Here, too, is a great peephole like a window, and by it an old piscina.

The dim but pleasing little chancel has linenfold panelling on the walls, and surmounting the richly traceried panels of the reredos is a deep border like lace in the delicacy of carving. The east window has a lovely Crucifixion and figures of St Helena and Paulinus, who is said to have baptised his converts in the Trent hereabouts. Beautiful glass shows St Edith of Wilton and St Elizabeth of Hungary, and

35

another window has Mary and Martha of Bethany. The pulpit and lectern were made from beams of the old roof.

On a stone tomb lies Robert de Jortz de Bertune, a 13th century knight of the powerful family who gave the village its name (Bertune Jortz). He wears plate armour, and his belt is of flowers. His head is remarkably small for his body.

The portrait of Sir Brian Stapleton, who died in 1550, is engraved on an alabaster stone, showing him in armour with dogs at his head and feet. His son Brian was one of the husbands of Alis Roos, whose figure has almost vanished from a very worn stone.

Calverton is a village north-east of Nottingham where much modernisation has been carried out in recent years. The colliery on the outskirts was opened in 1952, and this brought an increase in the population. The new shopping centre, which is designed on an open-plan basis with shops separated from traffic, was opened in 1963.

The village is perhaps best remembered for its associations with William Lee, who invented the stocking frame.

Though it is generally accepted that he was born here, some claim Woodborough as his birthplace. There is some uncertainty, too, as to whether it was of Calverton or Woodborough that he became curate after taking his degree as Master of Arts of Cambridge. And whether his invention was cradled in romance or in dire necessity depends on which of two stories we believe to be true—one telling how the constant knitting of a lady indifferent to his wooing drove him to the creation of a machine to take the place of her needles; the other how the poor curate found his inspiration in watching the nimble fingers of his wife whose knitting eked out his scanty income.

After working here with his wooden frame for about two years, using rough tools and wool spun from the backs of local sheep, Lee sought the patronage of Queen Elizabeth, who saw the frame at work but, disappointed that it did not make silk stockings, refused to grant a patent. Then the inventive parson made the frame produce silk stockings as easily as woollen, but the queen, fearing that it would throw the hand-knitters out of work, again refused a patent.

Blyth

The old school building
at Bunny

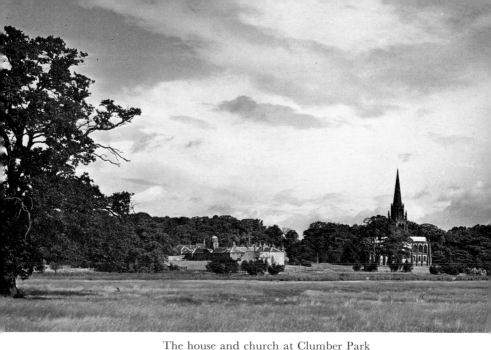

The house and church at Clumber Park

The Willoughby Almshouses at Cossall

Through the mediation of the French Ambassador, Lee in his despair accepted the invitation of Henry IV to France, and, with the help of his brother James and a few workmen, set up the frame at Rouen. There the help promised him did not materialise owing to the king's assassination, and Lee was left penniless in Paris, where he died about 1610 and was buried in an unknown grave. The frame was brought back to London, and eventually hosiery became a staple industry of Lee's own county.

His lasting memorial is in the great power machines which knit and make lace for the world today, for they had their beginning in his stocking-frame, one of the most astonishingly complete inventions ever devised at a single operation, and the first machine ever made to produce a looped or knitted fabric.

The church of St Wilfrid came into the Domesday Book, but only a few things are left of ancient days. The church the Normans left was made new in the 14th century and again in the 18th. Fragments of Norman moulding are in the north wall; the sides of the chancel arch are Norman, and on one of the capitals is a tiny panel carved with two figures believed to be St Wilfrid and a convert. There is a bell-ringers' gallery, and built into the belfry are seven stones carved by a Norman mason to illustrate the occupations of the months. January is represented by a man sitting at a table laden with food, while his hawk looks on; February is a man in a tunic, cloak, and heavy boots, warming himself at a fire under a tree; for March or April a man is pruning a tree with a big knife; another in June seems to be hoeing among growing crops; August is a man in a big hat, reaping corn with a sickle; and two panels represent September with two men threshing corn with flails. An eighth stone has a man on horseback with his hawk on his wrist, and a dog with tufted tail holding a hare or a rabbit. Recent improvements to the church include an annexe built in March 1962.

Carburton is a quiet little village lying close to one of the entrances to Clumber Park. Side by side through the village run the road and the little River Poulter till they enter Clumber Park. The river feeds the lake at Welbeck as well as that of Clumber, and the fine stretches known as Carburton Forge Dam and Carburton Dam remind us of the days when it worked an iron forge here, the iron being brought from Derbyshire and smelted by charcoal.

Its old church of St Mary is outlined on a rising slope, and it has a lovely view between the two parks. In a churchyard, bounded by the Flood Dyke is the small chapel of Norman foundation, with nave and chancel under one roof, a square bell turret at one end, and a little porch. The interior has recently been redecorated. A plain Norman doorway lets us in, and three tiny Norman windows are still here, a 13th century lancet between two of them in the east wall. The west window is 600 years old, and the tub font is Norman. There is a double sundial on a corner of the church, and just inside the door is part of an ancient gravestone.

The rare possession of the church is a register dating from 1528, said to be one of only three existing of this time. A second is at Perlethorpe three miles away, and the third is at Elsworth in Cambridgeshire. The date from which registers were kept by order of Thomas Cromwell was 1538, so that these three are ten years older than the oldest official record.

Car Colston. Not far from the Roman Fosse Way is this pretty village of many interests, its seclusion guarded by gates at the ends of the lanes that leads us to it. Cottages and little inn, fine houses and the old stocks, make a picture of old-world charm as they gather round the biggest green in the county. There is a handsome modern hall in Elizabethan style, and at the Screveton end of the village is part of the 17th century home of Dr Brunsell, who is said to have been a kinsman of Christopher Wren.

Here for many years lived Dr Robert Thoroton, whose famous *Antiquities of Notts* was published the year before he died in the village. He was born at Screveton in 1623, and after studying medicine in London he returned to his native county to practise. But his love was for antiquities, old churches, and old families, and he decided to interest himself more in the dead than in the living.

Round the church of St Mary runs an exceptional plinth moulding. The beautiful tower with slender belfry openings and a low pyramid roof belongs to the 13th and 15th centuries; other 13th century remains are the entrance to the south porch and the doorway within it which has an original door with later hinges. From the 14th century come the lofty nave arcades, the clerestory windows on the south, the north aisle windows, and its blocked doorway.

The glory of the church is its chancel, though its beauty is marred by the organ. Built in the 14th century, soon after the Black Death, it is typical of the fine work of this time in Notts, and has great gabled buttresses and lovely window tracery, the handsome sedilia and piscina being adorned with canopies, pinnacles, and finials. A grimacing man is peeping from one corner. The graceful altar rails are probably 17th century. There are a few old bench-ends, a poor box 400 years old, parts of the old chancel screen in a dado, and carved Jacobean panels in the pulpit and a desk. The oldest relic is the round Norman font.

Carlton adjoins Nottingham to the east of the city, and offers fine views of the Trent Vale. The parish church of St Paul was begun in 1885 and completed in 1891. It has a chancel with spire, vestry, nave of six bays with apse at the west end forming the baptistry, north and south porches and western turrets. Carlton now has a population of 41,260, its urban area being enlarged in 1935 by the inclusion of the parishes of Colwick and Gedling.

Carlton-in-Lindrick is two villages with one church, close to Worksop. There are old yews among the glorious trees in the churchyard, and from a mighty beech at its eastern end we have the prettiest view of the all-embattled tower and pinnacled church of St John. The exterior of the church has little of note except the ancient Saxon tower, which is of two distinct Early Saxon periods, with buttresses and top dating from the 15th century. Near the tower is the Devil-Stone discovered in 1937. Legend says that, if you run round it seven times, you will either have good luck or see the devil. Near the main doorway of the church is the base of the 14th century church cross. The doorway itself dates from about 1160 and was originally the Great South Doorway. It was moved to its present position when the south aisle was built in 1831. The arch into the nave is of a different period on each side. The western side dates from about 650 and the eastern from about 1060. When the latter work was done, the earlier work on the western side was left unaltered because the tower, being a place of refuge and defence against enemies, was full of materials for dealing with unwelcome marauders and was not regarded, therefore, as being part of the church.

The nave and north aisle roofs have heraldic bosses carved upon them. The font dates from about 1190. The Becket Chapel was built about 1180 and is much altered. The glass is all that remains of the old window over the high altar, damaged first by the henchmen of Edward VI, and later by the dismissed coachman of a former rector. The Chapel was restored in 1967. The relic altar, so named because it contains a relic of Saint Thomas of Canterbury (Becket), murdered 1170. It was re-erected by village workmen and reconciled on St Thomas of Canterbury's Day, December 29, 1935.

In the northern wall is an old arch of late mediaeval origin. It is possible that the Christmas Crib and Easter Sepulchre were placed here at the appropriate seasons of the year. The East window is 15th century but the stained glass is modern. The Hatchments on the south wall of the church are of Ramsden quartering Smyth of Heath Hall, Yorks (1753), and of Ramsden impaling Appleby of Wooton, Lincs (1783). There is an old wooden chest with three locks, about 400 years old.

The name of the village, Carlton-in-Lindrick, probably means the tun (enclosure) of the carls (freedmen) in the lind (lime) ric (wood).

Carlton-on-Trent is a quiet oasis by-passed by the A.1 road. The stone church of St Mary dates from 1851, and stands on the site of an old chapel of Norwell, of which the doorway is the only fragment left. It has a lofty tower and a graceful spire with two tiers of windows and a curious arrangement of rows of stone projecting like the spokes of a capstan. The altar table and two chests are 17th century, and a small old font, no longer used, looks like a huge egg cup with its bell-shaped bowl only 17 inches across. The Bell Inn, well known to 18th century travellers, is now a farm-house.

The quaint wayside smithy is picturesque with a great brick horse-shoe round the entrance, painted black on golden walls and pat-terned to show the nails, its old rhyme beginning;

Gentlemenl, as you pass by,
Upon this shoe pray cast an eye.

Caunton lies north-west from Newark. Its red houses and small grey church are gathered pleasantly about the willow-bordered Beck. It is the village of the man Tennyson called the Rose King.

Hiding in splendid trees near the church is Caunton Manor, a pleasant old brick house with a stone portico, where the Holes lived since the 15th century. Here Samuel Reynolds Hole lived for the greater part of his life, first as curate, then as vicar and squire, be-fore serving as Dean of Rochester. Here he loved and studied roses, grew them, wrote of them, promoted societies for their cultivation and shows for their exhibition, and made himself the most famous of amateur rose-growers. It was by his efforts that the National Rose Society came into being. He died at Rochester in 1904, and is buried in the churchyard at Caunton.

The church of St Andrew is lighted by windows from the three mediaeval centuries and a 15th century clerestory. The chancel arch, the font, and the nave arcades are all 13th century, the south arcade a little older than the north. A fine elm grows near the 14th century porch which shelters an elaborate doorway of the same time. The tower and its arch are 15th century. There are three old piscinas, a founder's recess, an ancient bracket carved with a curly head, and quaint corbels on the hoods of the windows.

In memory of the Dean the chancel is neatly panelled in oak, and the beautiful glass in the west window shines red, blue, green, and gold, having portraits of Elizabeth of Hungary with roses and lilies, St Andrew with a book and a cross, St Dorothy with a spray of roses, and an angel with golden wings holding a scroll with the words, "The desert shall rejoice and blossom as the rose."

Dean Hole gave the poor glass of the east window and three chancel lancets in memory of his parents, two sisters, and "a beloved friend John Leech", the famous Punch artist. The witty dean would help him with many of his drawings, and he enjoyed the strange distinction for a clergyman of being elected to Mr Punch's table.

Clarborough. It has three things to see, a church and a yew and a glorious view of the countryside to Sherwood Forest. Some say the yew is older than the church, and may have been growing a thousand years; it is still green and shapely, though its great days are gone and only half its hollow trunk is left. The much-restored church of St John the Baptist has a 15th century tower of two stages with a sundial on a buttress. From about 1400 come fine windows in the chancel and the very narrow aisles, the massive font with quatrefoils, and the south arcade. The 13th century north arcade is the oldest part. The only coloured glass glows richly in the east window, showing John the Baptist in raiment of camel hair, crying out as he sees Our Lord on the edge of a crowd.

A brass tells in quaint rhyme the virtues of George Mower, a boy of 14 who died in 1752; one of the Mowers gave the church an ancient silver chalice. A monument with a draped woman bowed over an urn has a long inscription to the Outybridge family.

Here there preached last century Parson Hodge, who proved himself a hero one terrible night. He was on board the *Royal Charter* when, after a voyage from Australia, she was wrecked off Anglesey in 1859. While a sailor tried to swim ashore with a rope, brave Parson Hodge calmed 500 terrified passengers by holding a prayer meeting. Before help reached them the ship was shattered on the rocks, and when morning broke only 39 people were left to tell the story of how Clarborough's parson spent his last moments.

Clayworth is a pretty village on the old Roman road north-east from East Retford.

Over the porch to the entrance to St Peter's church is a sundial with the words above it: "Our days on the earth are as a shadow." Looking up, one can see that the upper part of the tower, with eight fine pinnacles and eight quaint gargoyles, has been rebuilt, but in the base is some of the oldest work in the church, coming from early in the 12th century, or even from Saxon days. Part of the wall between the nave and chancel is of the same time, and has a little herringbone masonry near the arch. There are two Norman doorways, one with a later one built outside it, the other framing a fine old door with studded panels and restored tracery.

The 13th century nave arcades of wide and elegant bays have pillars on Norman bases, one pillar with five heads and three ornaments in place of a capital, another wreathed with foliage. A 13th century archway in the south wall of the chancel opens to a chapel shut off from the aisle by a simple stone screen which may have been set up about 1388, a rare possession for a village church. A 13th and a 15th century archway lead from the chancel to the north chapel, which has a 700-year-old arch between it and the aisle.

The clerestory is 15th century. The charm of many of the 14th century windows is enhanced by modern glass, saints and prophets and angels making a fine gallery. The upper half of the beautiful vaulted screen is new; the base, with its massive embattled rail enriched with floral medallions, is perhaps older than the Reformation. The new font has an old carved cover, and an old font has traces of painting.

The oldest memorial is a floorstone in the tower with a worn inscription to a rector of 1448. Under a great stone tomb carved with foliage and a shield of arms sleeps Humphrey Fitzwilliam, a Tudor judge, and on the tower wall is a memorial to William Sampson, a rector who founded a school and left behind 62 closely-written leaves of parchment giving a history of the parish from 1676 to 1701. Among the memorials of the Hartshornes who lived at Hayton Castle (now a farmhouse between the village and North Wheatley), is a quaint brass with the tiny figure of Time lying on his back; he has his scythe, and the sands are run down in the hourglass at his feet. The rhyme on the brass tells us of the virtues of John Hartshorne of 1678.

There are memorials in the church of a Yorkshire family distinguished in the siege of Scarborough Castle during the Civil War, the Ackloms. They had the neighbouring Wiseton estate in the time of Charles II, and half a century ago built the handsome hall on the site of the older house in which they lived through the 18th century till the heiress married Lord Althorp, a well-known politician and an honest one. Lord Brougham was a frequent guest, and it has been said that perhaps the first Reform Bill was outlined under his roof.

Across the road from the church is a road leading to Royston Manor, which is listed as an ancient monument. A memorial to two brothers of the Otter family of Royston Manor is in the church.

Clifton, some 12 miles north of Newark on the River Trent, is two villages, Clifton North and South, a mile apart.

The church serving these two villages is that of St George, which has eight tall pinnacles crowning the splendid tower. This tower is chiefly 15th century with some remains of the 13th; in its west doorway hangs a worn old door, and its fine arch to the nave is adorned with shields and embattled capitals. A porch made new and a 13th century doorway lead into the nave, where a beautiful arcade has 13th century arches resting on massive Norman pillars. The 500-year-old chancel arch has sides and carved capitals two centuries older. Worn heads adorn the hoods of the windows (many of which are 15th century), an old chest is like a trunk, and there are some old timbers in the aisle roof. Stone heads of kings and a queen support the modern roof of the chancel, which has a cornice of vine and grape.

The oak reredos, elaborate with paint and gilt, shows the Nativity. The old piscina is like a tiny font, its round bowl on a tapering shaft and set in a rounded niche; and very quaint is an old image bracket in the aisle, carved with flowers and a cat-like face with its tongue out and its pointed ears upright; seeming to watch us come and go.

Clipstone stands on the edge of Sherwood Forest in the valley of the River Maun. On a hillside overlooking the village are the remains of King John's Palace, the rough grey walling, with jagged openings once doorways and windows, is impressive in the suddenness with which it rises against the sky as we see it from a narrow lane. It is said that kings of Northumbria built it and lived here. It was built at any rate before the time of King John, who used it as a hunting lodge. Henry II improved it and gave it a park. An English and a Scottish lion met here when King Richard the Lion Heart talked with William the Lion on his return from the Crusades in 1194. Edward I held a Parliament at Clipstone in 1290. The building began to decay in the time of Henry IV.

Two miles away, in a grassy bay of the road to Mansfield, are the remains of another vanished glory—the lifeless fragments of the gnarled and twisted trunk of an ancient oak, supported by props and fastened by chains to a younger oak. It is called the Parliament Oak, because Edward is thought by some to have held his parliament here and not at the palace. Another story is that by this tree King John (who was staying at his hunting lodge at the time) had a meeting with his nobles after hearing the news which led to the execution of 28 Welsh youths at Nottingham Castle.

Between Clipstone and Edwinstowe is a fine Gothic archway known as the Duke's Folly or the Duke's Archway, built by his Grace of Portland in 1842 after the style of the old Priory Gatehouse at Worksop. With buttressed walls, and rooms with traceried windows on each side of the central arch, it breathes the spirit of the Forest in the splendid figures niched on its north and south sides, and the stone hares that sit above the projecting bays. Richard I is here in chain armour, with unsheathed sword; Friar Tuck with folded arms looking quizzically down; Allen-a-Dale with his harp; charming Maid Marian; Robin Hood himself with a feather in his cap, and Little John, like Robin, with his bow and quiver of arrows.

The arch looks one way to Clipstone, the other along an undulating grassy stretch, lined with oaks, running straight as the crow flies to the Mansfield road. It is said that the duke meant this broad turf ride to be part of a direct drive from Welbeck to Nottingham, passing through his Archway.

There is no church in this village, but new Clipstone, a mining village about a mile away, has a modern housing estate and church.

Clumber Park lies some 2½ miles south-east of Worksop, and extends to 3704 acres. It was created by the Dukes of

Newcastle out of heathland bordering Sherwood Forest, and is a notable example of 18th century landscape design. In 1770 Stephen Wright built Clumber House for the first Duke of Newcastle, but this no longer exists as it was pulled down in 1938 and its contents sold. In this lovely park there are two items of special interest, the first being the Duke's Drive or Lime Tree Avenue, which is over 2 miles long, while not far from where the lovely house once stood is the Chapel of St Mary the Virgin, built by G. F. Bodley for the 7th Duke between 1886-89. The Chapel is in two main sections divided by an elaborate screen. To the east of this screen, richly carved choir-stalls and a decorated chancel flank the path to the gold and white high altar of Nottinghamshire alabaster. The nave is quite simple with plain arcaded walls underneath the high windows. The Park was bought by public subscription, to which local authorities largely contributed, and is managed jointly by the National Trust and local authorities.

Coddington is an attractive village on a hill just outside Newark. On the outskirts stands the remains of a windmill which used to be seen for miles around, but now has no cap or sails.

The church of All Saints has a tower with eight fine pinnacles. It is a wide and pleasant place, entered by the enriched 13th century doorway inside a modern porch. The nave arcades are 13th century, the north a little older than the south. There are stone seats round the pillars of both arcades. The font is 700 years old. The modern chancel has a wagon roof painted in mediaeval colours with much gold. The traceried panelling of the sanctuary walls, and the reredos with roses among its carving, are adorned in similar style. Very beautiful are the oak sedilia with a coved canopy and a rich cornice. The lofty chancel screen, with gilded tracery and four figures of bishops, was one of the gifts of the Thorpes, who have been benefactors to church and village.

Among so much that is new in woodwork a little old is treasured in six traceried bench-ends.

With the farm buildings close to the churchyard is a gabled dovecote, one of the oldest in the county, and used now as a little house.

Colston Bassett is a picturesque village near to Bingham. In a road flanked by trees, where a stepped wall runs by the grounds of the hall in its park of 90 acres, a stone bridge spans the tiny River Smite.

In a delightful setting where the ways meet is the charming old cross, rising with slender grace from a flight of steps. It is 15 feet high, and was rebuilt on the ancient base about a century ago. By another road embowered in trees (planted in 1710) is the stone church built in 1892 in memory of a beloved wife and her son, looking across the park to the fine old house where they lived.

Rich with elaborate battlements and pinnacles, the church of St John's central tower rests on lofty arches and is crowned by a spire rising to 150 feet. The transomed east window glows richly with eight scenes from the life of Our Lord. The great attraction of the church is the fine carving in stone, especially notable in the undercutting of the capitals of the nave arcades and in the stone base of the oak pulpit, where the luxuriant foliage seems to be symbolical of the wealth of trees in the village. On the slender pillars supporting the roof are four angels, and the stone reredos has coloured panels of Our Lord and the Four Evangelists. The Hall pew has an elaborately carved oak canopy.

A lovely winged figure in the chapel, sculptured in marble, is to Alice Catherine Knowles; it was in memory of her and her son that her husband built the church. The son was drowned in Cumberland when 21, and there is an inscription to him and to a brother who fell in the Boer War.

High up on the edge of the park, in a glorious situation, are the pitiful remains of the 13th and 14th century church of St Mary, which once had the shape of a cross and was one of the most beautiful in the county. Of its famous peal of bells, five are now in the new church, and the old font has found a resting place in the new churchyard.

Colwick is a short distance from the city. Its race-course is well known to lovers of the turf, and its hall, attached to the race-course, is now a hotel. Built in 1776, and keeping still a splendid staircase and fine rooms with fireplaces in the style of the Adam brothers, the hall is full of interest, for the place where it stands is said to have been lived on since Saxon days. It was a home at the time of the Domesday Book, when there was a mill by the Trent. Among the many owners who followed were the De Colwicks, who held it for a rent of 12 barbed arrows supplied by the king when he came to Nottingham Castle; then came the Byrons and the Musters, through whom it became the home of Mary Chaworth, the ill-fated heiress of Annesley immortalised in Byron's poems. She was his early love but came here as the bride of the sporting squire, John Musters. She was here when the Reform Bill rioters looted and fired the hall, and the exposure she suffered then brought about her death a few months later at Wiverton Hall. The church which stood nearby and which held monuments of both the Musters and the Byrons is now a ruin. A new church in Colwick has replaced the old one on the race-course. It is St John the Baptist, the foundation stone of which was laid on February 26, 1950.

Cossall. They say the first coal in Notts was dug up in this border village seven centuries ago, and there are collieries still round about it, though the old village is in surprising seclusion on a green hilltop, looking to Ilkeston a mile away. It is a delightful picture as we come from Trowell, crowning a slope down which the canal winds like a serpent through the meadows.

Except for the 13th century tower and the low spire with dormer windows, the tiny church of St Catherine is now a centenarian, having been rebuilt in 1842. Under an arched recess in the sanctuary is a marble tomb of the Willoughbys, remembered for the fine almshouses near the church, founded by George Willoughby in 1685. In an aisle window is St Catherine in ancient glass. The bowl of the font is 15th century.

Cossall is proud of the great oak reredos, for its work was all done by village carvers. The cornice has roses, and among the fine bits of carving is a panel of passion flowers and leaves trailing over a cross, under a pinnacled canopy with a splendid finial.

There are a number of war memorials in the churchyard, and

48

one, to John Shaw (a Lifeguardsman), recalls his heroism at Water-loo. A giant of physical strength, it is said that he put out of action eight Frenchmen, refusing to retire from the field to have his wounds dressed, and only stopped fighting when he fell over from sheer exhaustion. He was born in 1789 at a farmhouse.

Costock is a pleasant village south of Nottingham with cottages and farms, a little church in a narrow lane, and a charming Elizabethan manor house.

The church of St Giles is mainly 14th century, including the bowl of the font, but a lancet window is 13th, and the aisle and the porch are 19th. In a richly canopied recess in an outside wall lies the battered figure of a priest in robes; it is said that his head was knocked off by soldiers in the Civil War. Built into the wall near this recess is a lovely fragment of a Saxon preaching cross.

The church has what we may call a garden of poppyhead benchends, six of them 15th century, and over 60 the work of a former rector. He was Charles Sutton Millard, and very good his work is, the ends well carved, and no two of all the poppyheads alike. The east window in the church with the Crucifixion is in memory of this man.

Cotgrave lies south-east from Nottingham, and its colliery, which is its chief industry, commenced production in January, 1964.

The Fosse Way skirts the village, and the remains of four Roman soldiers found in separate but neighbouring graves beneath its surface, with spears, daggers, and coins of the 4th and 5th century AD, suggests that the site at least of Cotgrave was known to the legions of 1500 years ago.

Its prettiest corner is in a leafy lane where great limes and elms guard the church of All Saints, and a lychgate leads to a burial ground.

A gnarled old walnut tree stands near the tower, and an ancient yew shelters the chancel. Like most of the old work left in the church, both tower and spire come from the 14th century, the tower buttressed to the battlements and opening to the nave by a lofty

49

arch. Of about the same time are the nave arcades with clustered pillars, and the chancel arch whose sides and capitals come from the close of Norman days.

The base of the tower contains many tablets recounting feats of bell-ringing. There are six bells of which one (treble) was added in 1906. Three (1651, 1827, and 14th century) were re-cast in 1908.

Under the tower hang King Charles's Rules:

Profane no Divine Ordinance
Touch no State matters
Urge no Healths
Pick no quarrels
Maintain no ill opinions
Encourage no vice
Repeat no old grievances
Reveal no secrets
Make no comparisons
Keep no bad company
Make no long meals
Lay no wagers
Do nothing in anger

Cotgrave finds its way into many parts of the country with marl for cricket pitches, which is found on the high ground on either side of the village.

Cotham overlooks the lovely Vale of Belvoir from its place between the River Devon and the Lincolnshire border.

The church of St Michael stands some distance from the main road, and is approached across a field. It is only a shadow of its old self, and at the time of writing was considered unsafe for people to enter. Towards the end of the 18th century it lost two aisles as well as its tower, from which two gargoyles now guarding the churchyard gate are said to have looked down for over 500 years. Some of the old aisle windows are in the nave walls, and two 14th century relics are the massive font and the charming piscina. Two marble tombs, one of which has lost its brass portrait of a 14th century knight, may belong to the Leekes, who lived here before the Markhams came.

The modest home of only a few folk, Cotham has little claim to distinction now, but it was a proud village five centuries ago when it became the seat of the Markhams. William was Lord Treasurer of Edward I, and in the church of East Markham, the village from which they sprang, lies the Judge Markham who drew up the document for deposing Richard II. Sir Robert, a supporter of the White Rose, was knighted after the Battle of Towton Field, and his son John set out from his home here to distinguish himself as a leader in the terrible battle when the White Rose met the Red for the last time at East Stoke, three miles away. No trace of their splendid house is left, but there is a monument in the church to Anne Warburton, wife of Robert Markham.

Cottam looks over meadows stretching nearly a mile to the Trent, dividing Nottinghamshire from Lincolnshire. Nearby is the new power station with its eight cooling towers, each 383 feet high and believed to be the highest in Europe.

The tiny church of Holy Trinity has a doorway 800 years old.

A lychgate at the end of a wayside path brings us to the simple building, with walls aslant, nave and chancel under one steep roof on four massive old beams, and a turret for one bell. A porch shelters the Norman doorway, which has crude chevron mouldings boldly carved, and pillars on each side with scalloped capitals. The bowl of the ancient font is outside the porch, set on a new base.

Creswell Crags belong to Derbyshire as well as Notts, the boundary running through them on the verge of Welbeck Park. At their foot are the famous caves where remarkable treasures made by the earliest men in Britain have been found. The caves proved to be packed with evidence of earlier ages, and at one time or another remains of reindeer, bison, bear, hippopotamus, wolf, rhinoceros have been found, as well as human remains. Some of the discoveries are now preserved in museums at Derby and Sheffield and the British Museum.

Cromwell is now by-passed by a new dual carriage-way on the east, and the Great North Road running through the village has become just a quiet village street. Its name is its distinction.

In the old house by the churchyard, once the rectory, are foundations which are said to be part of the old home of the Cromwells, of whom the last and most famous was Ralph, Lord Cromwell. Treasurer to Henry VI, Constable of Nottingham Castle and Keeper of Sherwood Forest, he was a man of wealth and a great builder. He built Tattershall Castle in Lincolnshire, and the greater part of Wingfield Manor in Derbyshire.

A 15th century embattled tower crowns the pleasing little church of St Giles, which was restored 60 years ago when the 14th century arcade of two bays was opened out in the chancel, and the chapel built on old foundations. From the 13th century come the south doorway, the nave arcade, and some lancet windows. Among other mediaeval windows are two in the chancel with the graceful flowing tracery of the end of the 14th century, and in a tiny roundel of old glass is a rose. The low iron chancel screen with gates and wrought iron altar rail were made in the village smithy in 1890. In 1967 a pair of gates was added to the altar rail in memory of William Dolman, a former Rector.

Cropwell Bishop was formerly known as Crophill Bishop, and takes its name from the rounded hill now known as Hoe Hill on the north side of the village. The church of St Giles stands in the centre of the village. Its fine tower dates from the 15th century, the chancel is 14th (and restored), and the nave arcades with round pillars are 13th. The font (with a 17th century cover) and two piscinas are 600 years old, and from the same 14th century come most of the windows, except for the 500-year-old clerestory. The only colour in the windows are a few fragments of old glass, and the memorial window of St Nicholas with a ship, St George in armour, a soldier helping a comrade on the battlefield, and an angel with the crown of life.

In the nave are ten gnarled oak benches of about 1400, their poppyheads carved with flowers, faces, eagles, and little men with

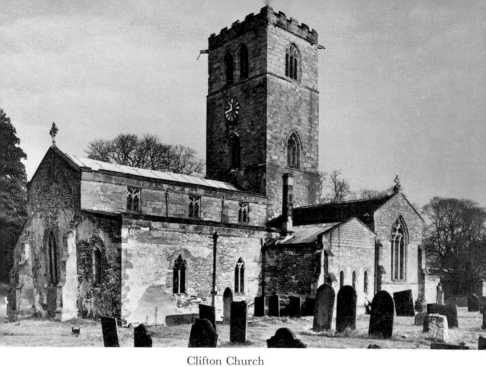

Clifton Church

e Norman north door at Balderton Church

The Norman south door at Laneham Church

The Easter sepulchre at Arnold Church

The west side of the font at Lenton Church

their legs doubled up. The chancel screen, a patchwork of old and new, has fragments of mediaeval tracery, faces of two men, and symbols of the Last Days in Jerusalem. Eight fearful stone grotesques support the lovely Tudor roof of the nave with its richly moulded beams and leafy bosses. It is odd that on a later beam than the rest the carpenter carved the date backwards, as if not quite sure how it would read from below: it runs 4671 instead of 1764. The oldest woodwork here is about 12 feet of wall-plate from the middle of the 13th century.

There is a gypsum works adjoining the now disused Grantham Canal, and marl is also produced here.

Cropwell Butler is less than a mile north of Cropwell Bishop. A smaller village than its neighbour, it derives its name from the same source, and likewise is mostly agricultural. It is a chapelry of Tythby. In pre-Reformation times it had a chapel dedicated to St Nicholas, but by Thoroton's time (1677) it had ceased to exist, and by 1832 no traces remained. In 1845 Mr George Parr built a small brick chapel at a cost of £400. It was closed in 1879, but bought by the parishioners for £200, restored at a further cost of £300 and re-opened in November, 1897. It is dedicated to St Peter, to whom Tythby church was originally dedicated according to ancient wills.

Cuckney is south-west from Worksop beside the River Poulter. Here many ways meet on the edge of the Dukeries, with lovely views of their woodlands. At a charming corner a shelving cedar stands facing an inn with cream walls and a swinging sign of the Greendale Oak. A mile and a half away, near Welbeck Abbey, is the famous tree to which the name belongs, so old that none can tell its age, its hollow trunk propped up. It has a strange tale to tell. In 1724, as the result of a wager by the Earl of Oxford, he drove a coach and four through one of his trees, an archway ten feet high having been cut in the massive trunk, which was then about 35 feet round above the opening.

Into Cuckney's old story comes a Saxon knight who was allowed to keep land here after the Conquest in return for shoeing the king's palfrey when he came to Mansfield, being given a horse if he did his work well but forfeiting one of his own if he did not please. In the 12th century Thomas de Cuckney, founder of Welbeck Abbey, was lord of the manor, and a moated mound in the churchyard is said to be the site of his castle.

The church of St Mary treasures fine Norman remains. It is rare to find Norman work in a porch, but, though this porch was made new 700 years ago, it keeps an original string of Norman ornament which makes a trimming for the top of the side walls, and also round the gable. A lovely Norman doorway, with zigzag and cable mouldings and a hood ending in grotesques, lets us into the church, where the long nave is divided from its aisle by an arcade of six round arches on pillars of varying shapes. Except for one round pillar which is earlier Norman, this arcade was built when the Norman style was changing to Early English, and the priest's doorway is of the same time. From the 15th century come the top of the sturdy tower (on a 13th century base) and many of the windows. There is an unusual piscina with worn ornament about 700 years old, and the broken remains of a fine stoup or font have been brought to the church after being dug up in a garden. Three coffin stones form windowsills in an aisle, and part of another is in the nave floor. There is some old tracery in the tower screen.

A stone in the middle of the chancel floor, so worn that its inscription is gone, marks the resting-place of Robert Pierrepont, who became Earl of Kingston-upon-Hull in 1628 and was killed in the Civil War.

In 1950 between 40 and 50 skeletons buried in three tiers and a foot stone coffin were discovered under the nave of Cuckney Parish Church. They were discovered by workmen who were putting in a concrete raft to offset mining subsidence. When the job was complete the skeletons were buried again near the old west door of the church. It is thought that they were young men killed in battle during the reign of King Stephen.

Darlton lies midway between Lincoln and Worksop, and has wide views of the countryside.

Two lofty limes guard a 19th century lychgate to the church of St Giles. The tower is old and unbuttressed and has a 700-year-old lancet. The great possession of the church is the lovely south doorway letting us in, built at the close of Norman days, and having a hood of fine moulding over a round arch resting on detached shafts. A tiny mediaeval arcade divides the nave from the aisle, and a big window a hundred years older lights the east wall. The old aumbry has flowers in the spandrels. A cup and its cover are Elizabethan.

On the wall of the chancel are fine brass portraits of a knight and his lady, both with praying hands, and standing erect on grassy ground. The knight is in plate armour with a sword, his hair falling on to his shoulders; the lady has a long gown with an embroidered belt from which hangs a chain with an ornament, while from her pointed headdress two streamers fall to her elbows. They belong to about 1510, and are probably Sir William Mering and his wife.

Daybrook is on the fringe of the city, situated on the busy Nottingham to Mansfield road. The church of St Paul's, its great tower, with fine windows, pinnacles, and a lofty spire, stands at a corner and forms a south porch with a vaulted roof. The great west window is between buttresses adorned with figures in canopied niches, and above it is an array of eight more handsome niches.

Attractive as it is outside the church is equally so within, where arcades of four bays divide the nave and aisles. It is so spacious and lofty that 15 windows glowing with countless figures do not rob it of light. The great east window of seven lights has nearly 70 figures; and shining in the west are the twelve Disciples. The only plain glass is in the clerestory. A charming feature of the church is the stone, which seems to burst into life in a wonderful mass of carving—in the alabaster reredos with its vivid scene of the Last Supper, in the three sedilia and the piscina, in the pulpit with figures all round, and in the font, which has on its seven sides figures of Faith, Hope, Charity, Courage, Truth, Purity, and Industry. Delicately beautiful is the ironwork on each side of the chancel, and on the gated chancel screen. The floor of the chancel is Italian mosaic in soft colours of

55

cream and green and rose; but loveliest of all is Sir Thomas Brock's marble figure of a beautiful woman in the sanctuary, a gentle smile on her lips, and a lily beneath her folded hands. She was the wife of Colonel Charles Seely and mother of Lord Mottistone; and the church, built by Mr J. L. Pearson, RA, architect of Truro Cathedral, is her memorial.

Bestwood Park, part of which is now a large housing estate, lies a little to the north on the opposite side of the road. Charles II gave this estate to Nell Gwynn's son Charles Beauclerk, whom he made the first Duke of St Albans when Nell Gwynn threatened to throw the brat out of the window. The tenth duke built Bestwood Lodge (now occupied by the army) last century, making it a handsome brick house with gables, and he also built the church in which he lies.

The **Dukeries** is a name given to the three large estates of Welbeck, Clumber, and Thoresby, and which lies some 25 miles north of Nottingham. Of the three estates Thoresby is the only one open to the public. Clumber House was demolished in 1938, but the park, which is now owned by the National Trust, is open to the public. Welbeck is now an Army College. For further details see under appropriate headings.

Dunham-on-Trent is a pleasant riverside village, much frequented by fishermen. Its toll bridge, which carries the road to Lincolnshire, was built in 1832.

The church of St Oswald is approached past the gay flower garden of a cottage, or through the old stone archway opening to the churchyard, its great capitals carved with grotesque animals and foliage. The tower is a noble tribute to the builders of the 15th century, and finds its glory in windows remarkable for their size and beauty. It is all that is left of an old church twice rebuilt last century. To this parish in 1856 came the Rev Henry Jubb, the first resident vicar for over one hundred years. He had the nave (apart from the south wall) rebuilt and a north aisle added, presumably on the site of the original, and the church was dedicated on October 1, 1862. Roughly

100 years later the church re-hung the bells, removed choir stalls from the chancel, and beautified the interior with soft furnishings.

Eakring has fine red-roofed houses lining the road, and fine views of the Forest countryside. At the foot of the village stands the church of St Andrew, much restored and made new. The tower has a 15th century top storey on a 13th century base which has a carved stone over its doorway showing traces of a figure. The sides of the tower arch are perhaps Norman, and there are three 13th century lancets in the chancel. There is a fine little Jacobean pulpit with a canopy, a poor box of 1718, a small old chest, and a 17th century font like a pillar. The arms of Charles II are in the church, and in the porch are those of Elizabeth, brought from a house in the village which was once an inn where the queen is said to have stayed. Two stone corbels on an outside wall show a woman's worn face and a demon with bared teeth.

A brass plate tells us of George Lawson who gave the church a silver chalice; he was rector here before the coming of a new rector who was told that he must not enter the village. He was William Mompesson, who from September of 1665 to October, 1666 had laboured in plague-stricken Eyam, ministering to his pitiful flock as they awaited their dread fate and perished one by one, till less than 40 of Eyam's 350 folk were left alive.

Three years had passed since the plague when he came to Eakring, but the people were afraid of infection, and Mompesson had to live for a time in a hut in Rufford Park. It is one of the saddest examples we have come upon of the superstition of country folk. He remained at Eakring for 38 years and died in 1708. On the chancel wall is the brass plate which used to be in the floor over his grave, and a modern inscription tells of his ministry at Eyam. The poor glass in three lancets is his memorial.

Perhaps the story of this brave rector comes nearest our hearts as we stand in the fields with only the sky above us, where a simple rustic stone cross marks the spot at which he used to preach during his pathetic exile from the village. Near the cross is a young ash tree which has replaced the old one under which he used to stand. It was known as Pulpit Ash, and was destroyed by lightning some time ago. From this rough cross, which stands at the head of a field at the top of the village, we have a pretty view of Eakring among the trees and a fine one of the countryside.

A short distance from the village are a number of oil wells. The first strike was made on June 8, 1939 at a depth of 1914 feet.

East Bridgford is approached from Gunthorpe by a steep hill which terminates in cross-roads with the village shop on the one side and the boundary wall of St Peter's on the other. There are several Georgian houses and cottages, in particular the Rectory close to the church on the Kneeton road *c.* 1700.

The church of St Peter was restored early this century, at which time 12 feet of Saxon walling 34 inches thick was found below the chancel floor, with other stonework which showed that the chancel of the church that came into the Domesday Book was only eight feet wide. Traces of fire here led to the belief that the ancient building had been burned by the Danes. Two fragments of a Saxon cross, and a 13th century headstone (buried in an upright position in the churchyard) were found at the same time, and are in the church for us to see. The chancel was rebuilt on a bigger scale about 1200, and was given its charming priest's doorway later in the 13th century. The middle portion of its 14th century arch is nearly a thousand years old; the 14th century sedilia and piscina were restored after being found in the rector's garden. A fine roof with angels at the ends of the beams looks down on the nave with 14th century arcades and a clerestory of the 15th. The porch with gargoyles and a niche with a modern figure, and some tiles with many patterns, are also 14th century. The tower was rebuilt in 1778.

Its great archaeological interest lies in the Roman village station of Margidunum, which was excavated by Dr F. Oswald. The remains discovered on this site are now housed at Nottingham University. The remains tell the story of a camp from its prehistoric days to the days when it came into history—from the days of the Early Britons to the days of its Roman occupation and its lapse into oblivion. It lies on the Fosse Way, the straightest road in England, midway between Leicester and Lincoln, and the camp covered about seven acres, enough to accommodate a thousand men and some cavalry. Here were found Roman coins from the first century to the fourth, a fine little sepulchral stone carved with two figures, one with a staff and one with a basket of fruit; great jars and cooking pots, and vessels moulded with human faces; fragments of glass, ladles, bucket handles, bone and bronze pins, and horse trappings (one engraved with a dragon); and many flint arrow heads, scrapers, and axes of the Bronze Age. But most remarkable of all these treasures is what we may be allowed to describe as a piece of Roman oak panelling, for it is nothing less than a complete section of the oak lining of a well of the time of Claudius. It is shaped like a square cage, and the roughly-cut oak planks still show the marks of the saw and the adze used by the carpenter 19 centuries ago.

East Drayton lies some seven miles from East Retford. Its church of St Peter and Paul is a fine example of the late mediaeval style of architecture with older interior details.

The tower is 14th and 15th century. The handsome porch of the 15th has elaborate buttresses and pinnacles, and a stone roof with ribs ending in tiny corbel heads showing grotesque and human faces. Other faces peep out from foliage in bosses of the nave and chancel roofs, where beams painted with scrolls and flowers are in rich contrast with grey walls.

The north arcade of the nave is six centuries old, and the south is five. There is a plain old font, and at the foot of the belfry stair is a small old door. Much of the lofty chancel screen is about 1500, and part of the old altar rails are in the south aisle.

East Leake lies some nine miles south-west of Nottingham, and a stream runs idly by alongside the main street of the village.

The church of St Mary the Virgin has two fine patches of herringbone masonry in the north wall of the nave, which come from early Norman or even Saxon days. The 13th century tower has a 15th century spire, and the nave arcade comes between the two. The clerestory is 15th century. The chancel, mostly made new last century, has a splendid 600-year-old east window and some 13th century lancets. The beautiful 14th century east window of the aisle contains glass in memory of a former rector, John Bateman.

The great font is over 700 years old; some of the poppyhead bench-ends and the splendid pelican on the pulpit are 500. The pulpit and the lectern are made of oak from the old belfry, and some open seats have been here since 1612. Part of a rare book called *The Dippers Dipt*, of 1645, is in the vestry; it was once chained.

East Leake's rarest treasure, in the church for all to see, is a long tin trumpet which is one of six left in English churches. Measuring nearly eight feet when extended, and 21 inches across the mouth, it was used till 1855 for the principal singers to vamp through, making what the Psalmist would have called a joyful noise unto the Lord. The other five are at Braybrooke and Harrington, Northants; at Charing in Kent; at Ashurst in Sussex; and at Willoughton, Lincs.

East Markham is a large, straggling village with a mixture of old and new houses set amid orchards.

It was at East Markham Hall that Elizabeth Cartwright, who went under the pen name of Mrs Markham, spent much of her early life. She wrote a history of England in 1823 and of France in 1828. She died in 1837 and is buried in Lincoln Cathedral. There is a memorial to her in the church here at Markham.

In the stone foundations of the manor house close to the church of St John the Baptist are remains of the old home of two famous judges of the Markham family, father and son. The father was Sir John, who helped to change the line of kings by drawing up the document for deposing Richard II.

It was Judge Markham who gave the deposition of King Richard its legal basis by drawing up the document, and here they laid him when his exciting days were over; he lies in the chancel under an alabaster tomb with an inscription and plain shields. His son John, known as the Upright Judge, is said to have lost office through carrying out his maxim that no subject can be arrested by the king for treason.

Set in a floorstone in the south aisle is a beautiful brass portrait of the first Sir John's widow, who after his death married William

Mering. The brass shows her in a high-waisted gown with hanging sleeves and a wide collar reaching to her shoulders. Her embroidered headdress is wired so that it looks rather like a canopy, and her hands are at prayer. The little dog at her feet, with bells on its collar, is charming.

In memory of the two Markham judges the east window of this aisle was renewed and filled with stained glass by their descendants last century. It has shields of arms and medallions of foliage; three of the shields are of old glass, and among old fragments in the tracery is St Scyth crowned.

The chancel is beautiful with its modern glass. The east window, shining silver and gold, blue and green, has Mary and Jesus, St Hugh and his goose, John the Baptist, and St Cuthbert. Splendid figures of St Alban, St George, and St Martin, with small scenes from their lives, look out from a window in memory of Kenneth Markham Rose, who fell in action in West Africa in 1915. He was the only son at the manor house.

A great delight inside and out is the clerestory of 16 triple windows, a glorious traceried lantern which helps to fill this spacious place with a blaze of light. It is a worthy part of a 15th century embattled pile which is one of the finest churches of this countryside.

Eight pinnacles and gargoyles like winged demons adorn the massive tower, which has transomed windows, a recessed doorway, an archway of great height opening to the nave, and a small figure in a conopied niche. Projecting far from the chancel buttresses are four extraordinary gargoyles—a winged animal, a grotesque with a rope round its shoulder, a creature in armour with a battle-axe, and another with staring eyes and one hand in its wide-open mouth. In the gallery of heads at the windows are a king and a queen, a bishop, a lady in a frilled headdress and a crusader. On a battlement is an old sundial.

Great heads look out from the nave arcades with channelled pillars. Much of the old work is left in the oak screen of the south aisle, the old pulpit has carved borders, an old pillar almsbox has iron bands, and worked up into the Litany desk is part of an old bench-end carved with the head of a bishop, vines coming from his mouth. He is hidden from the casual eye. The modern roofs have rich bosses and carved borders, and on the ends of the nave beams are angels and heads of human folk, one a man with his tongue out.

Very striking is the massive and unusual font, looking like a giant spider, with a bowl of 1686 and a 14th century base which has a central pillar and eight legs bent outward, their feet resting on a stone carved with four-leaved flowers. It is crowned by an elaborate pyramid cover.

Set up in the north aisle is the ancient altar stone. We read in the church that its presence near the chancel arch was revealed to a vicar in a dream the year before it came to light in 1897.

East Stoke has red-roofed houses gathered pleasantly round the cross-roads on the Fosse Way, and its meadows are by pretty reaches of the Trent. Only a name or two remind us of a black page of history written here, for on June 16, 1487, the Royal Army, under the personal command of Henry VII, met and defeated the insurgents, who supported Lambert Simnel, the pretended Earl of Warwick, and claimant for the Crown. The engagement was fought at Stoke Field, about one mile south of East Stoke. The rebels under the Earl of Lincoln were overwhelmed after a most sanguinary three hours, in which some 7000 men were slain. All the leaders of Simnel's army were put to the sword with the exception of Lord Lovel, who fled from the field, and was presumed to be drowned whilst attempting to cross the Trent. On the Syerston side of East Stoke Wood is a field with a stone slab commemorating the battle.

On May 28, 1646 the village was struck by the plague, and the first death was recorded in the parish register. By December 5 of the same year 158 more villagers had died of the disease, whole families being wiped out. Each name is marked on the faded parchment with a thick black cross. In a normal year, not more than ten people died in this particular village from all causes put together.

Stoke Hall stands back from the river in a thickly wooded park, with lofty beech, elm, and chestnut trees. It dates from the mid-16th century, and was much enlarged by Lewis Wyatt in 1821. The church of St Oswald is mainly from the late 17th and the early 18th century and is hidden from the road by a high wall. From the close of the 14th century come the west window of the low tower and its arch on 13th century shafts, and the east window. There are fragments of old glass, a mediaeval piscina, and a chest 500 years old.

On a wall is a framed copy of some extracts from Captain Scott's last message to the nation; Scott's friend Admiral Bromley gave it to the church when he left the Hall.

In the village is the Pauncefote Arms, named after a noted family, one of whom, Baron Julian Pauncefote, was first Ambassador to the United States. Born in 1828, he died at Washington in 1902, and a monument to him stands in the village churchyard.

Half a mile north of the village is the site of "Ad Pontem", a Roman fort or station. The site of this has been known for a number of years, and occupies the whole of a four-acre field. In excavations in 1953 and 1954, two brooches, a lead casket, and a beaker were found. Pieces of human bones were also found in September 1963, and on a site slightly south-west a Roman Ditch system was unearthed in 1965.

Eastwood is a typical mining town about eight miles north-east of Nottingham, and the River Erewash on its western boundary forms the dividing line between the counties of Nottinghamshire and Derbyshire.

The Parish Church of St Mary is a mixture of old and new. In 1963 the main body of the church was destroyed by fire, but the tower remained almost untouched, and the church was rebuilt in 1967. The registers date back to 1711.

Eastwood is perhaps best known for its associations with D. H. Lawrence. The author was born at 8a Victoria Street on September 11, 1885, and his book, *Sons and Lovers*, gives a vivid description of his early life in this mining village. Lawrence died at Vence, near Nice, in 1930.

The Sun Inn has historical interests, the most important being that a meeting of the Iron Masters and Coal Owners of the district resulted in the birth of the old Midland Railway.

Eaton lies two miles from East Retford on the River Idle. The church of All Saints built in 1858 stands high in a churchyard where fine sycamores and a great horse-chestnut grow, looking down on the river.

Yet this is the spot, it is believed, where more than 1300 years ago king met king in battle, one of them and the son of the other being slain. It was in 617 that the Battle of the Idle was fought in which Redwald of East Anglia slew Ethelfrith, the usurping king of Northumbria, but lost his own son Regnhere. Redwald had been sheltering Edwin, the true Northumbrian king, and as a result of the victory Edwin was restored to the throne. He married the beautiful Ethelburga, daughter of the Christian King of Kent, and was himself baptised by Paulinus.

At the entrance to the village is Eaton Hall College of Education, a County Teachers' Training College.

Edingley, between Southwell and Mansfield, is a trim little place abounding with orchards. The church of St Giles has something it has kept for 800 years in spite of much change. It has lost a south aisle, but two wide arches and other fragments of its 14th century arcade are still seen in the wall, and though the chancel was made new last century it has its old piscina and the priest's doorway, which is now blocked. There is a Norman west doorway with chevron and cable mouldings, and a small Norman window deeply splayed in the north and south walls of the nave.

A stream runs by the churchyard gate, and just within is a tremendous sycamore overhanging the road and sheltering a patch of ground 76 yards round.

Edwalton. Charming new houses and gardens line the busy highway, but the heart of the old village lies at the end of a leafy lane, three miles from Nottingham.

The church of Holy Rood is approached through a beautiful old lychgate with a shingled roof. The church was built by Robert Fitz-Ranulph, said by some historians to have been one of the knights implicated in the murder of Thomas Becket in Canterbury Cathedral. The chancel collapsed in the 17th century, and the new one, which was added in 1894, is of brick. The tower was added in the

16th century, and the pre-Reformation bells have been re-cast. The oldest part is the north wall in which can still be seen the outline of the Devil's Door which was left open during christenings to allow evil spirits to escape. The bowl of the font, curiously shaped like a trough, may be as old, but its base is modern and its cover is Jacobean. An old hooded doorway lets us in, and between the nave and the very narrow aisle is a 14th century arcade. In 1966 the church celebrated its 800th anniversary.

Edwinstowe. Pleasantly set on the River Maun, it is a gateway to some of the loveliest haunts of old Sherwood Forest.

Above the church and the charming hall the village opens out to a spacious common on the doorstep of Birklands and Bilhagh, two parts of a wonderful stretch of forest with a driving road between, and many a path which we may tread in the wake of Robin Hood and his Merry Men. Birklands has ancient glades and a wealth of oaks, beeches, and the graceful silver birches which give it its name; Bilhagh has the grandest remnants of the old Forest, with magnificent oaks which have seen mediaeval and probably even Norman days, splendid still whether in life or in decay. It is on record that in 1609 there were 21,000 oaks in Birklands and 28,900 in Bilhagh, as well as thousands of other trees.

Within a mile of the church is the Queen or Major Oak, an ancient tree of great renown; it is the glory of Birklands and perhaps the biggest oak in the land. No one knows how many years it has weathered, but it is hale and green and shapely yet in spite of having lost its top in a storm last century. Standing in a little clearing, with oaks and silver birches paying it homage at respectful distance, this Monarch of the Forest has a hollow trunk 30 feet round, strong enough to support unaided the mighty limbs which make a ring of about 260 feet. The branches are held together by a ton of iron bands, and are protected from the weather by 15 hundredweights of lead.

The tradition of the forest clings to the church of St Mary, for here Robin Hood is said to have made Maid Marian his bride. Beautiful inside and out, looking younger than its years with restoration, its

65

stone walls are of rosy hue with many delicate tints here and there. It came into the Domesday Book, but has nothing older than the plain Norman priest's doorway in the chancel.

The lovely tower, over 700 years old, is a landmark with its stout broach spire adorned with fine pinnacles and windows between them. The spire was much rebuilt about 1680 after a storm, and at the same time the people petitioned the king for leave to cut enough of the forest oaks to pay for repair to the rest of the church. Two extraordinary heads, one with great staring eyes and the other with open mouth, are on the tower arch. Among the heads on the 13th century north arcade and the 14th century south arcade are mitred bishops, a pouting face, some with curly hair, and one with smartly trimmed beard.

Most of the windows are mediaeval, one having a little old glass, and the clerestory is 500 years old. A window with Gabriel, Michael, and Raphael is in memory of somebody from Kent who died on a New Year's Eve. The fine font with quatrefoils is 14th century. A piscina in the south aisle is of this time, and two aumbries here have floors formed by the two halves of a 700-year-old coffin lid engraved with shears by the stem of a cross. The mediaeval stone altar, with two crosses, has been set up after being found on the floor of the belfry. Fragments of the old chancel screen are in the organ case and over the altar. The altar table is Jacobean, and under glass on a pillar is a Cavalier's spur found in or near the church. A dwarf pillar piscina, only 16 inches high, has a four-clustered pillar between its head and base; it is 13th century.

An unusual relic is a stone, about 14 inches long, projecting from the north aisle wall, carved along the middle with a kind of milling pattern. It is possible it may have been used for measuring land, and to have been originally 18 inches long, which was the length of a forest foot.

A stone marks the grave in the churchyard of Dr Cobham Brewer, who, while living with his daughter, died at the vicarage here in 1897. A great scholar, he is remembered for his *Dictionary of Phrase and Fable* and his *Reader's Handbook to Literature*, two volumes still used by working journalists. A stone telling us that a native of Scotland

lies here has a touch of the Scotsman's love of the land from which
he comes away.

Egmanton. It lies in a hollow with orchards and trees, the pretty
gardens of some of its houses reached by tiny bridges spanning a
wayside stream. It has a fine little church with something of Norman
days, and memories of a castle built soon after the Conquest. It
stood on the green mound near the church, encircled by a dry moat
and known as Gaddick Hill.

The church of St Mary is by the great chestnuts overhanging the
road in company with shapely old yews. The arresting thing about
the interior is its mediaeval air, which comes chiefly from the red,
white, blue, green, and gold of the modern oak screen, the organ
case over the doorway, and the open pulpit—a most unusual blaze
of colour for a church in this countryside. The handsome screen with
entrance gates has beautiful craftsmanship in its tracery and fan-
vaulting, and has a star-spangled canopy curving above a Crucifixion
group on the roodloft.

We come into the nave by a Norman doorway on which are small
crosses which may have been made by pilgrims. The panelled door
is old. The nave arcade has the English pointed arches on the round
Norman pillars, and the chancel arch, with a face at each side, comes
from the same builders, the men who saw the Norman style changing
into English. Most of the windows are mediaeval, old glass showing
roundels with wreaths and part of a bird, a glowing little figure of
St George, and perhaps St Michael. The massive Norman font has
a beautiful modern cover carved with symbols, the rebuilt chancel
has a 13th century piscina with two arches, and the 13th century
Savile chapel has a charming trefoiled piscina and an aumbry. The
old almsbox was made from a solid block of wood, the nave roof has
old beams, and there is a Jacobean table.

A stone in the sanctuary floor has on it worn portraits of Nicholas
Powtrell and two wives who lived at Egmanton Hall in the time of
Queen Elizabeth I; nothing is left of it now. Gargoyles of quaint
heads, a muzzled bear, and a grotesque with its hands in its mouth
look down from the tower.

Elkesley lies close to lovely Clumber Park, and is by-passed now by the busy A1 road.

The lofty 14th century tower of St Giles church serves as a porch with two doorways. One is 15th century, and in it hangs a fine panelled door of 1612. We come to its north doorway under an arch which is part of the 15th century nave arcade, left outside when the aisle was shortened. It is remarkable to discover that three of the bells have been ringing in this tower for 500 years, two of them inscribed, "I have the name of Gabriel who was sent from Heaven", and "This bell sounds for the praise of Holy Mary", and between the words are coins of their day.

The church was partly rebuilt last century, but it has some 15th century windows (including the clerestory) and a 14th century east window. The old nave roof has two bosses, and between the nave and chancel is an embattled beam. The chancel has no arch; near its entrance is an old niche, and above this is another niche which is the old rood-stair doorway with a new top. There is a Jacobean table, and a massive old oak bench like a glorified settle is crowded with carving. The small bowl of the old font has been set on a queer modern pedestal, after being used as a pump trough. The comical face of a man looks out from the nave arcade, and the quaint face of another smiles between two windows outside.

Elston lies to the south-west of Newark, and has associations with the Darwin family. The long grey hall at the junction of two roads was their birthplace. Here came William Darwin from Lincolnshire when he married the heiress of the Warings; and here to his son Robert (in whom began to develop the love of science which was to make the name a household word) were born two sons, Robert (who wrote the Principia Botanica), and Erasmus the physician, poet, inventor, and scientist.

Born in 1731, Erasmus had a successful career as a doctor in Lichfield. He won a reputation as a poet, and showed his love of living creatures in his *Loves of the Plants* (one of two parts of his *Botanic Garden*) in which he foretold steam locomotion and even the flying machine in these remarkable words:

Soon shall thy arm, Unconquered Steam, afar
Drag the slow barge or drive the rapid car;
Or on wide-waving wings expanded bear
The flying chariot through the fields of air.

He had wonderful powers of observation, and his mind teemed with far-reaching and potential ideas. He invented and suggested many domestic and industrial machines, and was a pioneer in sanitary reform as well as a great advocate of temperance in drinking. We remember him best for his anticipation of the theory of evolution, and for being, through his two marriages, the grandfather of the famous Charles Darwin and of Francis Galton. He spent his last years at Breadsall Priory in Derbyshire, and was buried in Breadsall church in 1802.

The almshouses founded by Ann Darwin nearly two centuries ago are facing the church, which has four tiers of battlements and a slender tower with elaborate pinnacles. Beyond a row of yews is the grey stone rectory, gabled and stately, with flowers in fine array, and a splendid cedar on its lawn.

Though the church is much restored, the two lower stages of the tower are 13th century, the time of three lovely windows in the chancel which have foliage capitals crowning their shafts. The tiny font may be 600 years old. Among the Darwin memorials is one to the father of Erasmus.

The old windmill still stands but is without its cap and sails.

In the lower part of the village is an ancient chapel standing in a field beyond a cluster of farms and cottages. Unused but cared-for, it has a lovely Norman doorway adorned with zigzag, two great 13th century buttresses, two 14th century windows, part of a coffin stone in a wall, and a pulpit with Jacobean carved panels.

Elton is twelve and a half miles south-east of Nottingham on the road to Grantham. The village consists of a number of well-built residences, a few cottages, and the ancient hostelry, The Manor Arms, now fully modernised. Outside this inn, three royal Princes, the Prince of Wales (Duke of Windsor), the Duke of York

F

(George VI) and the Duke of Kent were once photographed at a meet of the Belvoir Hunt.

The church of St Michael and All Angels is only 15 feet wide. Three round arches built up in a wall, coming perhaps from the close of Norman days, tell of a vanished aisle, and in the modern porch is a 14th century doorway which was set back when the aisle was destroyed. The plain font may be 700 years old.

The heavy altar rails are Jacobean, and worked up into the high pews are parts of the mediaeval chancel screen. Two modern oak choir seats are interesting for their carvings of four heads above the names of Knox, Latimer, Cranmer, and Edward VI, who is shown as a young king in cap and ruff. The oak pulpit is ornate with scroll-work panels, and the east window has Paul preaching on Mars Hill.

In 1780 the verger dug up some 200 silver pennies of the reign of Henry II, and was given £10 as a reward.

Epperstone, which lies in the vale of the Dover Beck, is about 8 miles north-east of Nottingham. In the Domesday Book it is referred to as Epreston, and the local entry states that its former owners, Ulviet, Ulvric, and Elsi were dispossessed by the Conqueror. It also notes that the two latter men had no hall, and that inference was that Ulviet (who also owned land at Woodborough) had one, but his share was the smallest and least valuable of the three. His land and mill were granted to Roger de Busli, the larger lands passing to Ralph de Limes and another Norman knight, to whom various estates in this region also went. There are earthworks on Solly or Holy Hill in Epperstone Park, but these are of an unknown date. In 1776 some 1000 copper coins of the 3rd century were turned up in an Epperstone field. A map of 1723 shows that the paper mill was then in operation, and was destined to make all the wads known as Bolton wads for the muzzle-loading guns used by the British Army during the Crimean War and the Indian Mutiny.

The ancient parish church which is dedicated to the Holy Cross, is but one of 83 such churches to be found in England. The first reference to it is in the Domesday Record of 1086, when it was probably built of stone. The present church was built between 1390 and 1450, and stands high above the road. It is approached by a flight of steps climbing up to the churchyard, which is graced by a large cedar tree. There is a small finial among the gravestones under this tree, shaped like a fleur-de-lys, which at one time came from the pinnacle of the church. The present chancel was built in 1776 and is a little narrower and lower than the original.

The 19th century saw numerous restorations take place. A porch was built in 1819 and the spire, which was struck by lightning two years later, was rebuilt at a cost of £49. The clock suffered considerable damage and was replaced by the generosity of John Litchfield Esquire and others in 1865. The years 1853–54 saw the old gallery taken down and new windows put in. Further work was carried out in 1877 and 1878, and between 1853 and the latter, £1140 was spent on restoration. Two oak angels with wings look down from the chancel, whilst close at hand is the altar table, which has an interesting story. In 1819 it was removed from the church and replaced by an altar given by the Baroness Howe. The present altar table was recognised in the laundry of the Manor by Captain Dufty, the agent, and came into his possession and was preserved by his family until 1953, when it was given back to the church by Miss Brett. A further incident is recorded which is worthy of note. An early nineteenth century Rector removed and buried the Norman Font and substituted a smaller one. No one knows the reason for this curious action, but the present font was restored in 1853.

An inscription tells of John Odingsells, who was a Member of Parliament for Notts in Barebones Parliament, which only lasted from July to December, 1653. At the east end of the aisle is a stone figure with praying hands, probably late 13th century and which may be one of the Odingsells family.

Epperstone Manor, which lies close at hand, has only a gateway bearing the letter "H" to remind us of its past glory when it served as an estate for the Howe family, whose admiral won such fame in his naval exploits and died in 1799. The Manor is playing a new role as a unit of the Nottinghamshire Combined Police Authority. Although the aids of modern science abound within its walls, Epperstone remains a very rural place.

Everton. Pleasant with its red roofs and winding ways, it lies in the the valley of the River Idle, and looks across miles of reclaimed fenland which stretch as far as Yorkshire.

The church of Holy Trinity has Norman remains and one treasure older still—an ancient tympanum belonging perhaps to Saxon days, crudely engraved with the heads of two dragons facing each other with tongues outstretched. It is over the doorway through which we enter.

The lovely chancel arch and the fine little horseshoe arch to the tower are Norman. Both are adorned with zigzag and thrown into relief by the dim backgrounds of a 19th century apse and the old tower. Except for its arch and a Norman window, the tower is chiefly 15th century. The Norman arch frames a splendid tub font carved with arcading and bands of zigzag and cable. It is a 19th century copy of the original Norman font, of which a battered part is now in the church after a sojourn in the vicarage garden. A fine little arcade of about 1190 divides the nave and aisle, and a capital carved with foliage crowns the pillar between the two bays. From the 15th century come the clerestory and the windows of the nave and aisle.

There are four old armchairs, and a huge and rather battered stone has the worn portraits of a 13th century knight and his lady.

There is a disused windmill at the south end of the village.

Farndon is close to Newark on the banks of the River Trent. In the middle of the village at the end of a quaint avenue of lopped limes is the church of St Peter with fragments perhaps from Saxon days.

The tower is mainly 14th century, with later windows. A beautiful 13th century arcade with pillars of grouped shafts divides the nave from the south aisle. The other arcade and its aisle have been rebuilt, but it is in the north wall that we find the oldest work, in crude herringbone masonry, seen outside, and a simple round-headed doorway. They are part of the first church on this site and are early Norman or Saxon. There is a broken stone coffin in the church.

The clerestory and a few windows are 14th century. The font is as old, but its richly pinnacled cover, like the oak screen, is modern. The simple oak roof of the nave has richly moulded 17th century beams, and the chancel has its old piscina.

There are yachting clubs and good fishing in the vicinity.

Farnsfield is an attractive village near to Southwell, with some traces of Roman camps in the area. One was Combs Farm Camp, one and a quarter miles south-west of Farnsfield, and the other is at Hexgreave Park.

Attractive outside with red stone walls, gabled clerestory windows, and a spire, the church of St Michael stands near the small three-cornered green. The lower part of the tower comes from about 1400, and is all that is left of the original structure, the rest being rebuilt in 1860. A curious feature of the tower is that its north wall, with an outside buttress, is enclosed inside the new building. The font is the only old relic. A tombstone in the churchyard to the village blacksmith, William Butler, who died in 1740 reads as follows:

> *Our tongs and hammers lie declined,*
> *Our bellows too have lost their wind,*
> *Our fires extinct, our forge decayed,*
> *And in the dust our vices laid.*
> *Our coals are spent, our irons gone,*
> *Our nails are drove, our work is done.*

It was at Farnsfield that Augustus Charles Gregory, the explorer, was born in 1819. At the age of ten he and his brother accompanied their father to Australia. Years later his exploration of this continent was recognised by the Royal Geographical Society, who sent him in 1855 on an expedition to the interior. 5000 miles of territory were added to the map by this work, which brought its leader the founder's medal of the society.

Finningley is Nottinghamshire's most northerly village, part of a curiously projecting bit of the county which makes a right angle

73

between Yorkshire and Lincolnshire. Three open greens adorn its winding ways, one shaded by a great oak, one where we turn by the school to find the church, and the biggest with its lofty elm in the middle of the village.

The manor house was Swayne's before the Conquest, and its most famous owner since was Martin Frobisher, the intrepid seamen of Elizabethan days. It was held by his family till the end of the 17th century, when Cornelius Vermuyden, the great Dutch engineer, acquired land here in connection with the attempt then being made to drain the fenland east of the village.

Before the little school and its schoolhouse were built the school was in the churchyard, which served as a playground. We may be sure John Bigland would know the old school, for he was master here some years. He wrote a host of educational books, and is remembered as one of our forerunners, for he wrote a fine survey of Yorkshire in a wonderful series of books known as the *Beauties of England* a century and more ago.

The church of Holy Trinity lies at the end of a little road overhung by fine trees. It is a fitting setting for the ancient church, which is of much more interest than its modest appearance suggests. Except for the embattled parapet, the Normans built the low tower with two tiny splayed windows in its west wall, belfry windows with central shafts, and a fine archway to the nave. They built the beautiful doorway letting us in, with simple mouldings and capitals with worn carving. The plain font and some masonry in the south wall are also of their day.

The porch with a stone roof was made new last century, and has a timbered and gabled front. Built into its walls are four coffin stones and fragments of others engraved with crosses, one with a pair of shears by the stem.

The nave arcade comes from about 1280, as does the fine arch on clustered pillars opening to the 14th century chancel, which has three sedilia and a piscina with two drains. The only coloured glass fills the east window with realistic scenes of the battlefield, stark tree trunks and shattered buildings, and angels with trumpets above a figure of Our Lord whose hand is on the shoulder of a soldier. It is a tribute to those who served in the war, and to 22 who did not return. The oak pulpit was made in the year after Queen Elizabeth died, and from the close of that century comes a wooden memorial with a canopied frame.

Perhaps the chief charm of this bright place lies in the open timber roofs, with much fine decoration. Six kingposts in the nave have curved and carved braces, and on the tie beams are medallions of flowers and floral bosses, one showing foliage coming from a quaint head. With the 17 floral bosses in the chancel is a crowned king with his sword and sceptre, and another has a bishop with staff and cross.

From the rear of the church can be seen R.A.F. Finningley, which is situated close by.

Fiskerton. With its leafy road running along a bank of the Trent, its quay-like promenade above the river, and its pleasant houses with look-outs, it is a delightful little village, and fishermen love it well.

The only church in Fiskerton is Methodist, and those who are Church of England go to the church at nearby Morton.

It is all very peaceful now, but it looked out on a bloodstained land over four centuries ago, when many men were drowned in the river. At East Stoke across the river was fought in 1487 the terrible battle which finally brought to an end the Wars of the Roses, when the army of Henry VII routed the Yorkists with the pretender Lambert Simnel. The rebels were driven from the old Fosse Way towards the river meadows, down a steep track which has since been known as the Red Gutter because of the ghastly slaughter here.

Flawborough. One of the smallest of Notts villages is this, where we see lovely views and hear that people never die. Into its panorama come Elston and Cotham, Shelton enshrined in trees, Sibthorpe and its fine dovecote, Thoroton's lovely tower, Belvoir Castle, and Bottesford's spire.

We can well believe the village is a good place for length of days, for, counting the ages on seven gravestones, we found the average to be 84. But someone found an answer as to why life even here must end, for another stone has the words:

It is no wonder we turn to clay
When rocks and stones and monuments decay.

The small church of St Peter was made new a century ago, but a fine Norman doorway with zigzag in its arch lets us into the modern tower. The bowl of the font, enriched with interlaced arcading, is also Norman, and has a cover of about 1660. A plain chest is over 400 years old. The chancel has its old piscina and mediaeval tracery.

Fledborough lies off the main road down a quiet lane leading to the Trent. When it was built in the 13th century, Fledborough was a thriving little port on the River Trent, at that time an important waterway connecting the Midlands with London and the Continent. With the decline of those waterways the village declined too.

So remote does it seem that we are not surprised to hear that it was a sort of Gretna Green in the 18th century, when a rector with the pleasant name of Sweetapple was willing to grant marriage licences to anyone. In the 19th century famous folk found their way here; Dr Arnold, the famous headmaster of Rugby, came to marry the rector's daughter in 1820, and nine years later came John Keble to bury the rector.

Flaede's burgh (as it was once known) was given by Lady Godiva to the church of Stow, Lincolnshire, but after the Norman Conquest passed to the Lisures who were liege men to the Lord of Tickhill.

Nothing remains of the Church mentioned in Domesday (it was probably of wood). It can be assumed that the Lisures built the first stone church towards the end of the 12th century. Of this edifice there only remains the tower. The nave was rebuilt with aisles in the early 14th century. One of the church's great possessions is the beautiful 14th century glass in some of the north aisle windows. The original chancel was pulled down in 1764, and rebuilt in 1891.

There are some fragments of an Easter sepulchre, an arched recess containing the tomb of a Canon of Lincoln who was at one time rector of the parish, and a wimpled female figure of the 14th century.

76

The register dates from 1562. There is an old stoup by the door, and the font is 600 years old. There is also a pillar almsbox dating from 1684. In the wall of the porch is an old sundial in pieces. The church has two bells, one dated 1310 and the other 1600.

Flintham. It lies by a fine belt of woodland stretching to the Trent a mile away. From the Fosse Way we have a glimpse of the hall in its splendid background of trees; it was built last century on the site of the old home of the Hose family, who were its lords from the time of Henry III to Elizabeth's day. From the road below the village we have a lovely view of the park.

The church is dedicated to St Augustine. The 13th century tower, with a pyramid roof, stands between the nave and the chancel, telling of the time when the building had the shape of a cross. The transepts were lost and the arches leading to them were blocked when the nave was made new over a century ago, but the two fine tower arches still left frame an effective picture of the chancel, with steps up to the sanctuary, some beautiful old lancets deeply splayed, and the old piscina. The reredos has old carving in the panels, the altar rails may be Elizabethan, a chest and the font cover are Jacobean, and the font itself is 14th century.

On a low tomb lies a battered stone knight in chain mail, his legs crossed. He belonged to the Hose family, and is precious to the village because he may have founded the 13th century church. A tablet tells us of Richard Hacker, who owned land here and was High Sheriff of Notts three years before his nephew led the king to the scaffold.

Gamston is trim and pleasant with many trees, and lies on the east bank of the River Idle, on the border of the old Sherwood Forest.

The all-embattled church of St Giles with its fine clerestory is a charming picture set in fields and woods, crowning a ridge which rises gently from the river. A round turret climbs at a corner of the nave. The massive tower, one of the finest in this countryside, has eight pinnacles 120 feet from the ground, and is a grand tribute to its early 15th century builder, who was perhaps Sir Nicholas Monboucher of 1385, owner of vast estates. The battered stone figure of a cross-legged knight lying in the aisle may be his.

Though much of the church is 15th century, the nave arcade, some walling in the aisle, and the chancel arch (one of its corbels having a face with bared teeth) come from the end of the 13th century. In the chancel lies a priest in robes, his tonsured head resting on a cushion held by two angels; and built into the chancel wall is a coffin stone showing the head and shoulders of a priest recessed in a quatrefoil.

The classical scholar, Henry Fynes Clinton, was born here in 1781. He was educated at Southwell, Westminster and Oxford, and was for a number of years Member of Parliament for Aldborough. In 1824 he published a great work on Greek Chronology and in 1845 a work on Roman History. He died in 1852.

Gedling. The fine view of the Trent Valley as we drop down the hill from Mapperley Plains is not to be forgotten, nor the charming picture of Gedling nestling below, with its church spire soaring above the trees.

The tower and its lofty spire is part of a beautiful old church built of stone from a local quarry. It is one of the earliest examples of a tower and a spire of the same time, for both are about six centuries old. The spire is renowned for the pronounced bulging of its eight sides between its tiers of windows, in one of its image niches is a mailed knight, and below the battlements of the tower are 24 quaint heads. In a niche by the west window of the south aisle is a saint.

Though most of the church comes from between 1250 and 1340, there are traces of an earlier one in the lower walling of the chancel, and in a small window high up near the tower arch. A splendid stone-roofed porch leads us inside, where stately nave arcades of about 1300, below a 15th century clerestory, divide the nave and aisles. The sedilia and piscina, richly moulded, are 600 years old, as is the font. A coffin stone by the altar shows a deacon, perhaps of the 12th century, and another near the tower arch has the head and feet of a mediaeval priest. The fine pulpit was made from old carved bench-ends, and there is lovely modern craftsmanship in the chancel screen, the stalls, and the organ case with a figure of St Cecilia.

In Gedling churchyard, lie two great cricketers, their graves separated by about the length of a cricket pitch. They were Arthur Shrewsbury, whom Dr W. G. Grace described as the greatest batsman of his age, and his friend Alfred Shaw, who was known as Emperor of Bowlers.

A short distance from the village is Gedling Colliery, which was developed by the Digby Colliery Company Ltd., and where shaft sinking was commenced in 1899. This was completed in 1902, and production commenced in 1904. Today this pit turns out more than a million tons of coal annually.

Gonalston. If you turn off the main Nottingham to Southwell road a little way past the Magna Carta Inn, you will come to the village of Gonalston. It can also be approached from Epperstone.

Its name is pronounced "Gunnalston", Gunnalston being the tun or farm of Gunnolf the Dane. Erbertus, one of William Peveril's men, was the owner of the village at the time of the Domesday Book. His daughter Emma married Ivo de Heriz. Their descendants owned Gonalston until 1527, when they sold it to George Monox of London. The present owner, Commander P. Francklin, is descended from the Monoxes.

The church of St Lawrence is Early English and is approached by a flowered walk and fine avenue of trimmed yew trees past the large old Rectory. A tower and spire crown the little church, which was rebuilt last century. Looking out from the hoods of the windows is a gallery of heads; a bearded man and a woman wearing a wimple (a mediaeval headdress) are to be seen at the porch, and a laughing boy with his tongue out is not far away. Most of the fine grey-walled chancel built about 1300 still remains, now three steps lower than the rest of the building, and having in its north wall a blocked arch which led to a vanished chapel. Up to 1787 the church had a northern aisle which continued eastwards to form a chancel chapel, and on the west gable was a wooden belfry. The fabric then was chiefly 14th century. In 1787 a diminution was carried out by Sir Phillip

Monox, who pulled down the aisle and chapel and flung the sepulchral slabs and effigies into a pit under a pew in the nave. Here they were found in 1848 by Mr. R. Westmacott, R.A., who had the satisfaction of recovering all three early de Heriz effigies, two knights in mail and a lady. In 1853 the church was again rebuilt, including a north aisle where the effigies again rest. Much of the old chancel remains with geometrical windows 1290–1300.

About half a mile to the east of the church on the Thurgarton Road is Spital Farm, which marks the spot of a hospital for lepers founded before 1179. It was about this time that William de Heriz left two water mills to the foundation. In 1289 (the spital being without a master) John Romanus, Archbishop of York, ordered John de Heriz, the owner of Gonalston, to appoint a new one, which John did. He also augmented the income and ordained that mass should be celebrated in Gonalston Church twice a week. Kirkby, who was the rector of Gonalston from 1527 to 1586, was largely responsible for its preservation through troublesome times of the Reformation, and the income formed part of the living of the rectors of Gonalston. The story goes that there is a tunnel linking the farm with Thurgarton Priory and it was used by the monks.

Between the village and Lowdham is a gaunt old mill by the Dover Beck, one of many once turned by this stream in the days of child slavery. In 1799 about 80 small children came down to one of the mills here. One of them who survived was Robert Blincoe, although he was crippled and deformed by the life. Robert was seven at the time he took up his employment, and his working hours were fourteen or sixteen hours a day at the machines. Although apprenticed till twenty-one, many died before they reached this age.

In the centre of the village there is a blacksmith's forge, built in the shape of a horseshoe.

With a population of about 150, this typical Nottinghamshire village lies sheltered by low hills in pleasant countryside where the Dover Beck flows to the Trent.

Gotham. Six and a half miles south of Nottingham lies the village of Gotham. The first part of its name tells of goats, of which the

Saxons maintained large flocks, whilst the suffix "ham" is old English for meadow or home—for goats. It is not known by whom the settlement was founded.

Just outside the village on a hillside was the place chosen for the hundred Moot, upon which at frequent intervals the Saxons and Danes and their mediaeval ancestors assembled in the open air, to dispense justice and administer the affairs of the 30 or more villages of the Hundred of Rushcliffe. Below the ridge is the reputed site of Rushcliffe Hall where the St Andrew family lived, who were lords of the Manor of Gotham for many generations. This Rushcliffe figures in the Domesday Book as Risecliff, and it has given its name to the Wapentake of Rushcliffe, and to the parliamentary division of the county in which it is situated. The village is also said to have had a castle, but little is known about it, and no vestige remains.

The fame of Gotham rests upon the old traditions of the follies of its inhabitants. Tradition goes that the villagers feigned madness on hearing that King John intended building a hunting lodge in their village, and because of the superstition that the ground which a king passed over must ever after be a public road. It was felt that if the King's messengers found nothing but fools in Gotham, then he would not choose to live among them. The Wise Men of Gotham therefore decided to try to fool the King. They tried to drown an eel in a pond, burned down a forge to get rid of a wasps' nest, built a hedge round a cuckoo in an attempt to cage it in, and then blamed themselves when it escaped, for not having built the hedge high enough. They also sent cheeses rolling downhill to go their own way to Nottingham. There are many more tales about the Wise Men of Gotham.

The alabaster men of mediaeval Nottingham achieved wide fame as makers of monuments and images, and though much of their gypsum came from Chellaston, no small quantity was obtained from the deeper quarries at Gotham, where large blocks of the finest quality were raised. The trade has been in existence for seven centuries, and late in the Victorian era the industry languished, but when the Great Central Railway was made, a branch line was laid to the quarries. To-day only one gypsum mine is operating, and most of the material goes by road.

81

The old village church dedicated to St Lawrence is chiefly 13th and 14th century, and has an unbuttressed tower and a sturdy broached spire of peculiar interest. They are believed to have been built from base to summit at one time, in the 13th century, the spire being one of the earliest stone spires in the country, and the only one in Notts to follow the design of the ancient wooden ones. It has two tiers of lights, and springs from a corbel table, its upper part having been made new. A 15th century clerestory crowns the nave with its arcades of the 13th and 14th centuries. One of the older capitals is entwined with foliage springing from four heads.

Of two monuments to the St Andrew family, who knew the village from the 13th to the 17th century, one has kneeling figures of William, his two wives, and their four children; the other shows John St Andrew of 1625, the last male of his line, kneeling with his wife under a canopy. With them are three daughters and a pretty babe in a cradle, the only son, who died 14 days old.

The chancel is striking with colour—a red and white panelled roof crowing grey walls and blue furnishings. The east window frames an Easter morning scene in rich colours, with the three Marys and the angel at the tomb.

Granby is a village of narrow winding lanes near the Leicestershire border.

The church of All Saints consists of nave, chancel, tower, and vestry, and stands in a closed churchyard in the centre of the village. Domesday Book records a church, built before the Norman Conquest by William D'Aynecourt, a priest, and another church at Sutton, which has long since disappeared, though the field in which it stood is still called the Holy Field. In 1155 Ralph D'Aynecourt founded the Priory of Thurgarton, and gave the prior the livings of Granby and other Vale churches. The roll of incumbents dates from 1253. At the dissolution of the monasteries the patronage passed from the prior to King Philip of Spain and Queen Mary, thence to Queen Elizabeth I, who gave it to John Manners, founder of the ducal line of Rutland. The present patron is the Bishop of Southwell.

The lower part of the massive tower, with its wide arch to the nave, is 13th century; the rest of it is 500 years old, with battlements and pinnacles above a fine band of quatrefoils.

A blocked doorway and the wide chancel arch are 13th century, and a blocked archway in the chancel, which led to a vanished chapel, is 14th century. The north doorway may be 600 years old, and has its original door on two splendid hinges. Projecting from the north wall is a built-up arcade which divided the nave from a lost aisle, and four heads with human faces are still here. The bowl of the 14th century font has been turned upside down to make a base for a new bowl, the panelled pulpit comes from 1629, and the altar rails may be about 1700. A tall lancet is one of several mediaeval windows, but the east window is modern. A floorstone of 1749 is to Abigail Anna Frost, sister of Archbishop Secker.

Granby treasures 14 old benches with quaintly carved poppy-heads, showing heads of women in horned headdress, animals and reptiles, grotesque heads with protruding tongues, and others with foliage coming from their grinning mouths. Most interesting of them all is one with a merman and a mermaid, she with her comb and mirror as she has been pictured since men have gone to sea.

In 1950 the tower was restored and three years later the five bells were refitted and a sixth bell added in memory of two church-wardens. In 1958 the south porch was opened and a vestry was built. In 1959 an oak screen was added, made of panels from Rufford Abbey. The altar has also been restored in memory of a former vicar. The churchyard contains some very finely inscribed slate head-stones. An old scratch dial is just discernible on the south buttress of the tower.

Greasley is some seven miles north-west of Nottingham, and from its hilltop there are fine views of the Erewash Valley.

The parish church is dedicated to St Mary the Virgin, and stands high above the main road. Four great beeches overhang the gate which leads to the church, which was much restored last century. Part of the chancel is old, and the fine tower, with a crown of eight pinnacles, is 15th century. The font, like a chalice, is perhaps as old as the tower. Among the memorials of the Rollestons of Watnall

Hall is a bust of Lancelot of 1685, a high sheriff beloved by all who knew him. We read of John Hides who was vicar for 51 years of last century; and we remember that William Warburton, a Bishop of Gloucester famous for his books, was vicar here for a short time, and that a pastor of the Pilgrim Fathers, John Robinson, was married in this church, his bride coming from Beauvale Priory Farm. There was a church on this site as long ago as 1086, and the list of parish priests can be traced back to 1254.

Gringley-on-the-hill. Halfway between Bawtry and Gainsborough is this airy village of lovely views and steep and dangerous ways. It climbs the hillside and spreads along a ridge at the end of a long range of low hills which stretch from Nottingham; and in Beacon Hill, a green mound at the very end of the ridge, Gringley finds its glory.

From this site of an ancient encampment, where Prince Rupert is said to have camped before riding to the relief of Newark, is a matchless panorama reaching for 20 or 30 miles whichever way we turn. We see the gleaming towers of Lincoln, the Great North Road riding straight through the land beyond the valley of the River Idle, and the Cars which carry the eye to Yorkshire, a flat area like a great sea of reclaimed fenland, but a beautiful sight from Beacon Hill when the sun lights up the golden corn and shadows make waves on the fields.

Strikingly set where the road divides to make a dangerous bend and a steep drop, is the fine old village cross, and near it, standing well above the road, is the church of St Peter and St Paul, which has been restored this century. The tower, with battlements and pinnacles which were all in a heap inside it till the restoration, is mainly 15th century, though a built-up arch in the outside north wall may be Norman. Against this wall is an ancient stone coffin. From the 13th century comes an arch to the chancel chapel and the north arcade of the nave, its leaning pillars on massive bases. Among many mediaeval windows are those of the 15th century clerestory, and the east window of the new south aisle shows St George with the dragon, St Michael with scales and flaming sword, and Christ crowned.

A treasure of the church is a beautiful shaft piscina 600 years old, with natural foliage encircling the top of a round column. Some old timbers remain in the roofs of the nave and the north aisle, and of four old bosses in the nave one shows the grotesque head of an animal with its tongue out, and another a man's face with a great moustache and a small beard. A quaint face with pursed lips and goggle eyes looks tirelessly out from the wall over the small doorway in the tower. The modern screens are neat and good, and a charming little angel crowns the modern cover of the font.

Grove is a pretty hillside village close to East Retford. As its name suggests, it is surrounded by trees.

A lychgate with stout oak timbers opens to the pretty churchyard, where the small aisleless church of St Helen was built in 1882 in the style of 600 years ago. Its fine tower has a spire with two tiers of tiny dormers, and is very neat inside with its vaulted stone roof and a charming arch to the nave. There is rich carving in the font, and also on a niche on the porch, sheltering a crowned figure of St Helena.

The only relics of the old church, which stood close by, are two floorstones in the tower, one showing a chalice by the stem of a cross, the other with splendid portraits of Hugh Hercy of 1455 and his wife Elizabeth, restored by a descendant. Hugh is a knight in armour with sword and dagger, with a Tam o' Shanter kind of hat on his head, and his feet on a dog. His lady has a long pleated gown and a head-dress at a rakish angle.

Gunthorpe. Once owned by Simon de Montfort, it finds its beauty by a wide peaceful reach of the Trent where the river sweeps on its way to Hoveringham. Opposite Gunthorpe's quiet meadows are woods and cliffs crowned by the pretty village of East Bridgford.

At one time these villages were connected by a ferry service, and in 1875 by an iron toll bridge. The latter was replaced in 1937 by a bridge of three spans and opened to traffic on November 17 by the Prince of Wales who later became Duke of Windsor.

The village chapel of St John the Baptist dates from 1849.

In the summer months Gunthorpe is a popular picnic spot with the added attractions of regattas and water ski-ing.

Halam is pleasant with its orchards and a stream flowing to the River Greet, and sheltered by the low hills between it and Southwell.

The church here is dedicated to St Michael the Archangel, and dates from 1100 AD. The bell that calls its villagers to worship is known in the countryside as the bell of a thousand years. It hangs in a sturdy 13th century tower with pinnacles and a squat pyramid roof, a muzzled bear and a dragon among its gargoyles, and an arch all askew opening to the nave. The bell is said to be Norman and is still sound, though its 18th century companion is cracked and never struck. The fine Norman chancel arch has scalloped capitals enriched with Van Dyck and diamond pattern. The font comes from the close of the 12th century; the beautiful little nave arcade from the end of the 13th was opened out when the aisle was made new half a century ago. A projecting piscina rests on a carved head, and there is a handsomely carved Elizabethan altar table. The oak lectern of our century has a splendid St Michael in a niche. We see the patron saint again in a 13th century lancet. Four lovely panels in other windows, by William Morris and Burne-Jones, show Gabriel bringing the good news, the meeting of Elizabeth and Mary, the Transfiguration, and the Ascension. A window rather like a page in a child's picture book has the Nativity with a choir of angels, roses and passion flowers climbing round the stable at Bethlehem with the oxen, an ass, and a lamb standing by, a dovecote and the doves, shepherds with an English sheep dog, and a shepherd with his crook. Four charming 15th century panels shining in a chancel window have Eve spinning, Adam digging, St Christopher carrying the Child, and St Anthony with his staff; birds are in the borders. On this window outside are two laughing faces, and on the north wall is a whistling boy.

Halloughton. Just off the highway to Southwell, its few farms and dwellings straggle along a winding lane, all up and down and buried in orchards, going to the pretty Halloughton Dumble.

The neat wayside church stands in a glorious company of elms and limes, silver birch and copper beech, an old yew, and a wide-spreading sycamore. It is said that Henry Kirke White loved to sit and dream in this charming seclusion. Here he may have sat and thought, as once he sat and wrote, that

Earthly things
Are but the transient pageants of an hour
And earthly pride is like the passing flower

Though it was made new last century, the church of St James keeps its original east end with two lancet windows. Its chief possession is the low 15th century screen, carved with tracery.

At one end of a farmhouse opposite the church is all that remains of a 14th century house associated with Southwell Minster, the home of a canon. Its stone walls are very thick, and some tracery is still left in one of its windows.

Harby is the most easterly Nottinghamshire village, close to the border with Lincolnshire. It was here that Queen Eleanor of Castile died on November 27, 1290. She came riding here with Edward I in September of that year, but was taken ill, and stayed at the manor house of Richard de Weston, where she died. Her body was brought to London and buried in Westminster Abbey. The resting-places on the solemn journey were marked by what have come to be known as Eleanor crosses, the last of which gave its name to Charing Cross.

In the next field to the churchyard is part of the moat which protected the manor house where she spent her last days, but nothing of the house is left. The old chapel in which the king founded a chantry to her memory has gone, save for two relics in the new stone church built near the old site. One is the plain Norman doorway opening to the vestry from outside; the other is the 14th century font. Here, too, are the only memorials Harby has to the queen, a small brass plate on the altar step telling us that she died here, and her little crowned figure in a niche above the tower doorway, with shields on each side of Castile and Leon, England and Ponthieu, as on her tomb at Westminster. Four tiles in the pavement near the brass inscription have similar shields.

The aisleless church of All Saints is made into a cross by the vestry on one side, and the tower (crowned by a shingled spire rising

87

120 feet) on the other. A tiny old chest has a mass of carving on the front.

Harworth lies north-west from Blyth amid beautiful woodland and river scenery.

The church of All Saints came into the Domesday Book, but, though fragments of Norman work remain, most of it was made new last century, when the Norman nave was pulled down, and transepts were added to give it the shape of a cross. The chancel was rebuilt in Norman fashion, but has still its lovely original arch, with unusual ornament and detached pillars, a very rare survival in two Norman sedilia, and the base of a Norman piscina given a new head. The fine south doorway, with its consecration cross, was built when the Norman style was passing into English.

All the walls are embattled, and eight pinnacles crown the tower, which has a modern west window in its 14th century base. Built into an outside wall is an ancient stone carved with a cross, and in a recess of another is a stone coffin.

We have from the road by Serlby Park a splendid view of the red brick hall at the head of terraced lawns, its gaunt lines softened by a frame of dense woods. The road becomes here and there a glorious aisle of beeches, then runs with the sparkling River Ryton to a stone bridge, where the river flows on to the Idle and our way goes to the Great North Road.

Oaks and beeches are grouped about the park in stately grandeur, and beech avenues come close to the house and thread the lovely woods. An old heronry in the park has many nests. The hall has been the home of the Galways since the 18th century, and was built on the site of the older house about 1770.

Haughton. So secluded is this place that it is hard to imagine the great days when the Longvilliers, the Manlovels, and the Stanhopes were its lords; or the 16th century days of pomp and splendour when it came into the family of Holles, who had found wealth in London bakehouses and honour at the Mansion House, for one was Lord Mayor.

They rebuilt the old homestead of the Stanhopes in splendid style, and made it one of the most famous houses of the county, known far and wide for its hospitality. They even kept a company of players. Denzil Holles, most famous son of his family, the statesman who held down the Speaker in the Chair while the Commons passed the Resolutions against the Crown, was born here in 1599. He was one of the Five Members Charles tried to arrest. His grand home fell into decay when the family, then Earls of Clare, made Welbeck their home; its only remains are in the moat and the stone foundations of the buildings of a farmhouse on its site.

A walk across the fields, in company with the little tree-shaded River Maun, brings us to the farm; and just beyond it, on the brink of the river, is the roofless ruin of the chapel of St James, with mighty trees in its mantle of beech and yew, chestnut and sycamore. It saw Haughton's great days come and go.

Open to the wind and sun and rain, and overgrown with weeds, it has still the old bellcote, herringbone masonry in the walls, a Norman doorway adorned all round with zigzag and cable, and the battered bowl of a Norman font. The traceried mediaeval windows are for the most part blocked, and in the nave wall are the short pillars and great capitals of an arcade which led to a vanished aisle. A fine pointed arch leads to the chancel, which has a tiny piscina and an image bracket. From the close of the 12th century comes an arch to the small north chapel, which has lost its east wall. A broken floorstone carved with a cross lies in the nave. One of three memorials to the Stanhopes is the broken figure of a woman in a long gown, her features worn, and her hands still at prayer; the others are gravestones, each showing the upper part of a figure recessed in a quatrefoil.

It is said that Sir William Holles, who died in 1590, was buried here. He was known as the Good Lord of Haughton for his display of hospitality; no one was ever turned from his door.

Hawksworth is one of the smaller villages in the county, and cottages and church line the long byroad.

The church of St Mary and All Saints has a tower, the lower part of which is 13th century, and the upper part 17th century. The nave, north aisle, and chancel were rebuilt in the 19th century.

Part of the Wars of the Roses was fought here, and a footpath leads across the old battlefield to the village of Thoroton. One field in the village bears the name of Butts, which reminds us that archery was once practised here. Yews were grown in the churchyard for bows and arrows.

Hawton lies well off the beaten track, where the River Devon flows two miles from Newark.

Its church of All Saints has some of the most exquisite 14th century stonework in the land. The house of the Compton and Molineux families has gone, but there is more than memory of them here, for a Compton gave the church a chancel of which a cathedral city might be proud, and a Molineux built a tower which is a landmark of compelling beauty.

Sir Robert de Compton's noble chancel was completed about 1325. A fine stringcourse runs under the windows and round the buttresses, in one of which is an image niche. The great east window of seven lights, with lovely tracery and shafts, is said to be one of the best of its time in England. It is difficult to do justice to the delicacy and richness of the sculpture in the chancel, thought to have been the work of that marvellous band of craftsmen who gave us the Chapter House of Southwell.

On the north side, under a carved cornice and all within a space 17 feet wide and 12 feet high, is Hawton's famous Easter Sepulchre, with a lovely founder's tomb recess and a most charming doorway, both with feathered arches. The doorway once opened to a now vanished chapel, and in the wall of the recess is the tiniest of peepholes, which gave the chapel a view of the altar. In the arch of the recess a man's face is peeping from the leaves, and two little women in wimples are reading books. On the finial stands a bishop, and within it lies the battered figure of Sir Robert de Compton in chain mail, his knees crossed. He died in 1330, and this glorious chancel is his lasting monument.

The Easter Sepulchre tells its story in three sections. At the foot four soldiers are crouching in sleep, each in a niche, and all wearing chain mail with helmets, swords, and shields carved with heads and dragons. In a canopied niche above them is Our Lord (now headless) rising from the tomb with one foot in the grave. At one side of Him are the three Marys, on the other side is an exquisite little niche where the Sacrament was kept from Good Friday till Easter Sunday. In the top compartment a fine scene of the Ascension shows the Disciples gazing up to catch the last glimpse of the Saviour's feet as they disappear into a cloud; an angel is at each side, and on the finial of the canopy below are His footprints.

In the opposite wall are the magnificent sedilia and double piscina, a gem of mediaeval art in perfect preservation. The three niches of the sedilia, with vaulted canopies and delicate leaf ornament in the hollow of the mouldings, are divided by shafted buttresses crowned by lofty pinnacles. Among their luxuriance of carving are two bishops and a king, two men on all fours among the foliage, two men gathering grapes (one cutting a bunch with his knife), and a fine pelican in her nest on the tree-top. Six saints, standing on little men and crouching animals, are being crowned by angels carved in the cornice above it all. A winged lizard and another winged animal are in the delicate capitals of the piscina, which has a quaint fiddler on one side and a harpist on the other.

The stately 15th century tower, wearing a crown of eight pinnacles and battlements above quatrefoil moulding and hooded belfry windows, was built by Sir Thomas Molineux. Descended from a warrior who came with the Conqueror, he was father of a famous judge, and ancestor of the Earls of Sefton. The original oak door, adorned with tracery and remains of a prayer, still hangs in the west doorway, which has Sir Thomas's arms and those of his second wife carved in the spandrels.

Some years ago bullets were found embedded in the old door, perhaps a relic of the Civil War, for only a mile and a half away is the Queen's Sconce, a famous fortification of the royal garrison.

The massive oak benches are as old as the tower, and so are the beautiful oak chancel screen (almost unrestored), a fine bracket and canopy over a lifesize figure in the south aisle, the clerestory, and most of the windows in the aisles. The east windows and a piscina in each aisle are 14th century, as is the font. From the close of the 13th century come the north arcade and the north doorway; the south arcade is a little later. The only colour in the windows is in a few old fragments of glass showing oak leaves in black and gold.

Hayton. It is three miles from Retford and one from the River Idle, a straggling village with surprisingly fine remains in its small church. In the churchyard lie three mediaeval stones with moss-grown figures carved in relief.

There is Norman masonry in the nave of St Peter's Church, and the lovely doorway through which we enter comes from the end of the 12th century, when the Norman style was passing. The splendid porch which shelters it is a rare possession for a village church; built about 1400, it has a stone-ribbed roof, and is enriched with pinnacles which are a study in themselves, for the crockets at the foot of every pinnacle are tiny sculptured heads of human folk and animals.

The beautiful nave arcade, 700 years old, has round arches and pillars, and one capital carved with foliage. The tower was built while Richard II was king. The fine font (about 1400) has a bowl carved with foliage and set on an arcaded stem. There are two old piscinas, a 13th century bracket carved with foliage, a Jacobean altar table, and a 500-year-old chest with a slot for Peter's Pence.

On a modern brass are angels in memory of Percy Hartshorne Cooper, a High Sheriff of last century. The old moated home of the Hartshornes (Hayton Castle) has gone, but the name survives in a farmhouse. Another brass tells of William Chapman Mee, who was vicar here for 53 years of last century.

Headon has a fine viewpoint from the little church of St Peter, where for 600 years two stone faces have been looking out from the tower on a patchwork of fields and woodland.

An unusually spacious tower, it looks almost as wide as it is high; it is thought that its builders meant it to be higher and perhaps to have a spire, and that the Black Death stopped the work, except for the addition of the embattled parapet. It has tiny lancets and a 14th century west window, and inside, with 17th century altar rails across its arch, it is a charming setting for the modern font mounted high on three steps, its bowl resting on a wreath of water lilies. From the 15th century come most of the windows and the arcades, their end arches on old and new brackets, and fine heads of women and bearded men. The lovely Jacobean pulpit, with two grotesque figures supporting a canopy, is daintily carved with arcading. There is a splendid dug-out chest shaped from the trunk of a giant oak, its wood seven inches thick in parts, the old hinges and hasps fixed on to a new lid.

At the foot of an oak crucifix hangs a small crown of thorns which were gathered near the spot where the Judgment Hall stood in Jerusalem when Christ was tried before Pilate. This crown must be very like the one He wore.

Sir Hardolph Wasteneys, the last male of his line, died in 1742 and has an inscription here. Headon had belonged to them from the 14th century, and Sir Hardolph rebuilt the old home, little dreaming that it would be pulled down before his century was done.

Hickling is on the edge of the Vale of Belvoir and seven miles south of Bingham.

The church of St Mary stands well back off the road among trees.

The tower has been rebuilt from its 14th century material, and a newel stair climbs from a small mediaeval doorway to the parapet, passing the works of the clock in a glass case. The chancel has been made new, but its arch, like most of the old work in the church, is 600 years old. The clerestory is 15th century.

The walls and arcades are leaning, and the tinted stone is charming against the plaster indoors. There is old timber in the roofs of the nave and aisles, and fragments of old glass are in a medley of new in the east window. A pillar almsbox is 1685, the font with angels under its bowl is about 1400, and three bench-ends of the same time have quaint heads on the arms and in the poppyheads.

One of the fine possessions here is the 14th century oak door letting us in, patterned all over with the delicate scrolls and leaves of the original iron hinges which have a charming lace-like effect. On the floor of the chancel is the brass portrait of a priest holding a chalice, one of only two priest brasses in the county. An inscription which seems to be upside down (for the head of the brass is toward the east instead of the west) asks us to pray for the soul of Master Ralph Babington of 1521, a rector here whose small figure we remember on his father's tomb in Ashover church, Derbyshire.

The oldest treasure, and one of the finest things of its kind in the land, is a relic of a 1000-year-old tomb, the coped cover of a Saxon coffin. It is 5 feet 6 inches long, showing in its mass of carving a fine cross, and animals enmeshed in interlacing knotwork. An animal at one end is biting its own tail. Very beautiful is a 600-year-old gravestone built into an outside wall, carved in relief with graceful branches of leaves growing from the stem and head of a cross. Some of the 18th century slate stones in the church are remarkable for the fine lettering of their inscriptions.

Not far from the church the canal comes to the edge of the road. It is called Hickling Basin and is a favourite spot for anglers.

Hockerton is a plain little village, with Southwell for a neighbour. It has two things left of Norman days, both in the church which stands by two old yews. One is the chancel arch, the other a small window in the nave, its deep splay making a fine frame for a bright modern St George. There is a 13th century lancet in the same wall, and most of the other windows are 14th century.

The low embattled tower is 500 years old. The unusual font, with eight sides and a round rim, may be 700 years old. The old stoup is in the porch, a tiny old almsbox is set on a new pillar, and one of the bench-ends has been here since 1599. Pleasing for its glass and for its story is a window showing St Nicholas (to whom the church is dedicated), the Madonna and Child, and St Cecilia with her organ. The face of Nicholas is that of a gracious old man, James Fuller Humfrys Mills, a former rector of this church.

Holme is a pleasant village with orchards and farms, which found itself at the end of the 16th century on the east bank of the Trent instead of the west, owing to the river having changed its course in a great flood.

94

Between the road and the river is Holme Old Hall, a creepered farmhouse with mullioned windows which has grown from the house where centuries ago the Bartons lived. With part of the fortune he made out of wool in the Calais trade John Barton rebuilt most of the church where he has been sleeping since 1491, and it is said that he put in a window of his house the words:

I thanke God, and ever shall,
It is the shepe hath payed for all.

One of his descendants married the Royalist brother of Lord Bellasis (who was Governor of Newark at the time of its surrender), and their son married Cromwell's daughter Mary. Lord Bellasis lived either at the Old Hall or in a house which stood where the red brick Holme Hall stands now.

The quaint church of St Giles underwent some restoration in the 1930's by a Nottingham man, Mr. Nevil Truman, a stained glass expert. This was cut short by the war, however, and no more work was done until about 1962. Since then work has been carried out on the exterior and interior. The original church probably goes back to 1150–1200, but it is noted for its restoration work done by John Barton, whose tomb is in the church, and who is also remembered by a stained glass window which records his death in 1491.

The handsome two-storeyed porch is part of John Barton's re-building, which included the addition of the south aisle and the chantry chapel. Over the entrance is a fine band of seven shields carved with heraldry, the initials of the Bartons and their badge of bears and tuns, the merchant's mark, with bales of wool, and the Staple of Calais with sheep below. Two gargoyles show a man with a book and a staff, and a grotesque struggling with a dragon.

The church still has 15th century furniture with fine wood carving and wonderful stained glass windows. One incident in the church's long history relates to the Great Plague and the unusual two-storey porch. In the upper room of this porch a woman named Nanny Scott took refuge when the plague was raging in the neighbourhood in 1666. With a stock of food she stayed there, and from the window she could see the villagers one by one being carried into the burial ground. When she eventually emerged from her refuge she found only one person left in the village, so, full of fear, she returned to the porch room and stayed there for the rest of her life.

Holme Pierrepont is a tiny village situated off the Radcliffe bypass. It is rather secluded and is approached down a narrow lane.

Its church is dedicated to St Edmund and is first mentioned in the year 1201. In the reign of Henry I the Manor of Holme was in the possession of the Manvers family, but in 1279 a daughter, who was the sole heir, married Henry Pierrepont of Hurst Pierpoint in Sussex where his family originally settled after the Norman Conquest. Very few traces of the original church remain, for it was almost completely rebuilt by the first Marquis of Dorchester about 1666. The present south aisle was the original nave and the organ chamber was the chancel, with the burial vault of the family beneath.

Among the interesting monuments in the church is a recumbent stone effigy of a pilgrim, lying just inside the door and along the floor by the south wall; but the most striking one is of beautifully carved Italian alabaster which commemorates Sir Henry Pierrepont who fought against the Lancastrians in the Wars of the Roses. Thoroton's History of Nottinghamshire (1797) mentions a brass figure near the vault which had no inscription. When the new floor was laid in 1960 this brass was discovered about a foot below the surface and has been mounted on the west wall. It is in a very good state of preservation and the experts date it about 1385. Two other mural monuments deserve particular mention. In the pier of the nave arcade facing the entrance is a very ornate tablet to the memory of "Young Oldham", a "poet of merit" buried here in 1683. It is reputed to be the work of Grinling Gibbons. Another memory of the Rev W. Saltern, Rector of Colgrave. It is by the well-known sculptor Flaxman. Inlaid in the front of the pulpit is a striking carving of the Sermon on the Mount, said to have been brought from Italy. In 1960 the main body of the church was given a new floor of Hopton Wood polished reconstructed stone slabs, and in the sanctuary a beautiful floor of Portland Purbeck marble. New oak altar rails provided the finishing touch to the beautifying of the church.

The hall, long the home of the Pierreponts, who became the Earls of Kingston, dates from the early 17th century, and stands next to the church.

Hoveringham. At one time this was known as the village on the hump. There are three pubs at Hoveringham, the Old Elm Tree by the river, and the Marquis of Granby and the Reindeer in the village. The total population of this village does not exceed 300, and its industry is chiefly farming. There are, however, some gravel pits which employ a small number of people. It was in August, 1952, that workman excavating gravel unearthed an old well. The farm on which it was discovered dates back to 1536, and the area in the immediate vicinity shows evidence of early human habitation over a period of some hundreds of years. The well is 7 feet deep and about 3 feet 6 inches in diameter, with wooden base 2 feet square. The sides of the well are stone lined, being cleverly interleaved.

In a field close by are the remains of a mediaeval village complete with sunken road.

Leaving the gravel pits and river behind and proceeding up the road in the direction of Thurgaton, one comes to the village and its church, St Michael and All Angels.

The small brick church has none of the beauty of the old one it replaced last century, but it has a few treasures. Built into the outside wall over the north doorway is a fine Norman tympanum showing St Michael flourishing his sword as he attacks two winged dragons with curling tails. He is defending the church (represented by a holy lamb) from its enemies; over his head is the Hand of God, and at the sides are Peter with a key and a bishop with his hand in blessing.

The font belongs to Norman and 13th century days, and was brought back to the church from the Ferry Inn last century. Set in a wall is part of an ancient coffin stone with the fine head of a cross carved in relief.

On an alabaster tomb lie the battered but still fine figures of Sir

Robert Goushill and his wife Elizabeth, the widowed Duchess of Norfolk. Her third husband was murdered after the Battle of Shrewsbury, and she married a fourth. Her father was the Earl of Arundel who was beheaded for treason in 1397; her second husband, the first Duke of Norfolk, who had been one of his accusers, was himself banished for treason.

From the church we make our way down the village street with its neat cottages, shops, Post Office, and village primary school. Many of the cottages can still boast a well in their garden, and some have fragments of the original church which have been put to ornamental use.

The River Trent is an added attraction to this typical Nottinghamshire village. The river is continually being dredged, which has meant that it is now much wider at this point. There was a ferry right up until about 1900, and some of the villagers can remember when the river was frozen over in about 1885, and a horse and cart were driven across.

Hucknall is a mining town midway between Nottingham and Sutton-in-Ashfield, and by virtue of its distance from the great Roman Fosse Way it must be assumed that Hucknall's origins are purely Saxon. Eighth century Saxon work was found in 1938 in the parish church building. Until recently the urban district had the name of Hucknall Torkard. The Torcards, or Torkards, were landowners in the area from the 12th century.

The parish church is dedicated to St Mary Magdalen, and is situated in the Market Square. The tower was raised to its present height in 1320, its lower part (with a beautiful wide arch, only slightly pointed) being all that is left of the simple church built at the close of Norman days. The nave and north aisle are 14th century, the aisle windows and the clerestory are 15th. The south aisle and the transepts are additions of last century.

This church is noted for its connections with the Byron family, whose members have been buried here since the first half of the century. Lord Byron, the poet, is buried here. Byron, a hero of the Greek War of Independence, died on April 19, 1824. His body was embalmed and reached England on June 30, when it lay at the house of Sir Edward Knatchbull at Westminster until July 12, when it was moved to Nottingham, arriving there on July 15. The body was on view to Nottingham citizens at the Black Moore's Head, Pelham Street, now the site of Boots the Chemists. On July 16 the body was moved to this church, where he is now buried in the family vault. Some years ago it was thought that there was an ancient crypt under the chancel, and to carry out the excavations meant opening the Byron Vault. On June 15, 1938 the vault was opened, and Canon T. G. Barber, then Vicar of the church, and others, were able to make many notes on the contents of this family vault. The lid of the poet's coffin was not fastened down, and the Canon was able to take a glimpse at the poet, who was in a perfect state of preservation, and was able to confirm that Byron was lame in the right foot. Among other coffins in the vault are those of the wicked Lord William, that of the poet's mother, of Lady Frances Byron, and Augusta Ada, the poet's daughter.

Perhaps the most famous name connected with Hucknall in recent years is that of Eric Coates, the composer. Born in 1886, Eric Coates was the son of Dr Harrison Coates, whose home and surgery were at Tenter Hill, Hucknall. His family were all musical, and their home became the centre of musical activity in the neighbourhood. He won a scholarship to the Royal Academy of Music in London, and later became leader of the viola section of Henry Wood's Queen's Hall Orchestra. In 1919 he gave up viola playing and concentrated on composing. His first national success came in his London Suite when the BBC borrowed a movement, the Knightsbridge March, as a signature tune to their programme "In Town To-night". Within two weeks 20,000 letters poured in to Broadcasting House asking for the name of the composer, and from then on Eric Coates never looked back. This great composer of light music died on December 21, 1957.

On the outskirts of the town is Hucknall Aerodrome, built at the time of the First World War. It was from this airfield in 1940 that Franz von Werra tried to make his escape by stealing a Hurricane, only to be foiled at the last moment when he found that there was no starter. Rolls-Royce have a test centre close by, and what was known as the "Flying Bedstead", their first vertical take-off aircraft, made its first free flight on August 3, 1954.

Kelham is perhaps best known for its Theological College which houses the Society of the Sacred Mission. The building dates from 1857, but the chapel, with its magnificent dome, belongs to this century, having being completed in 1927–28. The Society celebrated the centenary of its founder, Father Kelly, in 1960. He was born in Manchester in 1860, and after an undistinguished career at Manchester Grammar School and a year at Woolwich Royal Military Academy, he was ordained deacon in 1883. He undertook training men for the Korean Mission, which was eventually replaced in 1894 by the Society of the Sacred Mission. In 1903, Father Kelly moved to Kelham, the present headquarters of the Society. He died in 1950.

The old church of St Wilfrid is close to the college, in company with fine trees and playing-fields. A splendid elm overtops the tower, and a good old yew is near the porch, which shelters an ancient studded door; on the hood of the doorway are two quaint heads, inside the church.

Coming chiefly from the last years of the 15th century, the church is pleasing and light, with aisles, a lofty tower arch with embattled capitals, an old font, a few old glass fragments, a fine old roof in the north aisle, and stone corbels at the ends of the chancel beams, carved with flowers, heads of women, angels, and grotesque smiling animals. The traceried screens across the chancel arch and the south chapel are 15th century.

Here in the church we are reminded of the Manners and the Manners-Suttons who lived for a time at Kelham Hall. Robert Sutton was made Baron Lexington for his loyalty in the Civil War, and took his title from the name of his ancestors, three Lexington brothers famous in the 13th century. Robert Sutton, the second and last Lord Lexington, was a diplomat who, while ambassador at Madrid, lost his only son at 15: the boy's body was brought to England in a bale of cloth and buried here at Kelham. We read of him on the ponderous marble monument of his parents, where the more than lifesize figures of Lord Lexington and his wife are reclining on a mattress, both in richly ornamented robes and sandals, Lord Lexington holds his coronet, and a long inscription tells of his family and his career.

The Lexington Papers, comprising the correspondence of the second Lord Lexington with various public men, were discovered at Kelham Hall, and were published in 1851.

Keyworth. Its two things to see are the fine views of the Wolds and the wooded countryside, and the charming little church in a halo of trees. Though much restored, the church of St Mary Magdalene has an ancient story, told by a Norman font barely three yards round, and a beacon tower of rare design and exceptional beauty. Built about the end of the 14th century, and conspicuous for miles, the tower was used to guide travellers over the Wolds, and in times of danger as a signal station communicating with Nottingham, Belvoir Castle, and Charnwood Forest. Beautiful buttresses, stepped and gabled, strengthen it at the angles, and crowning it all is an embattled stone lantern with eight sides, little windows, and a tiny spire. Within the church the 13th century chancel has a 14th century window with a sill forming stone seats, but the east window and the arch are modern. The old arcade still divides the 14th century nave and aisle.

Keyworth Square is a meeting place of the Quorn Hunt, and there is an annual show held in the village in July.

Kilvington is only a few dwellings and a tiny church on a border hilltop, but it has a glorious prospect over the Vale of Belvoir and into Lincolnshire.

The church of St Mary was built in 1852, after the death of a rector who had allowed the old building to fall into ruin. With Staunton half a mile away, he thought Kilvington had no need of its own church, which was used for a time as a sheep-fold, and was actually offered for sale as building material. Its one ancient relic is a worn chalice and paten of thin pewter, dug up 40 years ago after

H   101 having been buried with a priest before the Reformation. The church lighting has been modernised, and the interior re-decorated.

Kimberley is 6 miles north-west of Nottingham. The rise of modern Kimberley dates back to 1816 when the Rutland estate was broken up and sold off in numerous lots, creating a number of new freeholders. Viscount Melbourne, destined to be Queen Victoria's first Prime Minister and friend of Robert Holden of Nuthall, and persons of the names Godber, Hanson, Smedley, Birkin, and Shaw were among the purchasers. In 1848 Kimberley was detached from Greasley and formed into a separate civil and ecclesiastical parish, and presently the living was restored to a rectory.

The church is dedicated to Holy Trinity and was erected in 1847. It is in the Early English style, consisting of a apsidal chancel, nave, south porch, and a western turret. Of the ancient church no trace remains. Cock fights were held within its crumbling walls, and by 1844 it had vanished altogether.

Kimberley's new Parish Hall was opened in November, 1967.

Kingston-on-Soar. About 10 miles south-west of Nottingham lies Kingston-on-Soar. There are a number of cottages with attractive gardens, making a pleasing entrance to the village, but they are quickly passed, and a row of more modern property follows before the village is reached and the property reverts to a more mellow look.

The approach to the church of St Wilfrid is past the village green and pump. This charming little church with its mullioned windows and its lychgate set in the wall dates in its present form from 1900, when it was rebuilt by Lord Belper. It is a small edifice of stone in the Perpendicular style, consisting of chancel, nave, south aisle, porch, and embattled tower on the north side, with pinnacles containing a clock and three bells. The register dates back to 1657. Perhaps the church's greatest treasure is the Babington Chantry, which contains no inscription, but round the capital of the pillars are carved numerous babes with their bodies half hidden in tuns or casks—a common monumental rebus on the family name Bab-in-ton.

Close at hand is a memorial to Algernon Henry Strutt, third Baron Belper, benefactor of this church and beloved squire of the parish, born May 6, 1883, buried at sea March 29, 1956.

Perhaps the best known of the Babingtons who lived at Kingston was Anthony, who at the age of 18 became page to Mary Queen of Scots, when she was in captivity at Sheffield Castle. He fell a victim to her charms, and in 1586 allowed himself to become the figurehead of the Babington Plot to murder Elizabeth and put Mary of Scotland on the throne. The scheme miscarried, and tradition has it that while Anthony was in flight from arrest he found shelter upon the canopy of the existing family monument in Kingston Church. He was later caught, tried, and condemned, and along with six other conspirators was executed in St Giles's Fields, London, at the age of 25.

Kingston Hall, the home of Lord Belper, was built in the middle of the last century by the first Lord Belper, a grandson of the great industrial pioneer, Jedediah Strutt, who came from the mining and hosiery town of Belper, north of Derby.

For many years now Kingston Hall and grounds have been the scene each August of the now-famous Kingston Agricultural Show.

Kinoulton lies on a hill with views over the Vale of Belvoir, and the Grantham Canal passes under the village street.

Its church of St Luke, standing opposite the old forge, was built by the Earl of Gainsborough in 1793. It is of red brick and is in the classical style of its period. The old churchyard (where the original church once stood) is on the hill close to the old Fosse Way. There are just a few headstones left, one of which is the finest in the county. There is an interesting story about a farmer who was reputed to have used gravestones from this old churchyard to mend his oven, until a farm labourer discovered the words "In Loving Memory" on his bread!

To-day there are many new houses in Kinoulton. The village cricket ground is said to be the best in Nottinghamshire, and the Neville Arms is the rendezvous of the Nottingham Old Crocks Car Club. There is an annual flower show.

Kirkby-in-Ashfield is some 10 miles from Nottingham and near to the Derbyshire border. Here rise three rivers, the Erewash, the Leen, and the Maun.

The town's main industry is coal mining. It came into the Domesday Book, and may have had a Roman settlement. The name lives in a group of places to-day, Kirkby-in-Ashfield, Kirkby Woodhouse, and East Kirkby.

The parish church of St Wilfrid is a recent structure and replaces the one destroyed by a fire in 1907. Some of the masonry of the Kirkby Church survives in the new one, and in the floor of the porch are old coffin lids engraved with crosses. The new church has a round north arcade and a pointed south arcade in the style of those destroyed. It is notable for a statue of St Wilfrid in a niche in the porch, and rich carving on the hoods, the capitals, and the corbels; for the beautiful oak stalls and pews, the handsome screen, and the organ case; and for windows glowing with colour.

The old market is no longer held, but a fragment of the tapering cross shaft of the old cross still stands on its old steps by the wayside in the oldest part of Kirkby, its distinguishing name of Ashfield reminding us that here was a clearing in the ancient Sherwood Forest, with ash trees abounding.

Kirklington lies between Newark and Mansfield. At one end of this village the little River Greet comes under the road from the millpool, and at the other lofty trees shade a lovely bit of road climbing towards Hockerton. The great house, an 18th century building modernised, stands in a park with a fine lake.

The church of St Swithin's has some of the old stone left in the brick tower, the hood of the south porch has heads of a king and a queen, and at the north door are two old faces amusing for their contrast, one a very fat man and one very lean. A lovely window in the chancel has most of its original 14th century work. One of the church's two treasures is the fine 12th century font, carved with a band of four-leaved ornament and interlaced arcading; the other is an ancient stone built into an outside wall, 4 feet long and perhaps as old as the font. Within a border are stars, zigzag, and nine round bosses in a block, and on one end of the stone is a sundial.

Kirton has little to show but a neat old church high above the road, looking over the housetops to a landscape bounded by the green depths of the Forest. Steps climb up to the churchyard, which goes on climbing higher still among fine trees.

The 500-year-old tower has a pyramid cap. From the 13th century come the north doorway with two worn heads, a window close by with two smiling faces, the chancel arch, and the fine little nave arcade of three bays, with stone seats round the pillars. Several windows come from the next two centuries, and there are a few old glass fragments.

Two treasures of the church of Holy Trinity are a splendid 14th century chest and a slender 16th century pillar almsbox stoutly bound with ironwork. The oldest relic is the small round bowl of a Norman font, long in the churchyard and now sheltered in the porch.

Kneesall lies about three and a half miles south-east of Ollerton, and the church of St Bartholomew stands elevated by the roadside. Its splendid 15th century tower has a striking parapet of pointed battlements and pinnacles like a crown, and between grotesque gargoyles at the corners is an angel on every side. Two smiling faces adorn the west window. The most remarkable of the huge gargoyles outside the nave has two figures with tiny bodies and huge heads, one sitting and one kneeling as they crouch close together. Their heads are touching, and they are looking out with wide eyes and eager expression, as if singing.

The south doorway comes from the close of the 13th century, when the tower arch was shaped; the nave arcades (with stone seats round the pillars and heads of human folk on the arches) are about 1400, as are the clerestory windows above them. Old lancets and fine 15th century windows light the chancel. A much valued possession is a fragment of an 11th century cross, 20 inches high and carved with knotwork. It was found in the tower wall at the restoration of the church in 1893.

Kneeton stands on the top of a steep wooded cliff some 200 feet above the Trent. The church of St Helen has been rebuilt many times, and most parts of it now date from 1879, the exception being the tower built about 1500. The registers are complete from 1592.

In 1967 the remains of a mediaeval encampment were found at Kneeton. Roman and 10th century pottery, bones and charcoal are among the objects that have been unearthed.

Lambley is one of those villages that has kept its rural charm despite the number of new properties that have sprung up in the area. It is sheltered by hills and watered by the little Cocker Beck whose stream winds idly through the village street. Its greatest claim to fame is its connection with Ralph, Lord Cromwell, who was born here about 1394, perhaps in the manor house which stood where the rectory is now. He was the last of ten generations to bear the name of Ralph, was a great statesman and financier, and as High Treasurer of England in 1433 may be said to have prepared our first Budget in his masterly statement of the national accounts. He built the castle and enriched the church of Tattershall in Lincolnshire, where he is buried. He left a lasting memorial in his birthplace, for he re-fashioned the beautiful church of Holy Trinity except for the tower and part of the chancel. His badge of office, a purse, is carved on stone panels by the east window outside, and worn stones in the chancel floor are in memory of his family. Other old coffin stones are in the stone seats of the porch, and its inner walls (like other walls of the church) are scored with marks which seem to have been made by bowmen sharpening their arrows. Most of the tower is 13th century; the top is 14th, but the arch opening into the nave is Norman. The north wall of the chancel was built in 1340 when the sixth Ralph Cromwell founded a two-storeyed chantry here. It has gone but there is still the peephole from its upper room. We come into the chancel through an old oak screen which has been here since 1377; it rises 11 feet high, and over it hangs a great wooden crucifix in memory of an old lady of Lambley who lived to be 95. The canopied pulpit is entered by an old winding stairway in the wall. The altar table is Jacobean, and there is Jacobean carving in the lectern, the reading desk, and the stalls. The font is 500 years old. The east window has fragments of ancient glass with a Crucifixion, a crowned Madonna and a saint in blue and gold.

Laneham has a high and low tide, though its fine reach of the Trent is miles from the sea. What is known as Church Laneham nestles close to the bank, which is like a seaside beach when the tide is out, and is picturesque with pleasure boats and barges passing to and fro.

Full of years and interest, the church of St Peter stands where chestnut trees overhang the road. Its 13th century tower has an 11th century square-headed doorway, and a crude round arch of the same time in the walling above. There is early herringbone masonry in the walls, and a lovely Norman doorway through which we enter has two detached pillars on each side supporting an arch with a handsome array of zigzag enriched with sunflower pattern. Rarer still is the fine old door it frames, for it is one of the oldest in the land, one of the very few Norman doors we have opened and shut on our journeyings, perhaps a dozen in all England. As old as the doorway itself, its plain weatherworn boards are still good, and it is swinging today on the hinges made for it eight centuries ago.

The Norman chancel arch has a shaft on each side. Between the nave and its aisle is a beautiful 13th century arcade of three graceful bays: at the foot of one of the clustered pillars is a great stone seat, and the base of the other is continued to make two steps for the massive Norman font. Almost the only coloured glass in the mediaeval windows are 14th century fragments of amber and red, showing a crowned queen with a kneeling winged figure at her side.

The church has two old chests, one 16th century, another an exceptionally fine one of the 13th, bound with iron and adorned with roundels carved with sunflowers. Another rare possession of the 13th century are 14 sturdy seats of oak shaped with the adze, their plain ends chamfered at the top. One or two have restored seats, but the rest are entirely original and remarkable, for very few churches in England have any like them. Three are nearly 12 feet long and the others 8. The registers are another treasure, for they are continuous from 1538.

From the old pulpit here preached Samuel Slinn Skene while he was vicar from 1904 till 1919. He had the remarkable experience of living to see seven sons ordained in the ministry.

Kneeling on cushions on an elaborate 17th century monument in the chancel are Ellis Markham, a judge, and his son Jervase, a soldier who died in 1636. Both have lost their hands. The judge, with a beard and long hair, wears a ruff, a tunic, and a mantle trimmed with straps and buttons. Jervase is in armour; his hair curls on to his shoulders, and an extraordinary long plait from one side of his head is tucked under his sash. He is said to be the Markham Queen Elizabeth mentioned in the couplet:

> *Gervase the Gentle, Stanhope the Stout,*
> *Markham the Lion, and Sutton the Lout.*

A farmhouse on the river bank is on the site of their old home, but its cellars are said to have belonged to the still-older palace of the Archbishops of York on this spot, in which Thomas de Corbridge died in 1304.

A good gift of this 20th century is the charming timbered porch which shelters the Norman doorway. It comes from a restoration which followed the 14th century design, and keeps the original timbered entrance arch to link the old with the new. It was the work of local craftsmen; the village joiner and his son did the timbering, the village builder set up the stone and brick and tile work, and the rich bargeboard was carved in the Laneham joiner's shop, so that all the work was done in the village. The joiner's son who helped to build it was the first to be carried through the porch to his last rest.

Langar lies to the south-east of Nottingham and its church of St Andrew is often referred to as the Cathedral in the Vale. It stands by an open field looking over the Vale of Belvoir. In the church is a nave of five bays with clerestory, north and south aisles, south porch, central tower, north and south transepts, and chancel. There is some fine carving on the pillar capitals of the Early English arcades.

Extending across the West end of the nave, where at one time there was a gallery accessible by a covered passage from the nearby Hall, is the panelling from the old screen. The reading pew and pulpit are Jacobean, and are said to have been made from the Howe family pew. The north transept contains monuments to three successive generations of the Chaworth family of Wiverton, two of them being of special interest as they illustrate the armour of the last half of the 16th century and the dress then worn by the ladies. In the south transept is a 17th century tomb of black and white marble, one of the finest examples of its kind and period, supporting carved effigies of Thomas, Lord Scroope, and his wife, above which is a marble canopy. There is also an Italian altar cloth of silk and gold embroidery made in the 16th century and taken from a French galleon by Admiral Howe at the Battle of the First of June in the English Channel, 1794, and given by him to the church. The south door is original work, and contains an unusual feature for a parish church, a small wicket door in the centre. The church registers date back to 1595.

The English novelist, Samuel Butler, was born at Langar Rectory in 1835. In his autobiography, *The Way of All Flesh*, he refers to Langar as Battersby-on-the-Hill.

During the Second World War Langar Aerodrome was the scene of operations by the R.A.F. and the United States Air Force. In 1950 the Royal Canadian Air Force took it over, and it was used by them until April 30, 1964, when they vacated it and left for Germany.

Langford is a small village four miles from Newark on the Gainsborough side. Its stone dwellings are on the highway, from which the big house is set back in lovely gardens and trees. Down a shaded lane leading to Holme, the small church of St Bartholomew stands in company with the vicarage, with the Tudor manor house, now a farm, nearby.

In this great seclusion a lonely knight, carved in stone, lies within the altar rails of the church. The arms of the Pierreponts are on his armour, his helmet is on his head, his hands are at prayer, and though his legs are broken there is something of the little dog on which his feet rested. He comes from the closing years of the 14th century, and would know the 13th century tower which still stands looking out over the pleasant meadows.

The chancel arch and the south arcade of the nave are about 1400; traces of an arcade which led to a vanished north aisle are in the nave wall outside. A beautiful archway which once opened to a chapel is enriched with flower medallions, embattled capitals, and a hood ending in heads. Mediaeval windows fill the place with light, and the fine old roof of the nave has curious bosses and faces pleasing and ferocious. The piscina is old; the splendid font of Sicilian marble is modern.

Close by the church the little stream known as the Fleet meanders among the willows in what was once the bed of the Trent. It is over three centuries since a great flood left the River Trent in its present channel on the other side of Holme, leaving the tiny Fleet to mark its old course.

Laxton. With houses dotted among a wealth of trees, on a ridge of land dropping down to a stream, quiet old-world Laxton has a unique interest as the last stronghold of the open field system of cultivation evolved in mediaeval England. The plough land is divided into three great open fields of some 300 acres each. These are divided into strips that are rented by the farmers. The strips are divided again by strips of grassland called sykes (pronounced sicks), with such attractive old names as Longwell, Hoxmoor, Foxmoor, Skittlepool, and Honey Hole. Each year, the bailiff and a jury of twelve go out into these fields to see if any of the farmers have encroached on either the sykes or clay roads. If they have (and the measuring is carried out to an inch), then a fine is imposed. On the same day the ancient Court Leet meets to discuss the affairs of the open fields. This meeting takes place in the local inn, and a portion of the fines exacted from the previous year are spent on beer by the new jury. Of the three huge fields, one is reserved for wheat, a second for spring corn (oats, beans, peas, and barley), and the third lies fallow. This rotation continues year after year. An interesting tradition is that after the crops are harvested, anyone in the village who "sends up smoke", that is, has a house, has the right of pasturing on the two fields that have been under crops. This is where the jury comes in. They say when the fields can be declared open. Visitors from many parts of the world have been to Laxton to see this feudal system of farming. It creates great interest everywhere, but by present day standards it is about the most uneconomic method of agriculture there is.

This interesting village has memories of great days when it knew the Everinghams and the Lexingtons. Three Lexington brothers who won fame in the 13th century were Robert, judge and soldier, John, Lord Keeper of the Great Seal, and Henry, Bishop of Lincoln.

Only the sites are left of its great houses. One of them stood south of the church, and traces of its fishponds are seen among the trees at the foot of a field by the old vicarage. At the end of a green lane facing the church is a big field known as the Old Hall grounds, where stood a Norman castle which became the home of the Everinghams. Since their day the land has been quarried for the buried stone, but a green mound, two courts, and a dry moat are still seen. From this site there is a fine prospect of the countryside, and a delightful view of the village.

With walls of mottled grey and amber stone the church of St Michael makes a charming picture by the wayside, in a churchyard with trim yew hedges, a bower of slender yews, and a draped column in memory of nine men who did not come back. Attractive as it is now, the church was robbed of much of its glory when it lost some of its length and width in the rebuilding of 1860. Then the sturdy, picturesque tower (with a pyramid cap on its crown of battlements and pinnacles) was rebuilt a bay farther east. The base of the tower comes from the close of the 12th century, with a doorway and arch of the 13th, and among its gargoyles are grotesque animals, a cross-legged satyr with cloven feet, an animal ready to leap down, another with pointed ears climbing on the parapet, and a crouching man.

Beautiful outside and in is the clerestory of six windows on each side of the nave, two long lines of light in a place already ablaze with light from the plain glass. Fine pinnacles crown its splendid embattled parapet enriched with a band of quatrefoils, shields, and flowers, and in the gallery of gargoyle heads are demons with bared teeth, a bear, a laughing grotesque, and two faces close together, one showing its tongue. This clerestory was built about 1490 by Archbishop Rotherham, whose fine sculptured figure with two roebucks at his feet is in a niche on the battlement. The lofty chancel screen may be his gift, though it is much restored.

The nave arcades (of about 1200) have slightly pointed arches on tall round pillars. The chancel has beautiful mediaeval craftsmanship in the sedilia (adorned with angels and a canopy with tiny bosses in the vaulted roof), the double piscina with a quatrefoil between the arches, and the Easter Sepulchre with flowing tracery. In the back of the Sepulchre is an aumbry with a lovely arch. In the south wall of the chancel (at its east end) is a tiny low window less than 4 inches wide and 20 inches long. The font is 14th century, and from its close come the clerestory of the chancel and some of the aisle windows.

In the north aisle are remains of a fine screen set up in 1532 by Robert de Trafford, a vicar whose name is on the rail. Massive old beams are in the chancel roof, and with the lovely old work in the nave roof are bosses of shields and flowers, and four figures at the ends of the spandrels. At the foot of the stone pilasters climbing between the clerestory windows in the nave are 14 small figures, some with books, a staff, or a chalice, others playing instruments, while some are animals.

The choir seats, the screenwork in the chancel, and the lectern with St George are in memory of a vicar for 40 years of last century; the prayer-desk is to a schoolmaster and organist for 40 years till 1927; the reredos and panelling of the east wall are in memory of the third Earl Manvers, lord of the manor. But it is in the monuments of bygone days that the chief interest lies.

The chapel on the north side of the chancel belonged to the Lexingtons, and the one on the south (now gone) to the Everinghams. All the figures which remain, all more or less battered, belong to the Everinghams, three actually resting on an open table tomb of the Lexingtons. The angels adorning this tomb are said to resemble those in the Angel Choir at Lincoln, which was begun when Henry de Lexington was its bishop. The three figures lying on the tomb are of

Adam de Everingham the Elder (who died about 1336) and his two wives. Adam is a knight in chain mail with a belted cloak and sword, his legs crossed, his feet on a lion, and his hands at prayer. His wives are in similar dress, but it is Margaret, the second wife, who arrests attention, for she lies carved in oak, and is the only wooden figure left in the county. So well does the oak blend with the stone of the other figures that its nature is not easily seen at a casual glance. Over her long gown she wears a mantle of many folds, the drapery caught up under her arm. Her hands are gone, her features are still discernible, traces of her wimple are seen, and her headdress, held by a band, falls on to her shoulders. Her head rests on two cushions, and a dog is at her feet.

Three knights of the family lie on the south side of the chancel. Two are of stone, with crossed legs; the other is a headless trunk with one arm but no hand, all that is left of Baron Reginald Everingham, the last of his race, who died in 1399. The middle one of the three is Robert de Everingham of 1287, the oldest of all the figures, and the last of the Chief Lords and Keepers of the Royal Forests. The third is a 14th century Adam de Everingham, perhaps the son of Adam who lies here with his wives.

Linby. Its collieries have not robbed the heart of the village of its old charm, for here are stone cottages with red roofs, an ancient church, and two fine crosses on flights of steps, with a stream flowing on each side of the spacious road between them. It is uncertain what the crosses were, but it is probable that both marked the boundary of Sherwood Forest. The older cross has a restored shaft on its original seven-sided steps; the other, coming from about 1660, is a charming picture spanning the stream, backed by tall trees and a flower-bordered drive.

The church of St Michael was in the Domesday Book, and there is much Norman masonry in the north wall. The Norman arch of the north doorway is over one of later time, and is sheltered by a pretty 16th century porch. A Norman doorway and the head of a Norman window are built up in the south wall of the 13th century chancel, entered by a lofty arch only a little younger. At one side of the arch is a peephole. The nave arcade, a piscina, and the corbelled arch of the 15th century tower are 700 years old. One of two old glass fragments in a 600-year-old window shows a crowned head.

On the outskirts of the village is Castle Mill with battlements to justify its name. It has now been turned into flats.

Littleborough is a tiny village looking across a fine sweep of the Trent to Lincolnshire's green fields and wooded hills.

On the approach from Sturton-le-Steeple where a road branches off to Cottam can be seen a hexagonal toll house.

Where the Normans built the church the Romans had been before them, for here they brought their road from Lincoln to Doncaster across the river, and founded their station known as Segelocum. Altars, urns, pottery, and coins have been found and one discovery here is famous. In 1860, while digging a grave, the sexton came upon a stone coffin, and on the raising of the lid there was revealed the perfect body of a young woman, wearing a garment fastened by a Roman brooch. It was a dramatic spectacle of a moment, for in the twinkling of an eye this Roman lady crumbled into dust.

In the summer of 1933 when a great drought brought the river to a very low level, there was revealed the ford made here in the time of Hadrian. For many years it carried traffic between the north and south. Here Harold and his Saxons crossed on their way to Hastings. Here, while Harold lay in his grave at Waltham Abbey, the Conqueror himself may have come on his way from York to capture Lincoln.

The quaint Norman church of St Nicholas, with a bell turret, is one of the smallest in the county, with a chancel barely 13 feet long and a nave only 24. The walls have an abundance of herringbone masonry inside and out, and rarer still are the Roman tiles built into them.

We come into the nave through a lofty Norman doorway, and into the chancel by a recessed Norman arch on carved capitals crowning detached pillars. The round Norman font has been altered so that it has now eight sides at the top. There is a mediaeval piscina, an Elizabethan chalice, and a carving of the Last Supper.

Lowdham. The loveliest corner of this Nottinghamshire village, growing round its busy cross-roads, is where the church of St Mary stands at the end of a little-frequented byway. With a brook flowing through the quiet dingle, and a background of woods, it is a beautiful picture outside, its 15th century spire crowning a sturdy tower built when the Norman style was passing. Inside it is full of light streaming through charming windows which are for the most part renewed, though the clerestory is 15th century.

The 13th century arcades have stone seats at the foot of their slender clustered pillars. The two bays between the chancel and its chapel are from the time of King John. The fine font is 14th century, a small altar table is Jacobean, and a studded oak door made in 1641 swings in the south doorway, which has a small consecration cross.

Lying in the chancel he founded in the 14th century is a cross-legged knight, Sir John de Lowdham, wearing chain mail and with a shield. The chancel was made new last century; on its south wall is a stone with the fine engraved figure of a 15th century priest in his robes.

On May 4, 1930 boys from the closed Borstal at Feltham, Middlesex, came to Lowdham and pitched camp. Now known as Lowdham Grange, this was the first open Borstal to be created in this country.

A house of particular interest which stands on high ground overlooking Lowdham has an upstairs made out of two American Central Pacific Railway carriages. The carriages are 54 feet long and are divided into bedrooms. They were brought to England for a railway exhibition in 1890 and later bought by the then owner of the property, who lived in them for a time before deciding to build them into a house.

It was at Lowdham that Cornelius Brown was born in 1852. On finishing his school days he went into the offices of the *Nottingham Daily Guardian* where he worked as a reporter, and at the age of 22 he was appointed Editor of the *Newark Advertiser*. He was the author of a number of books, but perhaps his most important was *A History of Newark*, which ran to two volumes. He died in 1907, shortly after completing this work.

Mansfield is a market town situated in the heart of the rich North Notts coalfields, and now has a population of more than 50,000. It probably takes its name from the little River Maun flowing through it.

There are old cave dwellings at Rock Hill. The Romans are said to have encamped here, and coins of Vespasian, Constantine, and Marcus Aurelius have been found. It was a residence of Mercian kings, and was for centuries a royal manor, Norman and later kings finding it a pleasant resort when hunting in the Forest.

Mansfield is proud of its schools. Brunt's School has modern buildings now, and is endowed partly by the bequest of Samuel Brunt of 1709, and partly by Charles Thompson, who was born here and became rich in his business career in Europe and the East. He settled down here after seeing Lisbon destroyed by earthquake in 1755, and became a local celebrity; and he has been sleeping since 1784 on a hilltop a mile away on the road to Southwell, a spot he chose himself because it reminded him of the place from where he witnessed one of the most appalling spectacles in history. He lies with trees about his grave in a stone-walled enclosure.

The scholars of Queen Elizabeth's Grammar School have a fine modern building on a new site, but the 16th century one still stands in St Peter's churchyard. A tablet over the doorway tells of its foundation in 1561, and it has links with not a few of the men Mansfield delights to honour. Two of its boys became bishops and another was the Earl of Chesterfield who wrote the famous letters to his son. One boy who trudged to this school was Richard Sterne, Archbishop of York and grandfather of the Laurence Sterne who gave us *Tristram Shandy*. Richard was one of Laud's chaplains and attended him on the scaffold. He founded four scholarships at Cambridge and two for natives of York and Mansfield, sometimes held by boys from his old school.

The Archbishop was a son of Mansfield, as were also Hayman Rooke, the antiquary who greatly loved his own corner of Notts; James Collinson, the artist who was a fellow student with Rosetti and Holman Hunt; and James Murray, inventor of the circular saw, whose father was "old Joe Murray", Lord Byron's servant. An old friar and a young footman are among Mansfield's most distinguished sons. The friar was William de Mansfield, famed in the 14th century for his knowledge of logic, ethics, and physics; the footman was Robert Dodsley who made a name as poet, publisher, and bookseller. Born in 1703, son of a master of the grammar school, he was apprenticed to a stocking weaver, but ran away to London and took a post as footman. While thus engaged he wrote a book of poems and a friend of Pope took him into his service. Later he started a bookshop and publishing business. A very delightful man, Dodsley was as modest as he was popular. *Tristram Shandy* and *Young's Night Thoughts* were two of the books he published. Dr Johnson called him Doddy, and Doddy suggested to the Doctor the scheme of an English Dictionary. The Annual Register owes its origin to him.

George Whitefield came here to preach, and George Fox spent the first four years of his mission work in the neighbourhood; he was imprisoned here for interrupting service in the church. In the cemetery on the edge of the town lies William Whysall, who played brilliant cricket for Notts and for England in 1930. A tall granite cross marks his grave, and on a granite shield are carved a bat and a ball, and a wicket with one bail off.

The only old church among a number of modern ones is the parish church of St Peter, standing in the middle of the town on a site where one of Mansfield's two churches may have stood when Domesday Book was made. The outside is embattled, the inside spacious and pleasing. The two lower stages of the tower come from the end of the 11th century, and a wide Norman arch opens to the nave; the top stage is 14th century, and the short spire with dormers is 1669. There seems to have been an earlier wooden spire covered with lead, for the repair of which the steward of the manor gave eight trees in Elizabeth's time. There is a fragment of Norman zigzag in a wall.

From a rebuilding of the church when the 13th century style was passing to the 14th come the lofty nave arcades and the chancel arch. The chancel chapels are 15th century, and the clerestory is about 1500.

In each of the two porches are two big and two small tapering coffin stones, all engraved with crosses. Against the wall of the south chapel is a great stone with remains of a Norman inscription, and the figure of a priest under a canopy; he was perhaps Henry de Mansfield, a 14th century vicar. In a recess of the south aisle a 14th century civilian lies sculptured in stone, wearing a long-sleeved gown, belted and buttoned. He has clear features and flowing hair, angels support his head, and his praying hands are broken. He may belong to the Pierrepont family. One of many brass tablets is to John Farrer of 1716, the Latin inscription telling us that he was skilful, prudent, and faithful. Another is to John Firth, vicar here for 45 years of the 17th century. He was followed by George Mompesson, son of the heroic William Mompesson who won immortality at Eyam during the Plague.

Standing in a fine situation just outside the town, at Harlow Wood, is a fine orthopaedic hospital.

Mansfield Woodhouse adjoins the county's western boundary and the northern boundary of Mansfield. The principal industry is coal-mining.

There is something to remind us of the past in the church of St Edmund, and in the great steps and base of the cross on the road leading to it.

Except for its 13th century base (with a modern west doorway and a window adorned with two fine crowned heads) the beautiful tower and its sturdy spire are 14th century, the spire unusual for its great dormer windows and the tiny ones at the top. The rest of the church was made new last century, and is interesting for its carving in wood and stone. Fine corbel heads of men and women, many of them crowned, adorn the windows and the porch; and among the great gargoyles are grotesques, a lion, and a dragon. On the fine sedilia are small scenes of the Sermon on the Mount, the Resurrection, and the Ascension; and in the arcade capitals of the chancel are flowers and angels. The big stone pulpit is of more interest than its plainness suggests, for it rests on a splendid corbel of Eve holding an apple, the serpent coiled round her arms.

There is abundant entertainment in the poppyheads of the bench-ends, which hide from the casual eye a host of tiny figures of animals and humans, full of humour. Among them are two-headed grotesques, an alligator, an eagle killing an adder, a fox jumping up at acorns, and a grotesque face with ears at the top of its head. One has the tiny head of a fox on one side and its tail on the other, as if it is creeping through the poppyhead; another is very quaint with a man at the top, a monkey at one side, and a grotesque animal creeping out from the other side.

Two relics of the 17th century are a shield of arms in a window, and a great stone monument with extraordinary standing figures of John Digby and his wife. John has flowing hair and is in armour with a sword, a thick sash of cord hanging from one shoulder; his wife has a quaint contented smile on her pursed lips, and wears a gown with puffed sleeves, flowing headdress, and a handkerchief tied under her chin.

A number of Roman remains have been unearthed from time to time. In 1786 a villa with hypocausts and a cold bath were discovered, while another villa revealed part of a mosaic pavement. All these discoveries were made a short distance from the church.

Maplebeck is a small village 4½ miles north-east of Southwell. The church of St Radegund stands high above the road in a setting of fine beeches, limes, sycamores, and chestnuts.

It is a mediaeval church restored. From the 14th century come the tower with its low spire, and the nave arcade. The 13th century chancel has two of its original lancets, and a 13th century doorway is in the aisle. The head of an aisle window is formed by part of an ancient coffin stone, and part of another is built into the aisle wall. Here, too, are four small pillars set in the wall, believed to have supported the 13th century stone altar. The fine old font bowl has been partly made new.

Most of the woodwork is Jacobean—the altar rails, the canopied pulpit, the neat oak benches with many of the seats renewed, and the chancel screen with balustrades to which has been added a 15th century beam. Fine 14th century timbers, grey with age, support the roof of the porch, and on one of the beams a wooden face near the door has been greeting all who have come this way for 600 years.

There are no shops in this picturesque village, but the Beehive is the smallest public house in Nottinghamshire. It is a characteristic English public house, and some years ago an American visitor to the village wanted to buy it and take it down brick by brick and ship it to the States. Situated on a slope of a hill overlooking the village, it has a Dutch tiled roof, and four small windows peep out from the brickwork. It dates back to 1803.

Markham Clinton, or West Markham, lies near the old Great North Road.

The old church of All Saints, mentioned in the Domesday Book, dates from Saxon times and is one of the oldest churches in the Diocese of Southwell. The present building is a mixture, for it embodies flint-like Saxon masonry, a Norman priest's door, early Gothic windows, a timber tower and half-timbered gables. The inside walls are all constructed in the Saxon herringbone manner, and a small portion has been left uncovered on the south wall. Until the restoration of 1949 the old mud floors were still in existence. Wooden platforms were later installed, but the original floor can still be seen at the west end of the church. The font is probably 11th or 12th century.

The old altar stone, more than seven feet long, was removed from the floor where it had been lying when the second restoration of the church took place in 1949. During the first restoration in 1930 a Norman piscina was discovered, and can be seen on the south side of the altar. Also discovered was a writing of the Apostles' Creed dating from the 16th century. The screen has been renovated, but the lower part is thought to be the original wood. There is an old oak chest, and the pulpit dates from Elizabethan times. There are some wooden benches and a ladder at the west end of the church, which are very old but their date of origin is unknown. On the outside of the church at the south side is an ancient sundial.

Between West Markham and Milton, off a road shaded by a fine avenue of limes, stands the Mausoleum Church, now in ruins. It is like a classical temple outside, with an outstanding portico at the east end and a tower in the centre crowned by a cupola which contained three bells. Sir Robert Smirke was the architect. Behind the altar are two chapels with vaults beneath. The chapel on the south side contains a beautiful marble monument to Georgiana, Duchess of Newcastle, who died giving birth to twins.

Marnham lies near Tuxford on the banks of the River Trent, and is really two villages, High Marnham close to the river, and Low Marnham which has the church. Europe's first million kilowatt power station dominates the village by the river, and was opened on October 5, 1962.

Perhaps the largest building this village had seen before the power station came into being was Marnham Hall, once the home of the Cartwright family and demolished about 1800.

There are a number of quaint gargoyles outside the church of St Wilfrid, where much that we see, including the tower, is 15th century. A 13th century doorway has deep mouldings all round, and a hood adorned with heads of a bishop and a queen with charming ringlets. The open doorway frames a delightful view of the interior, filled with light, its modern roofs looking down on 13th century arcades in nave and chancel. Very beautiful is the south arcade of the nave, with detached shafts and carved capitals. A similar pillar is in the chancel, which is entered by a 13th century arch.

The south aisle has a mediaeval piscina and a holy water stoup by the door. There is a Jacobean altar table and a 17th century chest. The old stone face of a man with a frightened expression peeps from a corner of the nave.

Wilfrid, the patron saint, is in old glass in the north aisle; and it is odd to note that he has two right hands, owing to the remains of the original figure having been made up with fragments. There is also an ancient roundel.

There are a number of memorials in the church, one a floorstone in the chancel to William Cartwright, 1781, who was responsible for rebuilding the Muskham road on brick arches above flood level.

He is best remembered, however, as the father of a group of remarkable sons, John, Edmund, Charles, and George. John was a Parliamentary reformer, Charles served in the Navy, George was an officer in the Army, while Edmund was to find his place in history as the inventor of the power loom.

Mattersey. It looks its loveliest from the fine little bridge carrying the road over the Idle, a picture of red and grey walls gathered round a venerable church.

The narrow bridge of three round arches, still showing mason's marks, is said to have been built by the monks of Mattersey Priory, founded in 1185. The only house of the Gilbertine order in the county, its ruins are at the end of a mile-long lane, in a delightful spot where the river swings sharply round in the meadows. In picturesque company with a farmhouse built partly with the stone of the monastery, the whole of the ground plan is laid bare, showing the buildings outlined in grey stone round the four sides of the cloister. There are parts of two walls of the refectory, a corner of a mediaeval tower or chapel which stood north of the small church, the bases of two altars, and several coffin stones.

The church of All Saints has a 15th century tower, with eight gargoyles of ugly little men, which stands partly in the nave, and its narrow arch rests on the heads of a boy and a girl. In the sculpture gallery adorning the north wall of the church outside are three gorilla-like gargoyles on brackets, and heads of human folk, grotesques, and a dog with long ears are on the hoods of the windows and the old doorway.

The nave arcades, with deep-pointed arches on short pillars, come from the end of the 14th century. Older still is the fine little chancel arcade of two bays with nail-head on the capitals and the letter A on a pillar; it is the initial of John Acklom, who repaired the chancel. The lovely 15th century east window of the chapel has blue and yellow fragments of old glass. A further window serves the purpose of a war memorial, showing five soldiers looking up to Our Lord holding a jewelled crown. The south aisle has a founder's recess; the modern font, with elaborate carving of foliage, has an extraordinarily high cover, like a hollow steeple resting on open arcading, crowned by a dove.

Two stone panels set in the walls of the vestry, elaborately carved with figures under canopies, were found under the chancel floor, and are rather battered. In one we see St Martin on horseback sharing his cloak with a beggar, in the other St Helena finding the Cross.

Misson is situated upon the boundary of north Notts, three miles north-east of Bawtry, with Yorkshire on its eastern side and Lincolnshire on the west.

The church of St John the Baptist is chiefly of the Perpendicular, probably 15th century. It was slightly restored in 1860 when the gallery with an organ was removed, and more fully in 1882, when the tower-arch was opened out. In 1892 the structure was severely damaged by lightning, but by 1894 an excellent restoration had been effected, and the old peel of four bells replaced by a new one of six, one bearing the legend "From Lightning and Tempest good Lord deliver us". The oak chancel screen dates from 1906. The lady chapel was erected in 1920 to serve as a memorial to those who lost their lives in the First World War.

Misterton, like Misson, is situated in that low-lying part of north Nottinghamshire that was once covered by a sea. This in time drained away, and left a huge morass stretching on one side into Lincolnshire and far into Yorkshire on the other. It was once known as the drowned lands.

It was lightning in the middle of the last century that led to the restoration and rebuilding of the church of All Saints. The tower was made new in its original 13th century style, and the actual stonework of its windows (with carved hoods) was replaced; the broached spire was added at the same time. Its 13th century arch still opens to the nave, but the glory of the tower is in another arch of that time leading to an aisle. Resting on two splendid corbel brackets carved with flowers and foliage growing from stalks, and framed by a fine hood, it is arresting as we enter the church through a lovely old doorway.

Three fine arcades add to the old array. The 14th century north arcade of the nave has foliage capitals, and two great heads supporting its end arches; one has curled hair, the other has grotesque ears and a beard all round a smiling face. The south arcade comes from the close of the 15th century, the time of the clerestory windows, the chancel arch, and the pillars of the arcade leading to the chancel chapel. These support three horseshoe arches of about 1200, the oldest remains in the church.

The east window with unusual tracery, a piscina with two drains, and the base of the font are mediaeval. A bell in the tower has an inscription older than the Reformation, saying "Let Gabriel's sweetest voice sound forth Jesus".

Among seven striking gargoyles looking out from the north wall are grotesque animals with manes, a griffin, and a creature with a bearded face, the body of a bird, and arms ending in claws.

Moorhouse is a tiny village near Laxton, Moorhouse Chapel stands at the rear of a farmyard. The old chapel was taken down in 1860 and the present structure with a bell turret was erected on its site. It is built of stone from the Laxton field with a dressing of Ancaster stone. The chapel which was opened in June, 1861 is lit by some charming oil lamps. The cost of the building was defrayed by the Rt Hon J. E. Denison.

Morton is a charming little village next to Fiskerton. The church of St Denis dates from 1756, and it is here that the people of Fiskerton also worship. No longer ivy-clad outside, the church has recently been re-decorated and re-pewed. The altar, though simple, has one stained glass window at the rear which is most impressive. Where a stream skirts the village we have a charming glimpse of the dovecote belonging to the manor house.

Netherfield adjoins Carlton and became an ecclesiastical parish in 1885. The church of St George built in 1887 in the Gothic style consists of chancel, nave, vestry, north aisle, south porch, and a western turret. In recent years the choir stalls have been removed from the chancel to the front of the nave.

Newark, or Newark-on-Trent, is situated near the eastern boundry of the county, and stands midway between Nottingham and Lincoln. It has many old and interesting buildings, especially around the Market Place. Its two great attractions are its parish church of St Magdalene and its Castle.

In the days of the first King of All England the Castle was the Key to the North. In Norman days it was rebuilt by the Bishop of Lincoln. In 1216 the wretched King John came here to die after being taken ill at Swineshead Abbey. It was made a ruin in the Civil War, when Newark made its greatest contribution to the story of our land, remaining steadfastly loyal to Charles. It withstood three sieges. South of the town are the Sconce Hills, the surviving fortification of the Royalists, and one of the most perfect examples of military engineering of the Civil War.

Dominating the entrance of the town from the north, the Castle rises between the canal and a garden of green lawn with flowers and trees. The north and west walls are more or less intact, with three corner towers; another tower is in the middle of the west wall, in whose great length are many arches and windows of Norman, Gothic, and Tudor styles. Three windows here belonged to the Great Hall (altered in the 15th century when the castle was a dwelling), and the lovely oriel here has the arms of Thomas Scot, who was Bishop of Lincoln till 1480. Other remains of the Norman Castle are the splendid north-east tower with its three-arched gateway, the south-west tower in which tradition says King John died, and the crypt. In the 13th century the west wall was completed and the six-sided north-west tower was built.

From the Terrace Walk we go down to the fine crypt with a vaulted roof springing from a row of pillars. Here is a big collection of ancient stones (some carved with zigzag and key pattern) which once adorned the castle walls and have been rescued from the canal. Here too is a slit in a wall nearly eight feet thick, and at the end of the crypt is a passage where the sentry could keep watch on the Great North Road. Close by we can see the groove for the portcullis, for here was the watergate and a drawbridge over the moat.

The ground floor of the 13th century north-west tower was the guard room, and in its walls are fragments of zigzag and beak-heads. Below is the dungeon, shaped like a commodious beehive, where one can feel something of the terror of the reign of King John.

It is pleasanter to remember the great days of the Castle, when Edward I and Henry VI came here; when Elizabeth walked through these great rooms, and Cardinal Wolsey called, a tragic figure, on his way to Southwell. Much that he saw we see still, for Newark has many witnesses of those spacious days. We may wonder if any other town so small can be more rich in ancient history. We look through gateway after gateway, along passage after passage, and think ourselves back in the corridors of time. At the entrance to Stodman Street is the house where Governors of the Castle lived during the Civil War, with three tiers of vaulted timber overhanging the street, and black and white walls at the back. At the corner of the market place, by the 18th century town hall, is a glorious peep of Tudor Newark; and at another corner is what many will think the best front Newark has, with overhanging storeys and a charming gallery of 24 painted figures under canopies—gems of antiquity which were looking out across the marketplace long before the first Stuart king passed this way. Once part of the White Hart Inn but now a draper's shop, it is 14th century, one of the oldest domestic buildings in the country.

Near it is the Saracen's Head, where they say Charles I slept, the inn which Scott made a resting-place for Jeanie Deans in his *Heart of Midlothian*. Next door is the Clinton Arms, where Byron stayed to see his first volume of poems through the press; and through its windows Mr Gladstone must have made one of his first political speeches to Newark men. Here he started that career in politics which was without a parallel for magnitude of power and length of days. Near the castle is the old Ram Inn where George Eliot stayed in 1868, and the attractive Ossington Coffee Tavern in 16th century style, built by his wife in memory of Viscount Ossington, Speaker of the House of Commons. Two old houses facing the post office in Kirk Gate, now shops under the projecting timbered storey, belonged to St Leonard's Hospital, a 12th century institution which has become one of the many charities of the town; it is thought that Henrietta Maria stayed here in 1643.

There are gabled houses of the 18th century, and a fine cross with a group of figures in niches round the top. Known as the Beaumond Cross, it is perhaps old enough to be one of the Eleanor crosses which marked the funeral procession of King Edward's queen from Harby to Charing Cross. In Carter Gate nearby Dr Warburton, Bishop of Gloucester, is believed to have been born in 1698, son of the town clerk. Like the musician John Blow (born here and remembered as the organist of Westminster Abbey), Richard Foster Sketchley (another native and a poet on the staff of *Punch*), Dean Hole of Rochester, and Dr Stukely the antiquarian, Dr Warburton was educated at the grammar school founded here by Thomas Magnus, a poor boy who attracted the attention of Cardinal Wolsey and became an ambassador. Now the scholars are in new buildings, but the old school still stands facing the east end of the church, set back from the road and partly hidden by a 19th century front. It has still its fine stepped chimney stack. We enter by the old doorway, and find the Tudor schoolroom restored as it was for the Education Department, with three walls of stone and one timbered.

By it is Newark's admirably arranged museum and art gallery.

The market place has still visible the stone to which bulls were fastened in the days of bull-baiting. Surmounting the town hall front are figures of Justice, a lion, and a unicorn. Rising behind another side of the market square are the tower and spire of the old parish church, second to none in the county. Beautiful indeed is this spire, climbing 252 feet (as high as the church is long) and making a charming end to a view along the narrow Kirk Gate.

There was a Saxon church here, and of the Norman church which followed there remain the vaulted crypt below the sanctuary and the piers of the central crossing, perhaps meant to support a tower which was never built. The lower part of the west tower is 13th century; the rest of it, and the spire, are early 14th, the time of the south aisle of the nave, with beautiful tracery in its great windows and fine heads on the hoods. After the Black Death there was a long pause in the building; the nave, the north aisle, and the chancel are 15th century, and the transepts were added in 1539. Thomas Mering's chantry chapel was founded in 1500; Robert Markham's is six years later, with a small peephole, and with paintings on two stone panels representing the Dance of Death. One painting shows a young man gaily dressed, a feather in his cap; the other is his lordly skeleton, holding a rose.

Looking at the church outside, we do not know whether to be more astonished at the wonderful detail or at its massed effect. The walls have a marvellous gallery of sculpture, with hundreds of gargoyles and figures and shields. Parts of the battlemented parapet are impressive with them, and the traveller will stand long by the war memorial on the green, looking at the tremendous east window with Mary Magdalene in the niche above it, the quaint figures ending the window arches, and a host of curious faces centred in the parapet's panelled tracery.

All the buttresses have gargoyles, all the pinnacles are charming, and the sculpture is remarkably varied. On one east-end buttress are two men in a boat with another man pushing them off; another has two men quarrelling, one pulling the other by the hair. There is another man evidently in distress. Two odd figures at the east window have their hands on their kness. All round the walls are these faces, many worn with time but their expressions still left; it is queer to see the stones still laughing though the face has disappeared. There is a fine corbel table round the walls. The tower has a parapet walk round the spire, statues of the Apostles in niches, and a lovely west doorway with carving in its mouldings and in the niche at each side. Indoors we find similar ornament adorning the massive 13th century arch of the tower, which has smaller arches opening to the aisles. Angels adorn the nave arcades, the arches resting on lofty clustered pillars with capitals carved with foliage and faces and symbols of the Four Evangelists. The splendid clerestory runs above the arcades in the chancel.

The west window of the tower has ten stately figures of familiar saints, the north aisle has a dozen figures from the Old Testament and little scenes from their lives, and in two Kempe windows of the south aisle are the Four Evangelists and Old Testament characters. The most precious window here is the east of the south chancel aisle, filled with a medley of old glass in red, blue, and silver; in the thousands of small fragments about 200 faces can be recognised, one piece showing two people whispering.

One thing stands out grandly in this place, the lovely screen carved in oak as the 15th century was closing. It crosses the face of the chancel and turns east to enclose the 26 stalls; black with age, it is enriched with tracery under a vaulted canopy with a cornice of vines. The stalls are fit to keep it company. They have arm-rests neatly carved with heads, quaint animals, and grotesques, and misereres among the best of their day, showing the humour and philosophy of the 15th century craftsmen. One has an owl carrying off a rat, dragons on another have crowns round their necks, a man on a monster is fighting a cockatrice, there are two lizards, and two birds are pecking grapes. In the fine poppyheads we see heads and grotesques, a bird in an oak tree, and lions and a dragon which seem to be fighting. At the end of the stalls on each side is a 19th century oak and brass screen, and there are old benches with carved ends in the chancel aisles.

Behind the high altar is a row of 13 stone seats in the lady chapel, their canopies enriched with tiny heads of animals and people. Running along the top are queer creatures, and above is a modern mosaic with 16 angels; it is a copy of Van Eyck's triptych of the *Adoration of the Lamb* at Ghent.

Enclosed by good modern screenwork at the east end of the north chancel aisle is the memorial chapel for those who never came back, with a tin hat worn in France, and a book of names on a bracket carved with a crouching hooded man.

The font was broken up in the Civil War, and repaired with a new bowl in 1660. The lower part of the stem is 15th century, and it is curious that each of the 16 figures round it is partly mediaeval and partly of the later time. Its fine lofty cover is 19th century. The pulpit was made to match the screen. The big painting of the *Raising of Lazarus* was once the altarpiece. There is an old pillar almsbox, and in the upper room of the south porch is part of a library left by a 17th century vicar. Modern stone figures of Mary and Gabriel are in niches by the east window of the lady chapel.

Two painted wall monuments have figures of 17th century men: Robert Ramsey, a servant of Charles I in his early days (with a moustache and pointed beard) and Thomas Atkinson, who lived to see the second Charles enthroned; very miserable he looks, with a cherub and a skull to keep him company. At the back of the screen in the north aisle is tucked away the painted bust of a man like Shakespeare, a mayor of Newark in Cromwell's day. Robert Browne's tomb in the lady chapel has shields of arms; he was a 16th century benefactor of Newark, and the glass in the clerestory windows of the church was paid for out of the rents of his charity for ten years of last century. A wall memorial in the south chancel aisle is to Hercules Clay, who gave money for an annual sermon and a dole of bread. A 16th century brass of an unknown civilian is in the north transept, and at the west end is the brass portrait of William Phyllypot, who died in the same century. Let in the wall at this end of the church are two very queer faces, one with three mouths, two noses, and three eyes, the quaint fancy of a mediaeval mason.

An extraordinary work of art that has survived the centuries is a colossal brass, one of the four biggest Flemish brasses left in England. It is much worn, but a tracing below enables us to see Alan Fleming, who founded a chantry here in 1349 for a priest to pray daily for his household. He stands with his hands at prayer, curls on this head, his cloak richly embroidered, and all about him traceried canopies and 50 small figures.

The reredos in the chancel, blazing with gold and reflecting the sunlight, is the work of J. N. Comper. In the centre is Our Risen Lord, and below and at each side are painted scenes and figures. We see the angels at the empty tomb, Mary Magdalene kneeling, the Raising of Lazarus, the anointing of Christ's feet at Bethany, the Entombment, Mary Magdalene announcing the Resurrection to the Apostles, and Gabriel and Mary with 14 other saints.

Who knows John Arderne of Newark? Yet five centuries ago he burst upon the darkened sky of England like a comet of learning and healing, than sank and left medicine and surgery to quacks and wizards. He was our first real doctor.

Where and when he was born is beyond discovery, but this fact we have in his writings: "From the first pestilence which was in the year our Lord 1349 till the year 1370, I lived at Newark in the county of Nottingham."

Arderne was a genius of the first magnitude two centuries before Harvey. He came to London from Newark in the plenitude of his powers, and seems to have taken all our princes and potentates under his care. His patients included the Black Prince, whom he appears to have accompanied at the Battle of Crecy; Henry of Lancaster and other warriors whose names blaze in the warlike annals of the age; and preachers, merchants, and others who formed the background of that warring era. All these he cites among the cases he had treated. He wrote books in Latin, but was not of the order of twaddling schoolmen. He seems to have known Hippocrates and Galen but nothing of his French and Italian contemporaries. How he got his skill and knowledge is a perfect mystery, but in an age which knew almost nothing of science, and appealed to magic and the moon for cures, he towers ahead of the rest of the world.

He was a brilliant operating surgeon, with a knowledge of anatomy astonishing for the period, and he taught by his books as gladly as he cured. He withheld nothing that study and practice had enabled him to perform.

There were no anaesthetics in Arderne's day, yet he insisted that the patient should be rendered unconscious before an operation, and then, "If you must cut, do so boldly; loss of blood is less, and shock minimised." Five hundred years before Pasteur and Lister he proclaimed the necessity of aseptic surgery. "Keep wounds clean (he said); they should heal without suppuration; but where this does occur assist the process by washing, that the wound may heal from the bottom upwards; otherwise do not dress too frequently."

Yet the teachings of this old seer, a miraculous man of his age with his miracles based on reason, were forgotten and lost for ages, and his work gave place to methods of gross superstition. It has remained for our own day to realise what a genius came out of Newark to offer health and healing to a disease-ridden realm.

Newstead, a much sought after residential area some nine miles north of Nottingham, is in beautiful wooded countryside. Newstead Abbey, or to give it its correct title, Priory, was founded in the year 1170 by King Henry II as an act of atonement for the murder of Thomas Becket. In the middle of the 16th century with the reformation and the enforced Dissolution of Monasteries, it provided ready cash and negotiable property for King Henry VIII, to whom Newstead Priory was surrendered in July, 1539. The following year Henry granted Newstead to Sir John Byron, and his accession to Newstead was the beginning of a long line which culminated with George Gordon Noel, the 6th Lord Byron and poet. He was born in 1788, but spent very little of his time within the walls of Newstead, and in November, 1817 the Abbey was sold to his school fellow and friend, Col Wildman, for £94,000. Col Wildman's executors sold the estate to Mr W. F. Webb in 1860, and Newstead remained in this family until 1931, at which time Mr C. I. Fraser, the grandson of Mr Webb, sold it to Sir Julian Cahn, who in turn presented it to the city of Nottingham. At the handing-over ceremony on July 16, 1931, M. Venizelos, then Prime Minister of Greece, came to honour the memory of Lord Byron, who went out to Greece to give active support to the revolution there in 1823.

For a small charge visitors are shown round the abbey, and among the apartments which are on view are the vaulted crypt, Lord Byron's dining room containing a carved mantelpiece of the 16th century (which is reputed to have come from Colwick Hall, near Nottingham) and the famous painting of Lord Byron by Thomas Philips.

The great drawing room (formerly the monk's refectory) now contains the Roe-Byron collection, bequeathed to the city by the late Herbert Charles Roe. There is also Byron's bedroom, with large four-poster bed, and the table on which he wrote *English Bards and Scotch Reviewers*, and adjoining it the supposed haunted room. It was here also that the prior could observe all that was going on in the abbey church below. Proceeding downstairs one comes to the

The church and bridge at Mattersey

Newark Castle

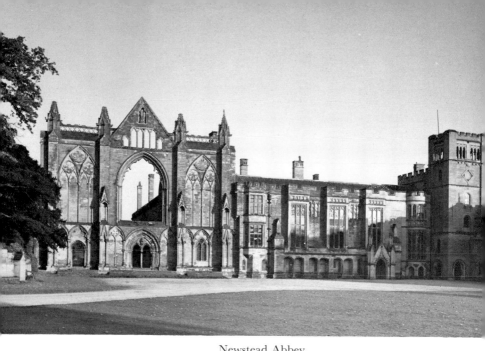

Newstead Abbey

A detail of the Gallery ceiling in Newstead Abbey

cloisters, and then the chapter-house, now furnished as a chapel. The crypt contains monuments to Sir John Byron (died 1567), that of his son, Little Sir John with the great beard (died 1604), and the third and fourth Byrons who died in 1623 and 1625 respectively. There are also some interesting relics of the Wildman family. David Livingstone was at one time a guest of the Webb family, and stayed for seven months between 1864–65, and wrote his book, *The Zambesi and its Tributaries*. A plaque recording this was unveiled on September 10, 1949.

The gardens, which are open throughout the year, cannot fail to delight all who visit them. The Japanese water-garden was constructed by Miss Webb, daughter of a former owner of Newstead, and the teahouse, as well as many of the plants, actually came from Japan. There is also the eagle pond, so named because of the eagle-shaped lectern recovered from it, and which is now in Southwell Minster. Close to the Abbey on the eastern side is the monument to Boatswain, Byron's Newfoundland dog, which died on November 18, 1808. Inscribed on the monument are the words that Byron wrote in honour of his beloved companion:

> *Near this Spot*
> *are deposited the remains of one*
> *who possessed Beauty without Vanity,*
> *Strength without Insolence,*
> *Courage without Ferocity,*
> *and all the Virtues of Man without his Vices.*
> *This Praise which would be unmeaning*
> *Flattery if inscribed over human Ashes*
> *is but a just tribute to the memory of*
> *Boatswain, a Dog*
> *who was born in Newfoundland, May 1803,*
> *and died at Newstead, November 18th, 1808.*

Near to Newstead is Fishpool, where, on March 22, 1962, the driver of a mechanical shovel unearthed a collection of coins which was probably the largest hoard of gold ever found in this country. It consisted of 1063 coins and nine pieces of jewellery. The total

K

value of the coins and jewellery was in excess of £250,000. It is thought that this hoard was buried just before or after the Battle of Hexham in May, 1464.

Normanton-on-Soar lines the bank of the Soar where it is for a long placid stretch the delight of river lovers.

The treasure of the village is the aisleless church of St James, almost wholly 13th century, with one of the county's two central towers crowned with a spire. The spire springs from a corbel table of heads much worn by time, and is lofty and beautiful. The transept forming the north arm of the cross is 19th century; the timbered porch is made new, but it shelters a lovely 13th century doorway letting us in.

Among the charming old windows are many lancets, one with a hood of four-leaved flowers. The great west window is a group of five. The east window, with quatrefoils in the tracery, is 14th century. The font was cut from a single stone and richly carved 600 years ago. The old altar stone in the lady chapel has still five consecration crosses, but the epitaphs on three old gravestones are worn with the feet of many generations. The panelled roof of the chancel has carved medallions, and five old tie-beams in the nave roof have carved bosses. Seven splendid oak benches are over 400 years old, there is an old chest, and the arms of Charles II are handsomely fashioned in plaster.

Normanton-on-Trent. It has on each side of it a stream flowing to the Trent, gay gardens, and a neat little church. On one side of the churchyard is a fine row of yews and beeches, through which we have a peep of the trim lawn and trees of the great house.

Though the church of St Matthew is much restored, some of it stands as it stood in mediaeval England, the nave arcades and the chancel arch 14th century, the tower and the clerestory 15th. The altar table is Jacobean, a stout ironbound chest is two centuries older, tracery from old bench-ends enriches new seats in the chancel, and there is old work left in the roof. The shallow bowl of a Norman font is set up in the churchyard.

North Collingham. It shares some things with South Collingham, its close neighbour. Both line a stretch of the road between Newark and Gainsborough, and each has a lovely old church set in its most charming spot, built of the limestone quarried on this eastern bank of the Trent.

Both belong to a neighbourhood of ancient story. South-east is Brough, the site of a Roman station on the Fosse Way. East of the villages, still on the Fosse Way, is the grassy slope of Potter's Hill with a tumulus, and just below the hill between 60 and 70 skeletons were found a century ago.

Its 14th century cross can be seen outside a local garage. Its three feet of shaft with traces of carving rests on a huge stone and a flight of three great steps, each 14 inches deep, the bottom one nearly three yards square.

High above a quiet wayside is the church of All Saints, looking down through a fine screen of elms, taller than the tower, to a pretty lane crossing the Fleet in the willows. This delightful spot has more than once been a scene of desolation, for in the churchyard wall are stones showing the height of floods which made this countryside a sea. One near the church gate is the base stone of an old cross, still with its socket, and it marks the height reached by the river in the devastating flood of 1795, when the Trent and the Witham joined owing to a sudden thaw after a seven-weeks' frost; it was about five feet above the level of the road. The other stone marks the flood height of 1875, which was 21 inches lower than in 1795.

The 15th century tower has a huge buttress at one corner, and the outer moulding of its fine arch to the nave rests on two heads, one with a tranquil expression, and the other grotesque with a toothless grin. The north side of this tower arch is the oldest part of the building, coming from the end of the 12th century.

In the 15th century north porch (with a stone roof) are two 14th century coffin stones carved with praying figures. The south porch is a little younger than the north; both shelter fine original doors, and another old door opens to the vestry. The glory of the church is in the 13th century nave arcades with clustered pillars: the north, the older of the two, has capitals carved with leaf and scrool, and one with two corbel heads.

Above the 15th century chancel arch is a row of seven heraldic misereres reaching from wall to wall; they are over 400 years old, and were placed here when the stalls were destroyed last century. Some old beams are in the chancel roof, and the beautiful modern roof of the nave has floral bosses. There are two old piscinas, and the massive 700-year-old font has a 17th century pyramid cover with a mass of carving.

North Leverton is east of East Retford. Its church of St Wilfrid is approached down a tiny lane overhung by lofty chestnuts, which appears unexpectedly between the houses.

The church is more attractive outside than in, and tells its oldest story in Norman masonry in the north wall of the chancel. Only a little later is the handsome doorway through which we enter, built when the Norman style was passing, the shafts on each side with capitals of stiff foliage. Among some fine 14th century windows still remaining are five in the chancel with flowing tracery. The embattled tower is 15th century, and the nave arcade comes from about 1300. There are two old piscinas, an image bracket, and buttresses with canopied niches.

At the far end of the village is a windmill built in 1813 to serve the surrounding district. It was increased in height and the present top was added in 1884. In 1958 it was struck by lightning for the third time in its history, and as a result four new sails had to be provided. These and other necessary repairs were completed in 1960, the cost being defrayed by grants, loans, and the generosity of gifts from friends and visitors. It was completely repainted and tarred in 1963.

North Muskham is the next village after South Muskham and is some three miles north of Newark. The ferry which once linked this village with Holme, across the Trent, no longer exists.

Like its neighbouring village the church is dedicated to St Wilfrid. Its embattled grey walls are adorned with many corbels, and gargoyles of grinning figures and grotesque heads. Two crowned women smile from a window, a winged grotesque shows two teeth, and a staring jester is holding his knee.

The lowest stages of the tower are 13th century, its small west window is a century younger, and the rest is 500 years old. A splendid door of studded oak opens to a delightful interior, where bright light streaming through plain glass in most of the windows falls on white walls and stone arcades, and on a wealth of lovely woodwork old and new. The south arcade is a little earlier in the 15th century than the north, which has fragments of a Norman arcade.

The shallow 15th century bowl of the font is on a tall Jacobean shaft; its fine cover of gilded oak is new, with winged grotesques, and a charming figure of John the Baptist. The bowl of an ancient font lies in the nave, and the chancel has its old piscina.

Among old glass fragments is the tun with a bar across the head, the picture name of the Bartons, who lived at Holme in the 15th century and were good friends to the church. They built this north aisle, which has a window with 28 of their small barrels, and three buttresses showing their initials and arms in panels carved with oak leaves and acorns; there are the three bucks' heads of their shield, and their badge of a chained bear sniffing at a barrel. In the aisle hangs a copy of the will of John Barton, who lies in Holme Church, his original will being in Nottingham Castle.

There is a lovely east window and many beautiful examples of old woodwork. The chancel roof with floral bosses is part of the modern woodwork completing the scheme.

A Crucifix shrine to eight men who died for their country was made from the wood of the old training ship *Britannia*. A curious memorial is an alabaster pyramid to John Smith of 1591, three of its sides filled with the terms of his will.

North Wheatley is 5½ miles north-east of East Retford. Set among limes and elms is the small aisleless church of St Peter and St Paul which has a 15th century tower, a chancel made new last century, a new timbered porch, and a story as old as the huge Norman font. A curious relic projecting from the wall, looking like a stoup, is really a mortar with stone bands. The nave has a mediaeval piscina and old tiebeams in its roof; the 17th century pulpit and the old rood beam across the tower are partly restored, and 25 traceried bench-ends come from about 1500.

A wonderful oak stairway to the platform where the bellringers stand is a fascinating possession; grey with age, it has 28 steps of roughly trimmed and quartered logs secured with wooden pegs to two stout beams, each of which is over a yard round near the top.

A brass inscription to a London wine dealer of 1445 is a memorial for a second time, for on the other side is an epitaph to Joan Cokesay. Adam Haket's 15th century floorstone has a cross and coats-of-arms. There are three Elizabethan chalices and three small Jacobean altar tables. Two 13th century shafts support stone tables under the tower and in the vestry.

There is a delightful view of the village from South Wheatley half a mile away, the home of a few folk who lost their church half a century ago. Its chalice and altar table are with those at North Wheatley, and its ancient font is in a Nottingham church. In the old churchyard stands the tiny Norman chancel arch, looking across what was once the nave to the 15th century tower, with its arch built up and two of its pinnacles gone.

Norwell lies 6½ miles north-west of Newark, and was once known as Northwell (distinct from Southwell).

The church of St Lawrence stands in a churchyard with fine elms and chestnuts, and a sundial 200 years old. It came into Domesday Book, and there are remains of Norman days in the fine grey pile. With transepts and a splendid western tower with a domed cap, it is beautiful indoors and out. Except that it was topped and pinnacled in the 15th century, the tower is 13th century.

The 600-year-old porch shelters a splendid Norman doorway with detached pillars. The north arcade is as old as the porch, but the south, with round pillars and scalloped capitals, comes from about 1190. Each arcade has a smaller arch at the west end, resting on 13th century corbels.

The village is proud of its church's mediaeval windows. The long lines of the clerestory on each side show quatrefoils in diamond-shaped tracery. The 700-year-old arch frames a lovely picture of the chancel with some lancets, and a 14th century east window with modern glass on delicate colours, showing the Crucifixion with Mary and John, St Lawrence, and Hugh of Lincoln.

The fine old roof of the north transept has moulded beams and carved bosses. On the arch from this transept to the aisle is the great head of a grotesque with pointed ears and a mouth showing three huge teeth. Two little heads adorn an aumbry, and lining its wall is part of a Norman coffin stone. A pretty effect is given by three steps leading to the narrow doorway of the old rood stairway. A handsome piscina in the south transept is carved with foliage and faces.

In three recesses are memorials. One is a loose stone carving of a head with wavy locks, another is a 14th century cross-legged knight with his sword and shield, and the third is a woman in a wimple with a charming face, her hands at prayer, and a dog at her feet.

In September 1967 a production of *Son et Lumière* was held at this church with the intention of raising funds for its restoration. This showing was the first of its kind in the East Midlands.

Nottingham. The Romans were hereabouts, but the town has no trace of them; the Saxons made it a place of importance (Snotinga-ham), and the Normans gave it the name we know. The Saxons are said to have built a tower on the summit of the great rock which rose above the marshes on the edge of the dense forest, and not long after Egbert had consolidated England the Danes came down the Trent and planted their standard on the Rock. King Alfred, after a long struggle, compelled them to come to terms, and in the division of the country which followed Nottingham became the chief of the five Danish Burghs. Alfred's son began the reconquest of Danish England, and recovered the old kingdom, his success in the Mid-lands culminating in the capture of Nottingham. He fortified it with a wall and a ditch, giving the wall towers and gateways, and cutting most of the ditch from the solid rock. He threw a bridge across the

Trent and built Bridgford. Athelstan, first king crowned for all England, set up a mint here, and his coins have the mark of the town.

In the days of the Normans the story of the town became closely linked with that of the castle, which the Conqueror ordered William Peverel to build on the precipitous rock. The Normans settled about the castle and left the people undisturbed, so that for a time there were two races in Norman Nottingham, the Saxons in the English borough on St Mary's Hill, the Normans in the French borough, each borough having its own laws and customs, its town hall, and its mint. Henry I rebuilt William Peverel's wooden fortress in stone, but his castle was burned down, and was rebuilt by Henry II, whose energy and goodwill Nottingham has reason to remember. He gave it its first charter in 1155, and in 1177 held in the town a council for establishing judicial circuits throughout the land. He helped the people to rebuild the town and closed it with more extensive fortifications, and encouraged the dyed-cloth industry which was growing. He held Nottingham Castle as a royal fortress and rebuilt it on a grander scale, and he loved to hunt in the neighbouring Sherwood Forest. He gave the castle to his terrible son John, to whom, in spite of his cruelty, Nottingham was always loyal. Yet the town has witnessed no more ghastly scene than that enacted on the castle ramparts in 1212, when John, furious at the news of another Welsh rebellion, ordered the hanging of 28 youths who were held as hostages for the good conduct of their fathers.

The son of the Norman founder of our Parliament, Simon de Montfort, became Governor of the castle in due course, and in the reign of Edward I the town elected its own mayor. Edward II lived at the castle, and in the early years of Edward III his mother, Queen Isabella, and her favourite Roger Mortimer, established themselves here. In 1330 they were captured by the young king and his followers, who secretly entered the castle by the passage through the rock known as Mortimer's Hole. We may go down it today. Edward held several Parliaments here where laws were passed which were to have a great influence on the growing trade of the town, the manufacture of wool into cloth. Richard II sat here in conference with his judges, and sought in vain to encroach on the liberties of the people. Henry IV found refuge here during rebellions and here he imprisoned Owen Glendower. Edward IV proclaimed himself king from the castle and here denounced Warwick the Kingmaker as a traitor. He lived here in sumptuous style and made many improvements in the castle which were completed by his bloodstained successor Richard III. We may still see part of a tower built by Richard; it is in a garden nearby.

It was from Nottingham that Richard set out for Bosworth Field, there to end the Plantagenet dynasty and to bring in the reign of the Tudors; and it was at Nottingham, when the Tudor dynasty was over, that Charles I raised his standard on Standard Hill, at a spot marked by a tablet in the roadway looking down to the castle grounds; it is near the entrance to the hospital. It was during the Civil War that the heroic Colonel Hutchinson held the castle for the Parliament, refusing the Duke of Newcastle's offer of £10,000 and the gift of the castle if he would join the king's side. His answer was that if the duke wanted the castle he must wade to it through blood, and the story of the colonel's courage in holding the town is nobly told by Lucy Hutchinson in her memoirs of her husband's life. When the war was over Parliament gave the garrison £1000, and the castle itself was dismantled and mostly demolished. The site was purchased by William Cavendish, the first Duke of Newcastle, and the building of a new castle was begun in 1674. Reform Bill supporters set it on fire in 1831 and it was a ruin for 44 years. The Corporation acquired the lease in 1875 and it was opened by the Prince of Wales (Edward VII) as the first provincial museum of the fine and applied arts.

Nottingham Castle became the property of the city in November, 1952 when it was purchased from the Oxford University Trust for £16,000, the Trust having previously bought it from the Duke of Newcastle.

The Market Place was for centuries the largest of its kind in England with an area of $5\frac{1}{2}$ acres. In the mid-twenties a decision was made to replace the Old Exchange which overlooked the Market Place with a more worthy building. In 1928 the market was moved to King Edward Street and provided with covered accommodation. Where the old stalls stood there are now lawns and flower beds flanking the processional way.

The Council House was designed by Cecil Howitt. The foundation stone was laid on May 17, 1927 by Alderman H. Bowles, and the building was opened by HRH the Duke of Windsor, then Prince of Wales, on May 22, 1929.

The splendid two-storeyed dome is impressive by day and by night, for at night it is floodlit. The plain lower storey has openings on four of its eight sides; the second storey adorned with four groups of sculpture by old students of the College of Art, the sculptures representing Law, Prosperity, Knowledge, and Commerce. We may climb up 70 steps to this colonnaded storey where we are rewarded with the sight of the bells and the spectacle of the Queen of the Midlands with the country round about her. There are five bells in this great dome, weighing over 16 tons, one of them (Little John), said to be the biggest of all tuned bells, weighing 10 tons. Except for great Peter of York, it is the heaviest bell in the provinces, and the hammer for striking the hours on it weighs a quarter of a ton.

The dome looks down from its 200-feet height to the floor of a spacious arcade of shops and offices, approached by great arches from the streets. Round the bottom of the dome we read that the Corporation of Nottingham erected this building for Counsel and Welcome, and to show Merchandise and Crafts. The spandrels of the dome are enriched with frescoes by a Nottingham artist (Noel Denholm Davis), showing in unfading colour four scenes in the city's story: the coming of the Danes, the Conqueror ordering the building of the Castle, Robin Hood and his band, and Charles I raising his standard.

On the ground floor of the Council House front, looking down on the great square, an arcaded portico guarded by two lions leads to the loggia. Above the arcade are eight columns supporting a pediment with sculpture representing the activities of the city. There are about 20 figures and a group of animals sculptured by Joseph Else, at one time principal of the College of Art. In the middle is Justice with scales and a golden sword, her eyes open; Education and Law stand beside her; Labour has a team of horses, and Agriculture has sheep and oxen. Another group represents Motherhood. A mason is erecting a column, a sculptor is carving figures of a woman and a child, there is an artist with his palette and a woman with musical instruments, and a reclining figure is bearing a model of the domed Council House.

Above the great windows of the reception hall, which look on to the square from behind the eight columns, runs a charming frieze with a procession of sturdy children engaged in the arts and crafts and industries in which Nottingham is or has been renowned. There are reapers, weavers, spinners, and iron workers with anvil and forge. Eight children carry a great bell, reminding us of the bell-founders famous here from the 16th to the 18th century; and eight little coal miners are hacking and drawing tubs of coal, reminding us of the days when such children worked in the mines. Children working on the tomb of a knight recall the alabaster carvers famous in mediaeval centuries, and leather workers represent an industry that is thriving still, 60,000 sheepskins being dressed every week in the city.

In the floor of the entrance hall is a mosaic of the city arms made up of 700 pieces. The balustraded staircase is lit by a beautiful dome of 144 panels of amber-tinted glass. At the top of the first flight of steps stands William Reid Dick's bronze figure of a woman holding out her arms in welcome, above her a fine wall painting by Noel Denholm Davis, representing Merchandise, Counsel, Welcome, and Crafts. All the floors have panelled rooms with lovely ceilings and hidden lights, or light shining from beautiful electroliers of bronze or crystal. The woodwork is walnut and oak. The reception hall has 20 fine columns and a panelled ceiling, decorated in cream relieved with pink and blue and gold. Its floor is oak, walnut, and pearwood, and at one end is a mirrored wall adding to the charm, while looking down from above are galleries for minstrels and guests. The Lord Mayor's Parlour has on each side of the fireplace and the door exquisite carving in limewood of flowers, fruit, and wheat, and some panelling from Aston Hall in Derbyshire. The handsome dining hall has walnut walls with a striking figured panel over the fireplace, and the room of the lady mayoress is in Adam style with green and gold walls. In the Member's Room the ceiling is enriched with vines, and on the table is the telephone which we are told was the 100,000th instrument installed in the North Midlands. The Council Chamber forms a semi-circle, where every member sits within 26 feet of the lord mayor's chair. The walls are panelled with walnut, with loose tapestry panels over a lining of seaweed, an ingenious device for helping the acoustics of the Chamber. One of the mottoes here is, "Laws are made for the good and safety of the State". There is a small mallet (for the chairman's use) made of oak from a pier of old Trent Bridge, and there are pictures of Old Nottingham by Tom Hammond on the walls of the corridors.

We may wish it had been possible, in the replanning of this heart of the town, to open up the view of the castle on the rock from the great square. It would have been one of the finest spectacles in the heart of any city. As it is, the castle is but a stone's throw or two up a street off the square, so that we step from the City Centre to the Castle Rock in a very few minutes. One of Nottingham's rare sights is at the entrance gateway to the castle, with banked lawns like velvet, rockeries and trees climbing to the terrace, and delightful flower beds.

There are magnificent views to the south and west from the terrace. On one of the lawns is Nottingham's memorial to Albert Ball, VC, the gallant airman who accounted for 47 enemy aircraft and was killed in action on May 7, 1917, three months after receiving the freedom of Nottingham when he was only 20.

By a broad path is part of an old bastion of the old castle wall, and here also is a lead cistern of 1681. At the end of a path leading to the inner moat is a square block, built up with original stones of the town wall which came to light when the Great Central Railway was being laid through Nottingham, and facing it stands a Georgian doorway. An old stone archway leads into the moat, now a charming walk and bowered with trees, from which rustic paths wind up the steep bank to the castle. An interesting relic in the moat is a great oak beam taken from a pier of a 17th century bridge over the Trent at Cromwell, near Newark. It was found in the river bed some years ago.

Down a flight of steps leading from the terrace one may visit the castle caves, the tour of which has recently been extended, which means that after descending to Mortimer's Hole, one does not return by the same route, but makes a circular tour. The guide points out many interesting features, e.g. the holes in the rock where cannon balls were secured prior to being fired. At the foot of the castle rock are some caves and evidence of a first line of defence. It is from this point that one continues up steps in the face of the rock to what is now known as the Western Passage. A chamber which was used as a chapel with altar is pointed out, and farther along one comes to what may have been a guard room. A new stairway has been fixed, which leads to a chamber with a brick arched roof, which was the original wine cellar of the Duke of Newcastle. From this point the guide takes one down a flight of steps to the dungeons, which consist of two chambers, one 12 feet by 24 feet and the other 33 feet by 14 feet.

We enter the castle under a crescent colonnade, where is an array of bronze memorials of renowned poets. Here is Albert Toft's bust of Philip James Bailey, with a plaque on the pedestal showing Festus. Oliver Sheppard's bust of Henry Kirke White has on the pedestal a bowed woman holding a spray of laurel. George Frampton's busts of William and Mary Howitt are delightful; Mary's cap is tied under her chin, and her arm is round William's shoulder, both looking at an open book. Byron's bust is by Alfred Drury. There are two sculptured panels by Ernest Gillick, one showing Thomas Miller, the basket-maker's apprentice who wrote *Songs of the Sea-nymphs*, the other showing Robert Millhouse with his quill pen; he was the weaver-poet who worked a stocking-frame when he was ten, sang in the choir of St Peter's Church, and lies in the General Cemetery here.

In the castle museum are to be found paintings by local artists such as Bonington, the Sandbys (Paul and Thomas), and Dame Laura Knight, as well as many by other artists. There is ironwork that once adorned one of Nottingham's famous buildings, and some of the stately coaches from the 17th century. On the walls is a fine collection of electro-type reproductions of coins from BC to AD. As re-development continues in the city, so are more caves uncovered. These have yielded pottery in the form of earthenware jars and beakers, some of which are now on display in the museum.

In May, 1928 two canoes reputed to be 2500 years old were found opposite Clifton Grove, and they are now exhibited along with various spears and other bronze age weapons. There is a collection of souvenirs of Captain Albert Ball, VC, and a section allotted to the Sherwood Foresters Regiment. Downstairs the rooms exhibit dress throughout the centuries and there are some models of early lace machines. A recent acquisition is the Gibbs collection of antique silver weighing in all some 6700 ounces, and including items from the 17th, 18th, and 19th centuries.

Outside the main gateway on Castle Green is to be found a statue of Robin Hood, who is surrounded by Friar Tuck reading, Little John repairing his bow, Will Stukeley singing and Alan-a-Dale accompanying himself on a harp as he sings to Will Scarlet. There are also four reliefs fixed into the Castle Wall. Maid Marian helps Robin and Friar Tuck in their fight against Guy of Gisborne's men, and in another King Richard the Lion Heart joins her hand with that of Robin. The remaining two reliefs show Robin and Little John fighting on the bridge, and Robin shooting his last arrow. The statue, which was a gift to the city by Philip Clay, was sculptured by Mr James Woodford and was unveiled by the Duchess of Portland on July 24, 1952.

Nearly two miles from the Council House and the historic castle is Nottingham University, rising on a green hill overlooking the Boulevard named after it. The antecedents of the University of Nottingham were the Adult School established in 1798, and the University Extensions Lectures inaugurated by the University of Cambridge in 1873, the first of their kind in the country. In 1875 an anonymous donor provided £10,000 to establish this work on a permanent basis, and the Corporation of Nottingham agreed to erect and maintain a building for this purpose and to provide funds to supply instruction. The foundation of the original University College building in Shakespeare Street was laid on September 27, 1877 by HRH Prince Leopold, Duke of Albany, although the Charter incorporating the University College of Nottingham was not granted until 1903.

After the First World War the College outgrew its buildings, and the constriction imposed by its site was removed when Sir Jesse Boot, afterwards Baron Trent, provided the spacious grounds on which the present buildings stand. The building which he provided, now known as Trent Building, was opened by His Majesty King George V on July 10, 1928. The grounds, which are open to the public all the year round, have a putting green and lido and a large boating lake making the centre piece in front of the main building.

Nottingham has been an industrial city for many generations. It was mining coal in mediaeval days. It has been linked with the hosiery and lace trades from their birth, for both owe their beginning to the genius of William Lee, a curate a few miles away, whose hand-frame for knitted stockings, invented in the time of Queen Elizabeth I, was the first machine ever known to make a looped or knitted fabric. The first of many improvements in the stocking-frame came in 1758 in Jedediah Strutt's invention for making a ribbed frame, and the next advance was the introduction of the "circular looped wheel" frame. Two centuries after its invention by Lee the stocking-frame was adapted for producing lace. John Heathcote's twist lace machine came in 1809, and the net-weaving machines of John Levers a little later. The coming of Hargreaves with his jenny and Arkwright with his spinning-frame had given a great impetus to the town's industrial activity, and Nottingham saw the first cotton mill built in England, in the year 1769.

The trades of Nottingham are numerous and varied. Boots, Players, Raleigh, and Ericssons are household names and known the world over. There is bleaching, dyeing, brewing, box-making, and thermometers, electronics, printing and stationery, leather, furniture, building, and among its uncommon industries is that of making glass eyes. Everywhere in its street names we are reminded of the old trades of the city. The wheel-wrights lived in Wheeler Gate; Bridle-smith Gate and Smithy Row echoed with the clang of the hammer and anvil. The tanners were in Barker Gate and the fur workers in Pilcher Gate.

Nottingham has much to offer in the form of entertainment and recreation. The Theatre Royal celebrated its centenary in 1965. Many shows are put on here prior to London production as Nottingham's theatre-goers are considered to be good judges of a successful show. The Nottingham Playhouse had its beginnings in Goldsmith Street, where it staged its last production in July 1963. With a small seating capacity and cramped conditions backstage a move to new premises was inevitable. Their new building, which stands in East Circus Street, was designed by Peter Moro, Associate Architect of London's Festival Hall, and was opened on December 11, 1963 in the presence of Lord Snowdon. Its main feature is its cylindrical auditorium specially designed to accommodate two different forms of stage, the "picture frame" type and the "open stage". It has a seating capacity of 750 with spacious foyers and a number of bars. Among the recreational facilities are the Ice Stadium, Lower Parliament Street, a Bowling Alley in Barker Gate, while the Harvey Hadden Stadium at Bilborough offers the athlete a fine running track, cycling track, and large arena for football pitch and field events. Nottingham is fortunate in having several fine parks. These include the Arboretum in Waverley Street, where band concerts are held during the summer months. There is a modern aviary here overlooking the duck-pond, and many beautiful trees and flower-beds. Within walking distance is the Forest Recreation Ground, which has many sporting facilities including cricket, football, and bowling and putting greens. On the first Thursday of October in each year Nottingham holds its annual Goose Fair on a site at the western end of the Forest. This fair, which had for many years been held in Nottingham's Market Place, was moved to its present site in 1928.

Thousands of city folk seek their recreation by the river, a most attractive place which may be taken as a model by many towns which waste their river banks. From time immemorial the crossing of the Trent at Nottingham has been an important link between north and south, but the first bridge of which we know was built of wood a thousand years ago. The mediaeval stone bridge had a chapel, and a shallow arch of it is preserved in the new traffic island.

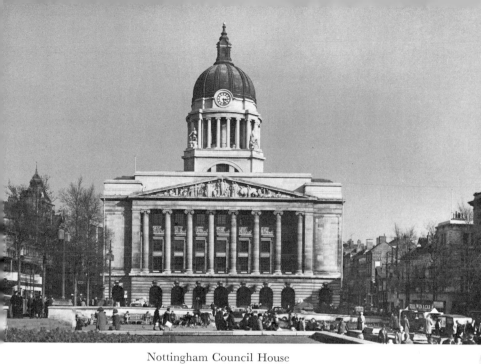

Nottingham Council House

Nottingham Castle

The Trip to Jerusalem inn at Nottingham

Ossington Church

The present Trent Bridge was built by M. O. Tarbotton, Borough Surveyor, in the years 1867–71. From this bridge to Wilford Toll Bridge a magnificent promenade runs for over a mile, covering 28 acres, shaded first by fir trees and then by limes. On one hand is green lawn and a fine flight of steps, while on the other side are wide playing fields, green spaces, and the attractive memorial gardens. The iron gates of the latter are enriched with scrolls of the city's arms and along the top of the gateway is the city's motto, "Vivit Post Funera Virtus".

Of Nottingham's great group of churches and chapels only a few are old. In the heart of the Lace Market, crowning the hill which rises 90 feet above the low land which was once green meadows, rises the stately church of St Mary's, its tower ten feet higher than the top of the castle to which it looks across the city roofs. It rises 126 feet, with eight pinnacles, and is as old as the Tudor dynasty. The church is a splendid example of 15th century work and has impressive walls richly adorned with buttresses and panelled battlements. The south porch, weatherworn but still beautiful, has a panelled gable and a vaulted roof, the inner doorway set between canopied niches with the great head of a lion above it. Its splendid double doors are faced with bronze scenes in the life of Our Lord and the Madonna, and over the doors is a Pièta, a sorrowing dove withdrawing behind a veil to appear again as a joyful dove, symbolising the weary soul finding new life; the doors are in memory of a vicar, Francis Morse, "Father, pastor, friend". Angels and flowers enrich the west doorway, which was put here when Sir Gilbert Scott restored the west end to its original style. Kings, bishops, and animals guard the windows on the north side. The fine panelled chimney of the old vestry is probably 17th century.

Except for the dim chancel, plainer than the rest of the building, the interior is full of light, the clerestory like a lantern with 12 great windows on each side. The lofty nave arcades have no capitals. Transepts open from the tower, whose massive pillars, 24 feet round, were twice rebuilt last century. The south transept is one of the oldest parts of the church; so, too, is the doorway in the north aisle, with crowned heads, probably those of Richard II and his queen;

the old studded door still hanging in its original iron fastening led to a chantry. In the stone seats along the aisle walls are stones from the earlier church, and there is part of a very old pillar covered by a movable board in the floor by the north arcade. Round the 15th century font is the familiar Greek inscription which reads the same both ways, meaning; "Wash thy sins and not thy face only." There are fragments of 16th century glass in the north transept, where is also a carved Jacobean altar table, and kept under glass in the south chapel is a beautiful fragment of alabaster of much interest. It shows a pope sitting under a canopy attended by two cardinals, and a kneeling bishop with his chaplains, and is said to represent Thomas Becket resigning the See of Canterbury. It was probably part of a mediaeval reredos. A rare treasure is a lovely Madonna and Child painted by Fra Bartolomeo, pupil of Raphael and friend of Savonarola.

Over 500 years ago John Samon left six-and-eightpence for a light to be kept burning forever in a chapel here. He was four times Mayor of Nottingham and lies on his canopied tomb in the south transept, a civilian in a loose-sleeved coat buttoned from his collar to his feet. His pointed shoes rest on a dog, and battered angels support the cushion for his head. His son Richard, who died in 1427, has a battered floorstone near the north-west door, with his arms on the stem of a cross. In the north transept is a handsome canopied tomb seeming to have belonged to three memorials. The canopy, which has rich niches in its gable, covered the 15th century tomb of Thomas Thurland, who was nine times mayor and four times MP, and is remembered in Thurland Street. The alabaster tomb below the canopy, with carvings of the Madonna, Gabriel, Peter, and John the Baptist, and with a lily carved with a crucifix on its stem may be that of John Tannersley, another mediaeval mayor. The marble stone on the top of the tomb, which has lost its brasses, may be that of William Amyas, a wool merchant. On this triple tomb we found resting the memorial of still another mayor, Robert English, an alabaster fragment with a mitred figure on it. The battered figure in the north aisle may be his.

One of the memorials in the north transept to the Plumptres is an

18th century alabaster medallion to a boy of ten who was greatly learned in history and mythology, Latin and French, and has on his memorial these words from Virgil's Lament for Marcellus:

> *Over the shade of him who was my son*
> *Heap I these gifts, and now my task is done.*

There is another delightful epitaph in the north aisle on a tablet to Ann Hollings of 1770:

> *Rest, gentle shade, and wait thy Maker's will,*
> *Then rise unchanged, and be an angel still.*

Two great alabaster shields and an inscription now in the south transept are all that remain of the tomb of John Holles, the Earl of Clare, who fought against the Armada.

Near the pulpit is a floorstone to John Whitlock, who was in charge of St Mary's during the Commonwealth, and helped to found the Unitarian chapel on High Pavement. The great west window with 42 panels telling the story of Our Lord from the Manger to the Cross, is in memory of one of Nottingham's most famous citizens, the 19th century lace merchant, Thomas Adams; and the 19th century glass in the south transept, with the parables in 48 panels, is in memory of the founder of modern banking, Thomas Smith, who was buried here in 1699. An 18th century monument with an elephant's head is to another of the Smiths. In a north transept window are 16 panels of the Miracles. A pathetic window in the south chapel is in memory of Catherine Monica Dalton, who was baptised here in 1899 and died a week after her marriage here in 1918; we see her in the bridal gown and lace veil in which she was married and buried; she kneels before the Madonna, with St Catherine and St Monica standing by.

In the south aisle is the best glass in the church, a modern gallery of 24 saints, bishops, and kings by Kempe; it keeps green the memory of the men of the Notts Regiment who fell in South Africa. A Scout window shows Scout badges, a knight in armour typifying courage, Christ with his arm on the shoulder of a pathfinder, a Scout setting out from home, and a camp-fire group in a field of bluebells. A window to the Notts veterans of the Crimean War and Indian Mutiny has for its theme: "Young men shall see visions and old men shall dream dreams." The dull window in the chancel of Gethsemane, the Last Supper, and the Road to Calvary, is said to be designed by Sir George Frampton (though it does not look like it).

In the tower hangs a peal of ten bells, all having been recast except one, which comes from 1595; the last of the great Nottingham firm which cast it, and which sent so many bells round England, lies in the churchyard near the vestry, George Oldfield.

At the High Pavement entrance is a memorial to those of the county who lost their lives in the First World War.

St Peter's, a stone's throw from the Council House, represents a fairly good example of early English architecture, and probably dates back from about 1180, being partly rebuilt in the 15th century. It was St Peter's and St Nicholas' that formed the two churches within the French Borough of Norman Nottingham. The tower contains eight bells, which were recast in 1771. The most interesting one is the seventh, presented in 1543 by Margaret Doubleday, a washerwoman, together with a legacy of 20/- a year for the sexton of the church so that he would ring the bell at four o'clock every morning to rouse the town washer-women so that they would not be late for their work. The church contains many memorials which give an insight into local history. Two sermons of particular interest are preached here annually: they are the Armada sermon preached on the nearest Sunday to July 28, and the Gunpowder Plot sermon preached on the nearest Sunday to November 5. Both these sermons take place at the morning service.

The church of St Nicholas stands near the new Maid Marian Way, and was founded about the time of the Norman Conquest. Of the Gothic building nothing remains, although a few fragments of the foundation were uncovered by the sexton of the parish while digging there about 1800. The present building dates back to the second half of the 17th century. The Civil War saw the end of the first church of St Nicholas. The Royalists, who were attacking the Castle, held by Colonel Hutchinson's forces, used the tower of the church as a platform from which to bombard the Castle. The attack failed and the supporters of the King considered that discretion was the better part of valour, and retired from their precarious position. Colonel Hutchinson decided later that the church should be completely destroyed to obviate a recurrence of this method of attack. The congregation were now without a church, and for a time held their services in a loft of nearby St Peter's Church. It was not until Cromwell was dead and Charles II had been restored to the Throne that any attempt was made to rebuild the church. Rebuilding began in 1671 and was finished in 1678. Since that time it has undergone several alterations and improvements. In the 18th century St Nicholas Church was known as the Drawing Room Church, a name it derived from those well-to-do people who lived in the parish and attended service there on Sundays. Laurence Collin, who had been a gunner in Nottingham Castle in the Civil War and lived at 39 Castle Gate, is buried in the south transept of the church. Its value was recognised in 1953 when it was scheduled as a historical church by the Ministry of Works.

St Andrew's 19th century stone church standing well at the top of Mansfield Road overlooks the Rock Cemetery, the entrance of which marks the spot where the town gallows once stood. The church has a tower with a spire, and there is some fine modern craftsmanship inside. The rich panelling of the sanctuary and the lovely alabaster reredos were the gift of John and Margaret Player in 1918, "for 25 years of happy married life", the reredos showing in high relief Christ enthroned, a charming Nativity in which the ass and the ox peep over the stall, Christ walking with two disciples, the Baptism, Gethsemane, and the Resurrection with an angel and two sleeping soldiers. All Saints in Raleigh Street comes from 1864, its tower surmounted by a sturdy broached spire, its apsidal chancel gabled on every face. The Roman Catholic Cathedral of St Barnabas on Derby Road, designed by Pugin in 13th century style, comes from 1842, its tower and spire rising to 170 feet from the middle of a cross. Close by is the Albert Hall, the headquarters of the Wesleyan Mission, and modernised in recent years.

There has been much development in the past few years with the result that Nottingham is losing some of its historical links, but the area round the lace market remains largely unchanged. Hollow Stone is perhaps Nottingham's most ancient street, and it was along this thoroughfare that the stage-coaches from London rattled past St Mary's Church before turning into Bridlesmith Gate to deposit their passengers and luggage at the old inns of the town. On Low Pavement is Willoughby House, built between 1730 and 1740. Just above is a narrow thoroughfare known as Drury Hill, since Alderman Drury lived here in the 17th century.

On High Pavement is the Shire Hall, a stone building with pilastered entrance and balustraded parapet, where even till 1864 criminals were publicly hanged. Remains of the old prison can be seen at the back, and below are the cabins and dungeons used as condemned cells. The hall is unique among Nottingham buildings, for it is the smallest civil parish in all England, a bit of the county within the town, having been left under the old jurisdiction when Henry VI separated the town from the county. Facing the Shire Hall is a fine house in which judges were lodged years ago and is now the Nottinghamshire Record Office.

The chapel in Castle Gate stands on the site of a much earlier one founded in Cromwell's day. The present building dates from 1863 and was the first church in the city to be wired for broadcasting.

At the other end of this ancient thoroughfare is Newdigate House, which was erected about 1675 and owes much of its fame to Marshal Tallard. In 1704 the Duke of Marlborough defeated the French Forces under Marshal Tallard at the Battle of Blenheim. The Marshal was brought to Nottingham and put on parole at Newdigate House, where he was to stay from 1705 to 1711.

One or two ancient inns remain in the city. The Trip to Jerusalem Inn is said to have been a calling-place for crusaders on their way to the Holy Land; it has rooms and cellars cut deep back into the castle rock, ventilating shafts climbing through the rock, a speaking tube bored through it, and a chimney climbing through the rock 47 feet above the chamber in which it begins. The Salutation Inn in Houndsgate, close by, has rock cellars which are believed to have been part of a Saxon cave dwelling, with a 70 feet well sunk in solid rock. In October 1956, new buildings were added to the rear, and it was during digging operations that workmen uncovered a number of earthenware tankards.

On Mansfield Road close to the junction with Shakespeare Street is the Midland Design and Building Centre, which was opened by Lord Snowdon on June 5, 1962. On the opposite side of the road the re-development of Victoria Station site is taking place. The station was opened on May 24, 1900, on Queen Victoria's 81st birthday, and was named in honour of the event. The last passenger train was the 5.34 p.m. to Rugby via Leicester Central, which arrived back in Nottingham at 8.04 p.m. on September 2, 1967. The station was both opened and closed without ceremony. The clock tower, a local landmark on the Mansfield Road, is to be retained as a feature of the new development, which will include shops and supermarkets, a bus station, a dual-level market hall to replace the existing corporation market, an underground car park, (one of the largest in the country), cinemas, public houses, and a crèche. The completion is due in the autumn of 1971.

In an ancient little graveyard called St Mary's Cemetery (now a garden of rest) on Bath Street lies a man whose name was once known far and wide. He was born William Thompson, he grew up to be the famous pugilist Bendigo, and he has been made familiar by Sir Arthur Conan Doyle as the Pride of Nottingham. His resting-place is typical of the old fighter, who was converted and became a popular preacher, and on occasion borrowed five minutes from the Lord that he might deal in his own way with the troublesome front row of the congregation:

> *But the roughs they kept on chaffin' and the uproar it was such*
> *That the preacher in the pulpit might be talking double Dutch,*
> *Till a working man he shouted out, a-jumpin' to his feet,*
> *"Give us a lead, your reverence, and heave 'em in the street."*

> *Then Bendy said, "Good Lord, since I first left my sinful ways,*
> *Thou knowest that to Thee alone I've given up my days,*
> *But now, dear Lord" (and here he laid his Bible on the shelf)*
> *"I'll take with your permission just five minutes for myself."*

On Bendy's tomb of rough grey stone crouches a fine lion as if about to spring, and the inscription runs:

In life always brave, fighting like a lion,
In death like a lamb, tranquil in Zion.

Basford has its old church dedicated to the little known St Leodegarius, and the church has 13th century work in the chancel, the nave arcades, the font, and the south doorway, and 14th century work in the south aisle and the south porch. The porch has a gallery of mediaeval heads. The west window with the Good Shepherd and the Light of the World is in memory of Henry Roger Pitman, who was vicar here for the whole of the second half of last century and two years of this. Built into the wall by the south doorway is an ancient Pax stone, which had some significance long ago in connection with the Apostolic injunction, "To greet one another with a holy kiss". Near the porch is the stone tomb of Henry Ward who is said to have died at 108.

Bilborough is a suburb of Nottingham, and translated means the fortified place of Billa, although of Billa nothing is known.

Domesday mentions no church here, but the embattled tower of the tiny aisleless church of St Martin comes from about 1400, to which period the square headed windows of the nave and chancel belong, but the fact that there was an earlier building is certain as the list of known rectors commences in 1306. There are no aisles, but the blocked up arch on the north side of the nave denotes the former existence of a chapel. In the 18th century the roof was lowered, and it may have been then that the flat ceiling and the singers gallery at the west end (both removed in 1877) were added. The porch is part of the original structure, but its roof belongs to later days. The font and the east window are 15th century, and a table is 17th. In the chancel is a marble memorial to Sir Edmund Helwys, who lived at Broxtowe Hall a mile from the church in Queen Elizabeth's century. So, too, did Thomas Helwys, who is said to have been chiefly responsible for the formation of the first Baptist church in England.

Bulwell lies to the north of the city. Its church of St Mary and All Souls stands on a hill just before you enter the market place. The present church, which dates from 1850, stands near a much earlier church. It has a fine alabaster reredos and alabaster panelling in the sanctuary. The whole of this work is Italian. A high altar of Derbyshire alabaster was given in 1945.

Carrington once had its own market place, but this has now disappeared under a large development scheme.

It was in 1825 that Ichabod Wright of Mapperley Hall purchased land from Robert Smith of Smith's Bank who was financial adviser to William Pitt, and four years later portions of this land were sold or let on lease for building houses for men of business who, for want of land in Nottingham, were compelled to buy land outside the city. To this land Mr Wright gave the name of Carrington in honour of his friend, Lord Carrington. He also gave the land for St John's Church and laid its first stone on May 12, 1841.

Clifton is about 3½ miles south of Nottingham's city centre, which at midnight on March 31, 1956, became part of Nottingham. It is approached via the Clifton Bridge which was opened by HRH Princess Alexandra of Kent on Thursday, June 5, 1958. The B579 road divides the new from the old at Clifton. On one side of the road is the new council estate, and on the other Clifton Village. Its famous grove of oaks, elms, and beeches planted more than two centuries ago stretches for over a mile along the top of a steep cliff overhanging the River Trent. It was the Nottingham poet, Henry Kirke White, who immortalised it in his fine poem:

> *Dear native grove, where'er my devious tracks*
> *To thee will memory lead the wanderer back.*
> *Still, still to thee where'er my footsteps roam,*
> *My heart shall point, and lead the wanderer home.*

At the head of the Grove stands Clifton Hall, once the home of the Clifton family, and now a Grammar School for girls. It was opened by the then Lord Mayor of Nottingham, Alderman J. Littlefair, on October 23, 1958.

The village green has lost none of its charm with its thatched cottages and a gabled dovecote which probably dates back to the 18th century. At one time May Day was celebrated with a May-pole dance on this village green, but this custom has long since been abandoned. On October 19, 1962 Sir Edward Boyle opened the Teachers' Training College close by, which stands in some 41 acres of ground and is bordered on one side by Clifton Grove.

The new estate has been well catered for with churches for most denominations, but it is to the village with its church of St Mary that we must look, for here are buried many of the Clifton family.

It is a beautiful building with a 14th and 15th century tower rising from the middle of a cross, and a lovely gable cross with a crucifix, over 400 years old, is on the west end of the nave. Like most of the church, the south arcade with finely carved capitals is 14th century, the clerestory coming from its close. The oldest part is the north arcade, with round pillars and pointed arches, built when the Norman style was passing.

Very charming is the effect of the lofty arches of the tower, framing a view of the much-restored 15th century chancel with its great windows and lovely roof. The roof was built in 1503 by a rector who signed it with his name and his quaint portrait. Under the brilliant east window is a splendid reredos of Derbyshire alabaster, coloured blue and gold. The stalls and screen are modern, and a fine chest is over 400 years old.

Most of the old monuments are in the north transept. The knight lying in an alabaster tomb with his head on a peacock, his feet on a weary lion, and the Clifton lion rampant on his surcoat, is either Sir Gervase, who died under Richard II, or Sir John, who fell at the Battle of Shrewsbury. The fine brass portrait of Sir Robert Clifton of 1478 shows him in armour with his head on a helmet and a greyhound at his feet; another brass is of his son Gervase, knighted at the coronation of Richard III. Very lovely is the smiling figure of his wife, Alice Nevill, who lies on an alabaster tomb, wearing a long-sleeved gown of smooth folds.

"Gervase the Gentle" lies magnificent with his two wives, all three in ruffs and wearing a remarkable number of rings, one wife having 11 and the other 8. On one side of the tomb are the five children of his first wife, and on the other is the second wife's son George, who was only 20 when he died a few months before his father, leaving the baby Gervase as the heir, who was to grow up to marry seven wives. We see George again in a brass portrait with the wife he married when he was only 14; he wears a short cloak and a big ruff, and she has a cap with her gown and embroidered petticoat. Close by is the floorstone of Dame Thorold, the grandmother who cared for the baby heir.

Grown-up, the much-married Sir Gervase set up an elaborate monument to his first three wives in 1631, showing their arms on a black sarcophagus with a medley of bones and skulls below; and built a vault in which he buried six wives, the seventh outliving him. At his own death in 1666 his bust and the arms of all the wives were placed over the chancel doorway to the vault. He is said to have left £1,000 for his funeral, which was attended with great pomp.

There are many later memorials to the Cliftons, and one more relic of old days is a leaden case thought to contain a heart, perhaps of Sir William Clifton, a crusader. They had a Negro servant in the 17th century, and it is said the initials J. P. on the entrance to the porch mark his height of 6 feet 4 inches. A floorstone in the south transept covers his grave, and tells us that Joseph, commonly known as the Black Prince, was converted to the Christian faith and died in the hope of a better life.

Lenton has an ancient monastery, founded in the first years of the 12th century by William Peverel, which rose proudly in the meadows where the little River Leen ran on its way to the Trent, and the monks would look up on one side to Peverel's castle on its high rock, and on the other to the green hills of Clifton. No man for miles around was so powerful as William Peverel. His priory was one of the richest, but it shared the fate of the religious houses seized by Henry VIII and its last prior was hanged with some of his monks.

Sir William Babington was buried here in 1455 when he was 99; he was Chief Justice and Baron of the Exchequer. Of all the ancient splendour, only a few fragments remain. The bases of two Norman pillars are in a back garden in Old Church Street. In the abbey church close by is Norman carving on an altar step, and part of a mediaeval gravestone showing a chalice and a book by the stem of a cross is near the west doorway.

This small church, with great chestnut trees for company, is on the site of a chapel of St Anthony which was attached as a hospital to the priory. The chancel and the vestry are part of the 16th century church built when the monastery was destroyed, but the nave was made new half a century ago, after being in ruins for 40 years.

The remarkable relic of the priory is the font, which was found at the close of the 18th century when foundations for a house were being dug. Then it was used for a time as a garden ornament; now it is in the spacious parish church, full of years and honour. It is indeed a wonder. It is almost square, and its sides are so richly carved that it is famed as the finest Norman font in the Midlands, and one of the best in the kingdom. On one side is the Crucifixion with the two thieves; on another a floriated cross; on the third two rows of rich arcading with angels, and the Baptism in Jordan; while panels on the fourth side may represent the Ascension, the Resurrection, the Church of the Sepulchre, and the three Marys. This noble font is the chief possession of Lenton's 19th century church, which has a lofty pinnacled tower, and a beautiful oak screen with a canopy rising from the middle of its single span.

Here is remembered one of the famous heroes of the Great War; it is thrilling to see his Victoria Cross engraved on his brass, with his other medals in the four corners of the plate. This rich brass, with a border of oak leaves, is a memorial to Albert Ball, the Nottingham airman who fell in France in 1917, a youth of 20 who won the VC, the DSO three times, the French Legion of Honour, and the Russian Order of St George.

At the back of the White Hart Inn are the barred rooms of the old Peverel Gaol, founded in 1113 for the imprisonment of debtors and left standing when the Court was abolished in the middle of last century. Other relics of the past are the mounting blocks at the front door of the inn.

Sherwood is a busy suburb and shopping centre which was incorporated in the borough of Nottingham on November 1st, 1877. The church of St Martin was consecrated in 1937.

Sneinton is within easy reach of the City Centre, and it was here that the founder of the Salvation Army, William Booth, was born in 1829. A plaque recording this is fixed on the wall outside the house at Notintone Place.

The Church of St Stephen is spacious and pleasing, with a central tower and lofty arches, a barrel roof to the nave, and good oak screens. The reredos in the chancel has canopied scenes in the Life of Our Lord. The oak reredos in the south transept chapel has canopied statues of the Madonna, Isaiah, and John the Baptist. The treasure here lies in the mediaeval seats in the chancel, which were cast out of St Mary's last century; the panelling on the walls has a cresting of shields and Tudor flower, and spandrels carved with two snarling dragons, grotesque heads with foliage coming from their mouths, a mermaid with her comb and mirror, and a quaint animal. In the rich carvings of eight of the misericord seats are heads, an animal with another animal on its back, a quaint creature like an ass, a chained monkey holding a pitcher, and an animal blowing a horn as it rides on a hound. The poppyheads have foliage and faces, human and grotesque.

In St Stephen's church, east of the chancel, lies a little-known mathematical genius who inspired Lord Kelvin. He was George Green, who was born in Nottingham in 1793, and in 1807 his father bought the mill which stands to this day on Belvoir Hill a short distance from where he is buried. He died at Notintone Place in 1841.

Wollaton takes its name from Saxon times, when it was known as Wulflaf's tun. With the City Extension Act of 1932, this delightful suburb three miles west of Nottingham was brought into the city boundary.

In old Wollaton village the pump still stands in its shelter in the square, and here, too, is the inn with foundation stones said to be part of the home of the Willoughbys, as is the stone cottage facing the church where some of them lie.

For hundreds of years the story of the Willoughbys has been the story of the village, beginning when one of them married an heiress of the Morteins. Some of them have helped to make the history of their county, and their country, and some of even a wider field; one of them built here as fine a house as any of his time. Sir Richard was Lord Chief Justice in the 14th century. Sir Hugh was the famous navigator who set out to discover the North-East Passage, and perished with his company off the coast of Lapland. Sir Francis of 1672 was a famous naturalist whose son became Baron Middleton. It was another Sir Francis who built Wollaton Hall in the time of Elizabeth, a splendid house with features of the Gothic, Tudor, and classic styles. Dutch gables and pinnacles crown its four corner towers, a fine Prospect Room looks out from the central block, and the Great Hall inside has a handsomely carved stone screen and a fine hammerbeam roof. We can well believe, looking at the towers and turrets, domes and parapets, that it has a window for every day of the year, for it seems to be covered with them. It took eight years to build, and cost Sir Francis £80,000, in addition to the cost of the Ancaster stone, which was defrayed by Wollaton coal. Its architect was Robert Smythson (who sleeps in the church).

The park, with nearly 800 acres, has long been the glory of Wollaton. It has noble trees in plantations and groves, lovely gardens, and deer browsing by the lake in a woodland hollow. The fine 17th century brick wall enclosing the park was given its last length when the village of Sutton Passeys disappeared in the next century.

We may all see this fine place today, for in 1924 Lord Middleton sold the estate to Nottingham, and the house is now the home of the city's Natural History Museum. The gardens are still fine, and there is a lovely cedar grove near a splendid flight of steps, with a peep of the golf links beyond. Unforgettable is the sight of the marvellous camellias in a house which cost £10,000 to build. Yet Wollaton holds nothing finer than the magnificent lime-grove, three-quarters of a mile long.

For many years the paintings on the north staircase and ceiling and the south staircase's ceiling were ascribed to Antonio Verrio (1639–1707) and Louis Laguerre (1663–1721). Research by Mr Croft-Murray of the British Museum has, however, established that the paintings are the work of Laguerre and Sir James Thornhill (1676–1734).

Wollaton Park through the years has been used as a setting for military tattoos, Scout Jamborees, the Bath and West and Royal Shows. The first Royal Show was held here in 1888, and the last in 1955, this latter being honoured by the presence of HM the Queen and the Duke of Edinburgh on July 6 of that year.

The church of St Leonard was much restored last century, when it was given a south aisle and a chapel to serve as the family pew. The three eastern bays of the north arcade are 14th century, the time of most of the old work. Two sides of the tower stand on open arches, through which we can walk outside the church.

Among the Willoughby memorials are the fine brass portraits of Richard of 1471 and his wife, he in plate armour and she in long cloak and gown. They lie on a tomb in a canopied recess, and below them lies a stone corpse. On a tomb between the chancel and the chapel lies Sir Henry Willoughby of 1528, with small figures of four wives beside him, and a stone corpse below. Three sons and three daughters are on the tomb, and it is thought that the third son may be Hugh, who was one day to be found frozen to death in his chair, with his will and his ship's log beside him.

On the death of Sir Francis, who built the hall, Wollaton passed to his daughter Bridget, who married her cousin, Percy Willoughby. Their memorial is a stone on the chancel wall, with a Latin inscription in beautiful raised lettering.

A priceless treasure, a rare gem for this village church, is the book of service and song which was used here for nearly a hundred years before the Reformation. Its great pages, about 22 inches by 15, are worn at the edges, but their rich illumination is almost as fresh as when they left the artist's hands 500 years ago. When Edward VI's

Prayer Book came into use this book was taken to the Hall and remained in the keeping of the family till Lord Middleton gave it back to the church in 1925. Here it lies in a glass case, the pages being turned over now and then. The book is almost complete. It was written and illuminated before 1460, for it belonged then to a rector of Wollaton whose executors bought it for ten marks and gave it for use in this church forever.

The window pictures are a pleasing part of the church, two in the chancel being the work of Christopher Whall. One shows St Francis surrounded by a company of 30 English and foreign birds, with the chaffinch, robin, thrush, blue tits, sparrows, love-birds, and doves among them, and St Nicholas with two children, one with a doll. It is in memory of a rector who loved birds and children, and who served here for 46 years. The chapel was restored in his memory, and has been given an oil painting for a reredos, showing in soft colours the scene in the Upper Room at Emmaus. The other Whall window is to James Cosmo Russell, who won the DSO and fell at Ypres in 1917; the window has figures of St George in gold and St Michael in silver, each standing on a dragon.

Nuthall has experienced many name changes in its long history, which goes back before the Norman invasion. During the early period it was known as "Nutehale". The Pipe Rolls of the years 1195–97 give a series of spellings which could be very misleading. In 1195 it appears as Nuchala. In 1197 it was spelt Niewehale, apparently to make sensible reading of it, but matters are made more confusing by the writer of the Borough Records spelling it Notehale.

Nuthall lost its great house, like an Italian villa, when it was demolished in 1929, but has kept a yew tree old enough to have seen most of the changes in this place. This tree may be nearly as old as the church of St Patrick, by which it spreads its shapely arms. The sturdy tower of the church was made new in the 18th century, except for its base which is mainly 12th century and the oldest part of the church, its pointed arch of a little later time resting on the original sides.

Like most of the old stonework, the lovely doorway letting us in (adorned with medallions and heads of a king and a queen) comes from the end of the 14th century, the time of the nave arcade and the windows with flowing tracery. The 15th century east window has old glass showing the Crucifixion and heraldic shields; other windows have old shields and fragments. The mediaeval chancel screen (with modern gates), and the old part of the screen hiding the organ, enclosed the east end of the aisle till half a century ago.

On a floorstone of 1558 are the engraved portraits of Edward Boun, his wife, and five children. A rector's stone has a cross, a book, and a chalice, and fragments of other coffin stones are in the wall outside. In a founder's recess in the aisle lies the alabaster figure of Sir Robert Cokefield, a 14th century lord of the manor. He wears plate armour and a jewelled sword-belt; his head is on a crested helmet, a lion is at his feet, and his hands are at prayer. His family were lords of Nuthall for about 200 years.

Ollerton. New roads and a colliery are making their mark on this old village, but it still stands at the doorstep of the Dukeries and Robin Hood's Forest, and it has one of the finest natural monuments in England. The village is on the bank of the little River Maun, near its meeting with the Rainworth Water which has come a lovely journey through Rufford Park.

Just outside the town is a colliery, and to house the workers a new model village, known as New Ollerton, has been built on the north side of the town.

Older than anything else in the village are the red bricks of the mill at the little bridge, by which is a garden of shrubs on an island made by the river as it turns the mill wheel; it is the Island of Remembrance, with a plain grey cross.

The parish church of Ollerton is dedicated to St Giles, and the present building dates from about the year 1777.

It is sad that where Nature is so rich the church is so poor. It was made new in the 18th century, and has little except a stoutly bound oak chest with three tremendous old padlocks, and a modern screen made from the oaks of Sherwood Forest.

M

Ordsall belongs to the Borough of East Retford and is straddled along the bank of the River Idle. It is mentioned in the Domesday Book, and has remains of three mediaeval centuries in its much restored church of All Saints.

The two lower stages of the lofty tower are 14th century, with a modern west window; the two others, with a crown of battlements and pinnacles, are 15th. The 14th century nave arcades have a little 13th century work in a pillar with slender shafts, two half-pillars, and some ornament. The only old windows, apart from the tower, are two of the 15th century in the chancel, one showing Paulinus with the model of a cathedral, Mary with a book and lilies, and Hugh of Lincoln with a swan at his feet. The other, glowing richly with a scene of the marriage feast at Cana, was given by Sir John Hall, Prime Minister of New Zealand, in memory of Joseph and Catherine Hall who were married in this church in 1696, a century before the first Englishman set foot on the great southern island.

The massive oak screen across the tower arch comes from the close of the 15th century, but has been spoiled. A treasure of the church is a chalice of 1517. The bowl of an ancient font lies in the churchyard.

In a canopied wall monument a man kneels at a desk on which is an open book. He has short hair and a beard, wears rich Elizabethan dress and a ruff, and is thought to be Anthony Bevercotes of 1612. It is recorded that during the Commonwealth Marmaduke Moore was turned out of the living here for playing cards with his wife, and also that he lost his estate through treason.

Orston is approached from Car Colston by a road shaded by trees, which goes over two bridges spanning the River Smite and a brook. The prettiest corner is by the stone church.

The church of St Mary has something from most centuries, the nave being 13th and 14th century, the chancel Early English, and the clerestory 15th century. The font dates from 1662, and is octagonal, and seems to be a Stuart copy of the Tudor font at Bottesford. The plain circular bowl of a Norman Transitional font is still in being. Now lying at the east end of the north aisle is the early

14th century stone effigy of a woman. She was probably Isabella, sole heiress of the D'Albini family, who were lords of the manor of Orston in the 13th and 14th centuries. Over the doorway into the tower from the nave is a painted panel of the arms of King George III. In a recess on a wall is kept a drum from the Battle of Waterloo.

In the churchyard is a stone to one Thomas Maltby who died in 1881 at the age of 101 years and 101 days.

About half a mile from the village is Orston Spa. This spring still exists but is much overgrown. Relics of the Civil War, a hoard of gold and silver coins, were ploughed up in a field nearby in 1952.

Osberton is situated about three miles east of Worksop. The hall was built by James Wyatt in 1806, and was enlarged and altered in the mid-19th century. The church of St John which is situated in the grounds, was built in 1833.

Ossington. The world seems far away in this delightful spot at the end of a charming ride from Kneesall. Its lanes are leafy glades; its few dwellings are trim with red walls and roofs. Not far from a group of stately larches, sheltering a bronze crucifix, a fine lime avenue leads to the church and the gates of Ossington Hall.

This hall was the home of the Cartwrights, who in 1768 sold it to William Denison; his brother Robert, a wealthy wool merchant, rebuilt the church. Ossington Hall, however, was demolished in 1963.

Built in Classical style, the church of the Holy Rood is also known as the church in the wood. It has a domed tower to which a Speaker of the House of Commons gave a clock, the church has rich glass filling its round-headed windows, and is interesting for monuments of Cartwrights and Denisons. Older than any of these are two brass portraits on a great tomb, one showing Reynold Peckham of Wrotham in Kent (who died in 1551) as a knight in armour, and the other his wife in a long gown and embroidered headdress. On a huge stone monument of 1602, adorned with arms, are William Cartwright (in armour) and his wife, both wearing ruffs. Under the projecting table on which they kneel are lifelike figures of six

167

sons and six daughters, most of them holding books, and two of the girls with skulls. They are charming.

Very fine are two statues by Nollekens of William Denison and his brother Robert, both in dress of their day. It was an ill wind for Lisbon that blew William's ship to good fortune in 1755, for it is said he owed much of his wealth to the fact that one of his ships arrived there after the city had been nearly destroyed by an earthquake. Carved at the foot of his monument is a scene of the ship unloading in Lisbon harbour; a group of men on shore have bales of merchandise, and in one corner sheep are grazing.

John Evelyn Denison, first Viscount Ossington and Speaker of Parliament, has a memorial of stone and coloured marble. He was one of a family of 14 children, of whom many won distinction. A beautiful plaque has the head and shoulders of W. F. Evelyn Denison in his soldier's uniform; he died from wounds received in the First World War. The handsome panels of the oak pulpit were carved by Lady Elinor Denison, lady of the manor.

Owthorpe is a small agricultural village sheltered in the Wolds near the Vale of Belvoir, and famed for its connection with the Hutchinson family.

Colonel Hutchinson was born at Nottingham in 1615, and passed from Cambridge University to the study of the law; but he preferred music and the arts, and followed no profession.

With all the graces of the age, he was a favourite in London Society, but his fine character preserved him from pitfalls, and at 23 his romantic love affair with Lucy Apsley ended in a marriage of unclouded happiness. He was, like his father, a member of the Long Parliament, but it was not without heart-searching that he denied the king's right to seize the county's store of gunpowder, and became Governor of Nottingham. There he played a heroic part, sustaining sieges and combating dissension in his own ranks, but remaining throughout triumphant. One of Charles I's judges, he signed the death warrant.

He lived quietly here between the expulsion of the Long Parliament and its restoration six years later. He drifted apart from

Cromwell, extended hospitality to oppressed Royalist relatives, and, becoming a member of the Convention which welcomed the return of Charles II, he was spared under the Act of Oblivion.

His enemies, however, falsely charged him with complicity in a petty plot, and in 1663 he was imprisoned in his wife's birthplace, the Tower of London, where he was subjected to cruelty and extortion. After six months he was transferred to certain death in a veritable pest-house, the ruinous and insanitary Sandown Castle, where he died.

The church of St Margaret's lies isolated in a field behind a farm and dates from 1705. It occupies only the site of the chancel of the former church, being only 50 feet by 24 feet. The screen, which is of about the same date as the church, came from Owthorpe Hall, the residence of the Hutchinson family, before it was demolished in the early 19th century. There is also a double decker Jacobean pulpit, a 15th century font, and some of the windows from the earlier church. Colonel Hutchinson is buried within its walls, his body having been brought there after his death while a prisoner in Sandown Castle, Kent.

Owthorpe has an annual fair and harvest supper.

Oxton is a quiet village that lies on the route from Nottingham to Southwell.

Rounding the bend in the village street there comes into view the parish church which is dedicated to St Peter and St Paul. Its entrance is overshadowed by the great yew, now some 600 years old. It is said that the churchyard has been a Christian burial ground for 1,000 years, and the oldest gravestone standing is dated 1674. There are numerous headstones to the Sherbrooke family (the name comes from the place of origin, Shirebrooke, Derbyshire) who settled in Oxton in the reign of Queen Elizabeth I. There is a family vault, the entrance being indicated in the floor of the nave. Some hatchments of the family hang in the nave. England's Chancellor of the Exchequer of 1868 became Viscount Sherbrooke in 1880, while the Governor-General of Canada in 1816 was Sir John Coape Sherbrooke. The church registers can be traced back to 1562, and there is an entry in 1659 which reads: "Robert, Sonne of Francisci Scothorn and Marie his wife, born March 21st; baptised April 23rd." Robert sailed to America in 1684 to join William Penn, founder of Pennsylvania.

The church is not without its war memorials, and two white ensigns hanging at the west end of the church are one flown in HMS *Tarantula*, by Captain Henry Sherbrooke, DSO, RN, and the other by his son, Rear Admiral R. St. V. Sherbrooke, the present squire, who in the Second World War was awarded the Victoria Cross and the DSO for distinguished and courageous service. Between the clerestoried nave and its aisles are 14th century arcades. The chancel of crazy stone has a fine Norman arch and Norman masonry in the wall close by, a beautiful 13th century lancet deeply splayed, and a 600-year-old east window with St George, St Nicholas, and a soldier at the foot of the Cross. The altar table is Elizabethan. In harmony with the rest of the church is the dark oak of the low chancel screen (with a quaint minstrel on each side of the entrance), and of the stalls with a Bible inscription carved round the top, all of our day.

Some of the possessions of Oxton have had their queer adventures. A rare relic is a Norman shaft piscina found in a wall in the village, and the 14th century font has been used as a pump trough. There is a 17th century font, and the round Norman bowl of a third is on the floor. In the nave lies a stone man in a long gown, who may have been a judge in the 14th century; his feet are on a dog, and two headless angels support his pillow.

Once a part of the Royal Forest of Sherwood, this parish has now only half the population that it had 100 years ago.

Papplewick. This is a village in Sherwood Forest with a hall dating from 1787, planned by the Adam Brothers for Frederick Montagu, then Lord of the Treasury. The church of St James was rebuilt by the same Frederick Montagu, except for its 14th century tower. It is an unusual and attractive little church, having a balcony inside running along the north wall and turning in an "L" shape to the west. The squire's pew at the east end of the gallery has a fireplace, and the story is told how Squire Walter, a proprietor of *The Times* who lived at Papplewick Hall for about 30 years, used to poke the fire noisily when he had had enough of the sermon! Other interesting relics are a number of coffin stones showing the occupations of the men they commemorate. One in the nave floor has the bow and arrow, the belt and hunting horn of the forester; and another has a cross and billhook. Two in the porch which are believed to be the graves of Sherwood Forest officials, have a pair of bellows, the symbol of the ironworker. The figures of Faith and Hope in the lovely east window are copied from Sir Joshua Reynolds's picture in a window of New College Chapel, Oxford. In the churchyard is a splendid old yew tree 14 feet round the trunk, with a seat round its base.

On the outskirts of Papplewick is a cave known as Robin Hood's Stable, where the famous outlaw was reputed to have stabled his horses.

Perlethorpe stands on the edge of Thoresby Park and in the Domesday Book is called Torp.

The church of St John which was built by the third Earl Manvers was consecrated in 1876, and a memorial to him can be seen on the north wall of the chancel. The church is beautifully proportioned; its walls are adorned with battlements, pinnacles, and buttresses, corbel heads, and gargoyles, and bands of quatrefoils, and rising to 128 feet from a lovely tower is a spire with two tiers of windows, like a needle in the sky seen from far around. It is lovely inside and full of light, and in its enrichment the oaks of the forest have a place, for the lovely stall, the benches and the pulpit have been shaped and carved from them by masters of their craft. The pulpit has a stone and marble base with handsome foliage capitals crowning the pillars. The bench ends have exquisite carving of fruit and the medallions in which can be seen a bird on her nest, a pomegranate, a water lily, and a passion flower. The stalls are a fine array of 16 crouching animals, and there is a fine door to the tower. There is rich stone carving in the corbel heads of bearded men on the nave arcades, and in their foliage capitals and in the splendid font on pillars of coloured marble. The beautiful stone work behind the altar shows the Good Shepherd with his flock in the centre and the four Evangelists, two on either side.

The rather unusual eagle lectern with wings ready for flight is thought to be of French origin. The window at the east end of the south aisle is a memorial to the late Earl Manvers. The picture of the Denial of Christ by St Peter, which now hangs in the north aisle, was behind the altar in the small church which preceded the present one, and is the work of Sir Benjamin West.

The churchyard is rich with shrubs and noble trees, two of them magnificent beeches and two splendid yews. The diamond shape of turf at the east end of the path running up the centre of the churchyard marks the spot where the altar in the former church stood. To the right of this will be seen its foundation stone, which being translated reads: "This Church of Peverelthorpe the Noble and Generous Prince Evelyn Duke of Kingston Knight of the Garter rebuilt in the year 1744."

Plumtree lies about seven miles south of Nottingham, and its historical associations are limited mainly to its church.

The Plumtree family so prominent in Nottingham history is said to have originated here. They were probably an offshoot of the local family called Plumtre, one of whom figured in a law suit in the time of Edward I.

The church of St Mary lies a short distance off the main road, and the approach is made past the war memorial in the church ground. The church dates back to the 9th century, and is probably the oldest church in the county. Early in the reign of Charles I the rector of Plumtree charged two men, two women, and two children with religious ignorance combined with refusal to attend church services, but the offenders got off lightly by a warning and the matter was dropped. On entering the church perhaps the first thing that strikes one is a painting on the opposite side which is called "The Descent from the Cross", and is a copy of the painting by Rubens which is in Antwerp Cathedral. It was presented to the church about 80 years ago by a former rector, the Rev William Burnside. The Burnsides were responsible for much of the restoration of the church. Among the monuments in the church is one to Sarah, wife of Richard Cole of Normanton, and daughter of Sir Thomas Parkins of Bunny Park, who died March 8, 1821.

The church was repaired in 1818. The gallery was enlarged and the nave re-pewed. Two years previously, the Rev Thomas Beaumont, who had been appointed rector in 1813, had obtained permission to live outside the parish because of the dilapidated state of the rectory. The chancel was restored in the 15th century. The church was restored in 1873–75, when the gallery was abolished and the Norman arch of the tower was opened to view. The chancel arch and walling were raised, and a fine stained-glass window took the place of the old one which was removed to the new north aisle. The plaster ceilings were destroyed, and a new roof supplied to the chancel, and the whole of the flooring relaid with white Mansfield stone. The tower was rebuilt in 1906, and it was then that the Saxon work was discovered. The coat of arms over the doorway inside the church is the royal coat of arms of George I, while the font close by is comparatively modern. The stonework from the old Trent Bridge is on the north side of the nave, and was used in the restoration of the church in 1873.

Radcliffe-on-Trent is a large village adjacent to the A52 Nottingham to Grantham road, and is perched on the steep wooded banks of the Trent. The beautiful cliffs stand 100 feet above the river, and from their summit a bird sanctuary extends for some two miles while the Rockley Memorial Park offers both visitor and resident a delightful walk. The views are extensive and there is much activity at the foot of the cliffs in the summer months, for this is where many of the yachts are moored.

In the Domesday Book the village is referred to as Radclyve, and here in 1487 Henry VII heard masses before leading his men over the Malkin Hills to defeat his enemies at East Stoke. The present church of St Mary dates from 1879, the old church having long since gone. It is a roomy church with many arches and a saddleback tower over 100 feet high. One relic of the old church it replaced is a brass engraved with the figure of a lady wearing a ruff and a long

173

veil as she kneels at a desk; she was Anne Ballard who died in 1626, and her epitaph runs:

> *Ask how she lived and thou shalt enow her end,*
> *She died a saint to God, to the poor a friend.*

An inscription to Stephen de Radcliffe of 1245 brings to mind the story of his oak figure, which lay in a recess of the old church. It is said that the villagers, in their great excitement at one of the victories over the French, fetched Stephen from the church, dressed him up to represent Napoleon, and committed him to the flames.

Close to the church are the old village whipping posts, and the Hall and Manor House nearby remind us of the past.

Ragnall lies 4 miles north-east of Tuxford close to the Trent. The church of St Oswald is much restored, and nestles among great trees.

There are pleasing windows of the 14th and 15th century still here, and in the little gallery of sculptures adorning them are a woman in a wimple, a praying angel, a knight with a shield, and the bust of a lady in a headdress. The font has roses in quatrefoils. One of two elaborate 17th century wall monuments is to William Reason; the other is to William Mellish, a London merchant who was brought to this village to lie with his wife.

Rampton lies a mile from the Trent, beyond which is Lincolnshire. The old church has something of Saxon England, and the lovely old gateway reminding us that families famous in the county made this village their home. De Ramptons, Malovels, Stanhopes, Babingtons, Eyres—all have been here.

Nothing is left of the old hall to which the Eyres came in the 17th century, built in the time of Henry VIII and pulled down two centuries later when they went to live at Grove. But its fine Tudor gateway, adorned with the Stanhope and Babington arms, still stands at a corner of the churchyard. A 19th century gateway in similar style stands by the wayside, and from it a long avenue leads to the house they built when they came back to the village in the middle of last century.

Fine limes and chestnuts surround the church of All Saints. Its high tower, looking all the taller for having no buttresses, is 14th century except for its west window, which is 15th, and under its battlements are ballflowers. The mediaeval porch has two charming windows, a sundial, and two worn figures said to represent an angel carrying a soul to paradise and a demon bearing away a soul lost. The old doorway into the church has heads of a king and queen. The church's most venerable possession is a strangely crude piscina, a tiny recess formed by overlapping courses of the walling; it is in the north aisle, and is thought to be Saxon. A massive square pillar in this aisle, and some masonry in its north wall, are also believed to be Saxon. This ancient walling was taken from the original north wall of the church when it was pierced by the north arcade about 1290; the south arcade is a century later.

The bowl of the font is Norman, its splendid arcading re-worked at a later time, and it rests on a 15th century pedestal. There are two mediaeval piscinas, and the south aisle has a tiny peephole to the altar. A pillar almsbox may be 15th century, and the altar table in a chapel is Elizabethan, with a strip of the old chancel screen fixed on to it. The present screen is modern, with beautiful carving of roses, vine, and thistle, and gilded medallions with emblems.

The chancel walls are lined with memorials of the Eyres, a soldier race who came here when Sir Gervase married the heiress of the Babingtons. Two floorstones with crosses may be 15th century, and over a doorway outside is a stone medallion to James Twist, a former vicar.

Ratcliffe-on-Soar. A lane winding with the river brings us to its neat cottages with hooded windows, and a brook flows under the road which ends at the church and the old manor house, now a farm. The churchyard is filled with the murmur of running water, and from a great ash tree we catch a glimpse of the river leaping the weir, and of Red Hill where it falls into the Trent.

Much of the church of Holy Trinity dates from the 13th century. Its glory is in splendid tombs, in bright light streaming through mediaeval windows, and in the feeling of simplicity and age which restoration has not disturbed. Time seems to have stood still within these grey walls.

The tower is from the end of the 12th century, and the 13th century spire springs from a corbel table with corner pinnacles which are miniatures of the spire itself. The spacious chancel is remarkable for being longer than the nave; some of its walling and part of the south aisle is also 13th century. From the 14th come the porch with its old roof timbers, the doorway and the lovely windows of the south aisle, the arch and east window of the chancel, and the nave arcades. The chancel has its old sedilia and piscina and a founder's recess. The 600-year-old font has a cover of about 1660. The mediaeval stone altar is still in use, and there is an unused Jacobean altar table. The altar rails are 17th century, and splendid old beams are left in the nave and chancel roofs.

The battered but still magnificent tombs of the Sacheverells are remarkable for the beauty of their detail. They are of four generations, and bring to an end the Ratcliffe branch of this famous family. On a handsome tomb with an elaborate canopy lies Ralph Sacheverell of 1539 and his first wife Cecilia, he in plate armour and SS collar, his head on a helmet and his feet on a lion; she wearing a cape, a lovely headdress, and round her neck a triple chain with a cross. On a splendid tomb between the chancel and the chapel, with figures of their 17 children, Sir Henry Sacheverell of 1558 lies with his wife, who wears a close-fitting gown with puffed sleeves, a cap, and a triple chain. Henry has tiny ruffs with his plate armour, and a double chain with a cross. His bearded head rests on a helmet with the crest of a goat, and his gauntlets are at his side.

Under the adjoining arch lies the next Henry Sacheverell with his wife, both in ruffs, with their six children carved on the side of the tomb. Henry's head is on a helmet and his gauntlets are at his feet; and his lady has a bit of lovely lace at the top of her gown. We see the last of them, Henry Sacheverell of 1625, lying in armour on the tomb of a monument in the chancel. Under the canopy above him kneel his three wives, their dress showing how fashion changed in the early part of the 17th century. On a panel are a son and two daughters. One of the daughters was grandmother of little Anne

Columbell, who died when she was 15; her floorstone is in the chancel. A stone with the portrait of a priest of 1497 perhaps belongs to John Prescott; another shows Isabel, the wife of Sir John Babington.

Just outside the village stands an enormous power station, it has eight cooling towers and a 650 foot high chimney. Water is drawn from the Trent at the rate of 13,000,000 gallons a day. It has a total installed capacity of 2,000 megowatts, which is equivalent to 2,000,000 kilowatts and cost £75,000,000 to build.

Rempstone is a Notts village lying close to the Leicestershire border. It takes its name from the Rempstone family, and it was Sir Thomas Rempstone who helped to put Henry IV on the throne.

The church of All Saints dates from 1773. In 1962 the remains of a lost church and an ancient moated manor house were excavated. The discovery was made about half a mile from the village, and probably marks the spot of the original settlement. The remains of what was St Peter in the Rushes consisted of a Norman tower, and also fragments of stained glass and 15th century tiles. The church was pulled down in 1771, and stones from it were used to build the present church three-quarters of a mile away. The remains of the manor house are thought to be at least 900 years old.

An annual event started in 1956 and held each July is the Traction Engine Rally.

Retford is divided into two, East and West, by the River Idle. On one side of the market square is the 18th century Town Hall, in front of which stands the Broad Stone, said to be perhaps the base of a cross which stood on a little hill called Dominie Cross, and believed to be one of four similar boundary stones in the neighbourhood.

The glory of the town is the church of St Swithin near the marketplace, built like a cross with a central tower; the lovely exterior is adorned with battlements, lofty pinnacles, and panelled buttresses, and a splendid clerestory adds dignity and charm to the nave and chancel. The pinnacles are a study in themselves, for their lowest crockets make a fine gallery of about 254 heads of human folk and animals, with faces young and old, pleasant and grotesque. Other faces are on the hoods of the windows, and there are grotesque gargoyles here and there. In an outside recess is a modern figure, seated and crowned, said to represent Henry the Third.

Founded in 1258 by Roger, Archbishop of York, the church is for the most part 15th century in style, but is much rebuilt and restored. The tower collapsed in 1651, destroying most of the chancel, and both were made new. Two centuries later the chancel was enlarged, the north aisle rebuilt, and all the exterior re-faced.

The tower, 90 feet high, has its old base with four 13th century arches, and the nave arcades are chiefly 13th and 14th century. Very lovely are their capitals, carved with flowers and foliage—bluebells, thistles, berries, oak, and acorns. One has vine and grapes growing from the mouth of a grotesque face, and two little figures are leaning on the branches. The middle pillar of two lovely bays dividing the north chapel has exquisite foliage.

Among a few old glass fragments are three heads of bishops, and a curiosity in a window of the same transept is a penny set in the glass. St Swithin (whose great statue is over the door inside the church) is a pleasing figure in a lancet. Two beautiful windows facing each other from the ends of the transepts are memorials to the Sherwood Rangers.

The beauty of West Retford's church of St Michael is outside, in its churchyard of lawn, and in its tower and spire. The tower, which becomes eight-sided at the top, has fine windows, and buttresses ending above the battlements in four lofty pinnacles. From these spring flying buttresses, and from the top of these four more slender pinnacles rise. About 120 graceful leaf sprays climb to the tip of the elegant spire.

A stone-roofed porch leads to the dim interior, with a mediaeval south arcade, a 19th century north aisle, an elaborately carved cover to the modern font, and an alabaster reredos showing the Ascension, its sculptured figures painted red, blue, white, and gold. An engraved floorstone comes from 1485, and in a niche on one of the old pillars is a fine modern figure of St Oswald.

Near the church is Holy Trinity Hospital, founded in the 17th century for 16 poor bachelors or widowers, and made new in 1833.

It is a charming block with a chapel, in a setting of lawn and shrubs and trimmed yew hedges.

South of the town is the church of St Alban built in 1901. The walls inside are of cream Bath stone, the nave arcades have clustered pillars, and the chancel is entered by a wide lofty arch. Lancet windows light the aisles; the fine east and west windows and those of the clerestory are in 15th century style. The beautiful east window is by Kempe.

Near this church is King Edward's Grammar School, built in 1854. The school shared in Scott's immortal expedition to the South Pole, for it gave the sledge drawn by the pony Michael.

Rolleston is near Newark on the River Greet. It was the home of the Neville family from the 13th century until the time of Queen Elizabeth I, but the old manor house where they lived was pulled down over 100 years ago.

Rolleston has another claim to remembrance. It is the village where Kate Greenaway, the artist, whose studies of Victorian children and countrymen in smock frocks have given delight to thousands, lived as a girl.

The base of the old village cross still stands, but the smithy which was next to it is no longer there.

The church of Holy Trinity has something of Saxon England. There is early herringbone masonry in its walls, and fragments of Saxon crosses came to light in 1895. Three blocks carved with knotwork are believed to be parts of a shaft, and a smaller fragment built into the wall is remarkable for having the name of the maker of the cross in neatly cut Saxon capitals, and small letters which mean, *Radulf made me.*

The outer walls of the splendid tower have been faced with new stone, but the original work of the Normans is seen in its lower walling inside; the rest of the tower is 15th century. The Norman south doorway has been rebuilt stone by stone; on it is what may be consecration cross, and a stone with remains of a sundial which may be Saxon. In a niche in an aisle is the fluted bowl of a Norman shaft piscina.

The chancel arch and the nave arcades with clustered pillars are 13th century. Among the mediaeval windows is an unusual one like a quatrefoil in each aisle, about 600 years old. There are two mediaeval coffin lids, and fragments of others in a wall. The tiny font is 17th century, the chancel screen has a 15th century base and and a new top, and the tower screen is the good work of a local craftsman of our day.

A rare treasure is a portion of the original paper register which was continued after the day of parchment registers had come. It has nearly 40 leaves stitched together, covering the years 1584 to 1615, and is full of quaint notes made by Robert Leband, a vicar who was drowned by falling from a bridge. His notes tell of current events, local gossip, the weather, the price of corn, and odd things about his flock. He had a good habit of sometimes putting unfavourable comments in Latin. We read that Joane Peele was "so singular a housewife as Rolston could not match". The good vicar must have known less noble types, for we read again that we must not trust a woman, even when she is dead.

A memorial of 1706 is to John Twentiman, a vicar who made interesting entries in the registers in beautiful handwriting.

Ruddington is situated about five miles south of Nottingham, and is west of the main Nottingham–Loughborough road. The name of Ruddington appears once in national history, because Henry VII's army camped there in 1487 on the eve of the Battle of East Stoke, the last one of the long Wars of the Roses.

The church of St Peter dates from 1887, and takes the place of a mediaeval one.

Imposing outside with battlements, roofs of green tiles, and a spire crowning a tower in which much of the older one survives, it is dignified inside, with a finely timbered roof looking down on the lofty nave arcades. There is rich carving of wood in the modern chancel screen, and of stone in the pinnacled sedilia. With the stained glass filling many of the windows are the Twelve Apostles in the south aisle. The face of the Good Samaritan in one window is that of a village doctor who died at the end of last century.

Between the village and Edwalton is a deserted graveyard with a few headstones, reminding us of the lost village of Flawforth which was once important enough for its church to be the mother church of both Ruddington and Edwalton. When the church fell into disuse its windows were used in the rebuilding of Ruddington chapel, and when it was finally pulled down in 1773 much of the material was used in making Ruddington's churchyard wall. Flawforth will not soon be forgotten, for three wonderful alabaster figures once in its church are preserved at Nottingham Castle.

Rufford Abbey, which is situated 2 miles from Ollerton on the main Nottingham to Ollerton road, was formerly the seat of Lord Savile until it was sold in 1939. The original abbey was founded in 1148 by Gilbert de Gaunt. On the dissolution of the monasteries the estate was granted to the Earl of Shrewsbury. The present house was first built in Elizabethan times, and was enlarged by the Marquess of Halifax. Among its most notable visitors were King George IV when he was Prince of Wales, and Edward VII, who would arrive here for the Doncaster race week. Little of the building remains, but that which does is in the process of restoration by the Ministry of Public Building and Works. Rufford Abbey is owned by Nottinghamshire County Council.

Saundby lies some 3 miles from Gainsborough and half as far from the Trent.

The approach to the church of St Martin, which was rebuilt in the last half century, is made through a farmyard.

The tower, with eight pinnacles, is 15th century; the nave arcade of two bays is 13th, and separated from it by seven feet of wall is a 700-year-old arch leading to the chapel. The beautiful font with a band of diamond pattern on the bowl comes from the close of Norman days, and a mediaeval piscina, elaborate with pinnacles and a finial, has a head carved on the projecting drain. The altar table is Elizabethan, and a Bible of 1611 has a leather cover with tiny flowers engraved on its metal bosses and clasp.

One of the windows has St Martin giving half of his cloak to a beggar at the gate of Amiens; in another he is asleep and dreaming, seeing in a vision Our Lord wearing the other half of the cloak. In a medley of old fragments in the tower are the small figure of a woman and the tiny face of a man. The screens, the roofs, and the door with splendid hinges letting us in, are good craftsmanship of our own day.

A battered stone knight of the 14th century lies in the nave, wearing armour and a helmet; his feet are gone, but the lion on which they rested is still here. There is a floorstone with a brass inscription to William Saundeby, who made the church new before he died in 1418, and a canopied monument is to John Helwys, lord of the manor till the end of the next century.

Scarrington, a quiet village with trim houses and wayside lawns, lies two miles north-east of Bingham.

Its church, dedicated to St John of Beverley, has a fine 14th century tower with a spire lighted by two tiers of dormer windows. Its lofty west doorway is adorned with ballflowers and a string of four-leaved flowers. Still ringing in the tower are three bells believed to have been ringing before the Reformation. Standing by the old forge is something which has now become a feature of the village. It is a pile of 50,000 horseshoes standing some 17 feet high, and thought to weigh about 17 tons.

Screveton is an old-world village less than a mile from the Fosse Way.

The parish church of St Wilfrid dates from the early 13th century. There are a number of interesting memorials in the base of the tower, which were moved there from the chancel when it was restored in 1881. The most interesting of these is the alabaster tomb on which lies the effigy in plate armour of Richard Whalley, who died in 1583. He had three wives, who in all bore him 25 children, and these are to be seen behind the effigy of their husband and father. The Whalleys lived at Kirketon Hall, which stood close by until its demolition in 1823. Above this memorial are the royal arms of King Charles II dated 1684. There are two misericords in the chancel, both beautifully carved, one depicting St Wilfrid, and the other, mediaeval, generally supposed to represent Winter. The sundial outside the south porch bears the date 1732.

Scrooby is a small village clustered round the Great North Road just before it leaves Nottinghamshire and enters Yorkshire. It is also within a short distance of the Lincolnshire border. Here lived the leader of the Mayflower Pilgrims who founded a new England overseas. It was the home of William Brewster and the meeting place of the old Fathers of New England. Alongside the church is Brewster Cottage, believed to have been the home of William Brewster from 1588 till 1608, leader of the Pilgrim Fathers. Of greater antiquity is the site of the Archbishop's Palace.

Here were seen the retinues of many a knight and squire. Margaret Tudor called here on her way to Scotland to be made a queen. Here Henry VIII held a Privy Council, and Cardinal Wolsey spent some months here on his last sad journey north. Archbishop Sandys, friend of Lady Jane Grey, often stayed here till his death in Armada year.

The waters of the Ryton were diverted to provide a moat around the palace walls, and the extent of these can be judged from the now dry moat which can still be seen. Another place of great antiquity and possibly of earlier date is that known as Monk's Mill or Wolsey's Mill, but whether the Cardinal had any connections with it we are not certain. However, it was certainly worked by a Brotherhood.

St Wilfrid, to whom the church is dedicated, was a monk born at Ripon. He became Bishop of York, and is believed to have built York Minster, and set up a number of Benedictine Monasteries in this country. He died at Oundle in 709.

The church itself, set in a churchyard of beautiful lawn, was made new in 1390 and much modernised last century. Adorned with fine battlements, it has some Tudor windows, a 14th century porch with a stone roof, and a 14th century nave arcade. A massive spire twice struck by lightning rests on a lovely old tower of rare design, its four angles chamfered near the top to make it eight-sided below its crown of battlements and four lofty pinnacles. Two fine pinnacles on the chancel have tiny heads at their base.

We know that William Brewster worshipped in Scrooby church, as did others who became Pilgrim Fathers; and we know that what is called Brewster's Pew was certainly, in one form or another, part of the church furnishing in his day. The handsome bands of vine and grape which make the back of the pew, and other pieces in two charming little chancel seats, were part of the chancel screen of about 1500. The pew has a massive 15th century traceried bench-end, and the two chancel seats have smaller old ends in similar style.

The font he knew has been sold to America, and the old stocks have gone there too. A floorstone to Penelope Sandys recalls the Archbishop whom Brewster would know in his younger days, and his son, Sir Edwin Sandys, who became Governor of Virginia and granted the Pilgrim Fathers the tract of land on which they settled.

Selston has lovely views out to the Derbyshire hills and Crich Tower high in the west, and one of the best vantage points is from the churchyard. It is a fitting resting-place for one who loved the open country, and under the shade of a lofty lime near the 15th century tower lies Dan Boswell, King of the Gipsies. On the broken stone now flat on his grave a few words are still seen, and though the epitaph is gone it was odd enough to be remembered:

> *I've lodged in many a town,*
> *I've travelled many a year,*
> *But death at length has brought me down*
> *To my last lodging here.*

The church of St Helen is old and beautiful. The entrance arch-way of the porch has capitals carved with grotesque faces, some with foliage coming from their mouths; it is about 1200. The splendid south doorway has a round arch on shafts with rows of ornament between them. The round arches and pillars of a Norman arcade divide the nave and north aisle; the south arcade, the plain chancel arch, and the arcades between the chancel and its chapels, come from the first years of the English style.

The clerestory and the east window are 15th century, and a pretty recessed window in the chancel comes from the end of the 13th.

The Norman font was returned to the church in 1900 after being a trough at one of the local inns.

On an ancient floorstone is the crude figure of a priest holding a chalice. A great stone in the tower has a rare cross, and in an outside wall is a stone engraved with a dog gnawing a bone. A little old work is left in the roofs, and among the quaint stone heads supporting the beams in the nave are a man and a woman like Darby and Joan. The oak pulpit, with rich vine borders, is of our century.

On an alabaster monument lie the great figures of William Willoughby and his wife, he a young knight in 17th century armour.

Each year there is a tower service, a Feast Sunday festival, when the Minister preaches his sermon from the tower of the church.

A landmark in this colliery countryside is the 50-year-old stone church at Underwood (2 miles away), a shingled spire crowning the tower.

Shelford, which lies by the Trent, is approached by a long narrow road from Gunthorpe Bridge. It is a pleasant village amid charming Trent valley scenery.

Shelford at one time had a priory which was founded by Ralph Hounselyn sometime in the 12th century during the reign of Henry II. There is nothing outstanding in its history, however, until 1536 when like most priories and monasteries it was dissolved. In 1537, Michael Stanhope obtained the lands of Shelford and he and his successors lived there until 1645.

During the Civil War, Shelford was a strong Royalist holding, and during the Roundhead attacks on Newark they held off the besieging army many times. However, in 1645, the Roundheads held a campaign to overcome Shelford, and Major-General Poyntz, Colonel Hutchinson, and 2,000 men proceeded from Nottingham to Shelford. When they arrived, Philip Stanhope refused to surrender, and decided to defend his King and home with about 200 men. The house was well fortified with palisade and moat but the attackers found a weak spot in the defence and forced an entrance. There followed a ghastly massacre when some 140 Royalist followers were slain, including Philip Stanhope. That night the house was burnt down. Shelford Manor was rebuilt in 1676.

The first mention of a church at Shelford is in the Domesday Survey of 1086, at which time Shelford possessed a priest and a church. Its population then was 250, and is about the same now. The present church of St Peter and St Paul has a Perpendicular tower, and forms a conspicuous landmark in the valley of the Trent. The registers date back to 1563 and contain many interesting entries, including baptisms, marriages, and burials of members of the Stanhope family, who became lords of the manor after the dissolution of the 12th century priory. The registers are now in the care of the County Archivist. On the window sill of the Stanhope Chapel in the church is a fragment of an old Saxon cross, the suggested date of which is 1050. It was discovered built into a buttress on the south side of the church during the 1877–78 restoration. It is a fine example of early carving, showing the Madonna and Child on one side, and a winged Byzantine Angel holding a book on the reverse side. Knotwork adorns the edges. It is regarded as a precious possession.

The two painted shields of arms at either end of the chancel are possibly the arms of William, Viscount Beaumont, Lord Bardolph, and Lord Beaumont, lord of the manors of Stoke Bardolph and Shelford, who died in 1507. These shields are made of heavy oak, and were originally in the chancel ceiling, but were removed in the restoration of 1877–78 carried out by the Earl of Carnarvon. The chancel was entirely rebuilt in the Early English style, while the monuments of the Stanhope family were removed to the east end of the south aisle, and a screen erected to form the Stanhope Chapel.

The last great work of restoration to the church was carried out in 1954–55. Since then, the organ has been removed from the chancel and placed by the north wall of the church, while the appearance of the chancel has been greatly enhanced by the walls being painted white. There are five bells; 1702, pre-Reformation, 1592, 1754, and pre-Reformation.

A feast is held on the first Sunday after St Peter's Day.

Shelton. Mantled in trees and bounded by the River Smite, this quiet home of a few people is part of a wide countryside which is golden in summertime with waving corn.

The big house and the small church look across a stretch of fine parkland, the lawn of the house and the churchyard coming in friendly fashion to low grey walls by the wayside. The house has two sundials and on the lawn is a great beech.

The church, which is dedicated to St Mary and All Saints, is one of only 24 in the whole of England so named. It lost its old tower a century ago. The chancel is made new, but it has two 13th century lancets, and over the modern east window is the old hood adorned with heads. A charming row of three old lancets in the aisle has tinted glass shedding a mellow light, and above them is the mediaeval corbel table.

The arcade of slightly pointed arches on round pillars comes from about 1200. A face smiles from the rich hood of a lovely piscina in the aisle, and the 14th century font is like a chalice. There are two Jacobean coffin stools, and old work remains in the restored chancel screen. Its embattled cornice is fixed on to the wall above the wooden chancel arch. A modern door with beautiful ironwork hangs in the south doorway, which has in its parts of two Norman doorways.

The great treasures of Shelton are two exceptionally fine Saxon stones carved with knotwork, perhaps from two coped tombs. Fragments of old carved stones are built into the vestry wall, and in the churchyard is a stone coffin.

Shelton was the birthplace of A. O. Jones, who captained Nottinghamshire Cricket Club and also a team to Australia.

Shireoaks is a mining village two miles north-west of Worksop. The church of St Luke was built by the Duke of Newcastle in 1862 in 14th century style. It has a lofty tower with a short spire, aisles and an apse, and steep roofs painted in mediaeval colours.

Edward VII, as Prince of Wales, laid the first stone, and he and Mr Gladstone gave some of the poor glass in memory of the duke who died two years after its building. Other memorials to him are the reredos, the sedilia, a table (all elaborately carved in marble and alabaster), and the mosaic lining the walls of the apse. The reredos has a group of 16 figures in the Crucifixion scene, also four angels, four saints, and symbols of the Evangelists.

Nothing is left of the ancient oak which gave the village its name, and threw its shade into Yorkshire, Derbyshire, and Notts. The boundary itself has changed, and the spot where it grew is now wholly in Notts. John Evelyn described the old tree as being 94 feet round, covering a patch of about 700 square yards.

Sibthorpe lies about 6 miles south-west of Newark.

The church of St Peter has lost its north aisle and the chapel where masses were sung, but the arches of the old arcade are still seen in the wall. The sturdy tower of about 1300 has a modern parapet, and Georgian work is in the nave and the porch. The beautiful 14th century chancel has windows with leaf tracery, and its lofty 13th century arch rests on shafts with foliage capitals. Over a founder's recess in the chancel is an elaborately carved Easter Sepulchre. The font is 17th century, a plain little chest is over 500 years old, and there are solid oak benches a century younger. There is a magnificent alabaster tomb to Edward Burnell made in 1590. The yew trees in the churchyard are reputed to be 1,000 years old.

At the rear of the church stands a dovecote about 31 feet in diameter, 60 feet in height, and containing 1,260 nesting places in 28 tiers. This is now the property of the National Trust.

Skegby village has grown on the steep sides of a valley and is some 3 miles west of Mansfield.

Standing on a lofty hill above the road is the church of St Andrew. Much of the old church has been lost in the rebuilding of 1870 which was made necessary by the mine running under it, but there is old work left in the base of the tower, a 13th century arcade in the nave, and a tiny 700-year-old piscina which has a woman's face carved on the drain. Built into the walls inside and out are 12th and 13th century coffin stones, carved with crosses, a chalice, a sword, and shears; one is only 27 inches long. A mediaeval stone on the wall has on it a kneeling priest. At the west end of the nave are the church's greatest treasures, two fine stone figures, once lying down but now standing against a wall. One is a lady with a wimple and a long gown, her hands in prayer and her head on a cushion held by angels; the other is a forester with his hunter's horn. They are thought to be Edmund Spigurnell of 1296 and his wife. Part of their home still survives in the 12th and 13th century remains in the ruined building by a farmhouse near the station. Also in the nave is an interesting brass to one John Miller, with a couplet telling of his death in 1915 at Suva. The altar is new, being placed here in 1947. Other items of new furniture include the vicar's stall, lectern, choir-stalls, bishop's chair, and the credence table, which show up well against the new blue carpeting. The church, which has three bells 1684, 1737, and 1830, has registers dating back to 1571.

Sookholme is a tiny village 5 miles north-east of Mansfield. The church of St Peter and St Paul has its share of Norman England in a wide chancel arch with roll mouldings and a font bowl shaped like a bucket. It has lost a third of its old length, but there is still much Norman masonry in the north and south walls, and a few windows are mediaeval. A fine piscina and a crude stone bench for the priests are 600 years old. There is an old chest, and the nave roof has two fine old beams and two ancient bosses, one carved with a quaint face with a pointed ruff all round it.

South Collingham is a delightful neighbour for North Colling-ham, with its gabled houses, wayside lawns, overhanging trees, and winding roads revealing odd corners of unexpected charm. On the three-cornered green is an ancient elm 17 feet round its trunk, which is now a mere shell with rustic poles filling the gap between its yawning edges.

Perhaps its most charming spot is where the church of St John the Baptist stands in a garden of roses and shrubs, with beech and sycamore trees shading the lawn; it is a beautiful churchyard, and on one side of it a holly arch frames a picture of the rectory garden.

The church is neat and lovely in and out, with old and new happily blended. Some of its oldest work is still its chief possession.

Exceptionally fine is the Norman arcade of the nave with rich mouldings and carved capitals, and an extraordinary corbel showing the head of a dragon-like creature with the bearded face of a man in its wide-open mouth, the face seen only when we stand below the corbel. The head of a man with his tongue out (as if at the beast) looks across the nave from the English arcade of the 13th century.

The tower is 13th and 15th century. It is a charming bit of the church inside, with its cream walls, its rows of benches, and a lovely arch with detached pillars. The massive font is 13th century and there are three old piscinas. In the 13th century doorway through which we enter hangs a splendid door, which is part of the excellent modern woodwork throughout the church. The benches have traceried ends and some linenfold, the pulpit has carving of vines, and the nave roof has floral bosses. A little old timber is in the roof of the north aisle.

Most of the windows are 15th century, and corbel heads with a striking family likeness adorn them outside.

South Leverton is 5 miles east of Retford.

The church of All Saints has a high unbuttressed tower which is mainly Norman, with 15th century battlements, and is charming inside, where its pointed arch opens to the nave and the lovely glass of its 13th century lancet sheds a rainbow light on the great Norman font. The windows shows Our Lord blessing the children, and is in memory of Maria Overend, whose gifts helped the restoration of the church at the close of last century.

One of the finest possessions of the church is the great Norman doorway, its detached shafts supporting an arch with handsome zigzag enriched with sunflower pattern. It frames a modern door with beautiful hinges, and as it opens to let us in the walls are seen like masses of mosaic, tinted buff, orange, green, and gold.

The 13th century nave arcades have pillars of grouped shafts crowned by foliage capitals, and among the corbels are two pairs of curious animals seeming to be fighting. Under the south aisle roof inside is a huge gargoyle-like head with staring eyes and open mouth. The chancel is made new, but in its side walls are eight 13th century lancets.

A tapering stone with traces of carving is the oldest possession of the village, for it is believed to have been the lid of a Roman coffin. A floorstone with a cross is only two feet long, and the fragment of another ancient stone has crude carving of feet and a shroud. The chalice is Elizabethan, and three bells are 17th century.

A pleasant house called the Priory has an old gabled end whose walls, four feet thick, may be part of a monastic building.

South Muskham is now a greatly enlarged village, with many new houses and bungalows. The Newark Bypass keeps most of the traffic away from the village, but the sound of the diesel trains from the nearby railway can be heard close to the church.

The massive tower of the church of St Wilfrid beckons long before we reach it.

It is the glory of the village. Its 13th century base has narrow lancets, 14th century windows light the stage above, and the splendid top storey is 500 years old. The belfry windows have embattled transoms, and hoods adorned with finials and heads; and one of them has a niche with a robed figure, perhaps St Wilfrid, holding a crozier and blessing all who pass by.

The oldest work in the pleasing little church is herringbone masonry seen inside and out of the north wall of the chancel, the carved bowl of a Norman font (with a 17th century cover), and the small north doorway of the 12th century. Less than six feet high, the arch of the doorway is almost round, a blending of the Norman and English styles.

The beautiful mediaeval door which lets us in is heavily ribbed and studded, and has two holes (now filled in) made by bullets of the Civil War. The nave arcades and the wide chancel arch are about 1400; the chancel has six 13th century lancets; the east window is 15th century. There are a few fragments of old glass, the piscina and aumbry are mediaeval, the south aisle has a few old roof beams, a table is Jacobean, and there is an ancient almsbox. Three bench-ends and four splendid poppyheads in the chancel seats were found under the floor during restoration; they are 15th century, the poppy-heads carved with roses, a double-headed pelican, winged and crowned grotesques, and four crabs with nippers and claws.

On the walls of the church are two glass cases holding musical instruments, one a bassoon and the other a clarinet. They were used in the band of the church many years ago to accompany the singing, and have recently been on exhibition in London.

South Scarle lies north-east from Newark on the borders of the county. In addition to the charming old church are several houses dating from the beginning of the 18th century, and a stone dovecote with a pyramidal roof. From the edge of the village there is a fine view of Lincoln Cathedral.

The church of St Helen shows its loveliest work as we open the door; it is in two Norman bays of the north arcade. Their arches are richly adorned with remarkable elaboration of zigzag ornament, their hoods are of tiny chevrons carved point to point, and the capitals have foliage and scallop.

These two bays are the original length of the Norman nave. A smaller arch at their east end comes from the 13th century, when the church was enlarged by transepts and the present chancel was built. This small arch, and the corresponding one in the 13th century south arcade, became part of the arcades when the transepts were opened to the aisles two centuries later; separating them from the other arches is eight feet of walling which is actually part of the Norman chancel. Between the Norman arches is the fine stone head of a man looking well content to have a place in so lovely a scheme; and two wide eyes have been looking across at the Norman work for 700 years. There are stone seats round some of the pillars. Fine 13th century arches to the tower and chancel, a 15th century clerestory, and a mediaeval roof with bosses and angel corbels with shields, complete the nave.

The rest of the sturdy tower is 600 years old, with battlements and pinnacles a century younger. The beautiful double piscina, the bowl and base of the font, and two lancets are 13th century. The

500-year-old screen is much restored, and a massive old ladder climbs to the belfry. A great chest, a pillar almsbox, and some bench-ends with tiny poppyheads, are other old relics. Under the tower are two ancient floorstones with crosses. Another in the chancel is engraved with the portrait of Sir William Mering of 1510, in armour and with his sword. In a niche over the 15th century entrance to the porch is the tiny crowned figure of St Helena, the patron saint, and from the windows happy little stone faces smile down.

Southwell is pronounced South-well by the locals, while to most other people it is known as Suth'l.

It lies some 13 miles to the north-east of Nottingham, and stands on fairly level ground near the little River Greet, which is a tributary of the Trent. It is renowned for its roses, and all who visit Southwell are charmed by its attractive houses and numerous colourful gardens. Notable among its rural crafts is the centuries old trade of saddlery.

The Saracen's Head is the oldest inn in the town, and was at one time known as the King's Arms. It was here that King Charles I stayed immediately before raising his standard in Nottingham in August 1642, and again after his engagement at Naseby in 1645. There he spent his last night of freedom before giving himself up to the Scottish Commissioners and being turned over to Cromwell.

In coaching days the Champion Stage Coach from Lincoln via Newark would clatter into the courtyard to change and collect passengers and mail before continuing its journey. Byron the poet was a frequent visitor to the inn, and on hearing of the death of John Adams, the carrier, who died of drunkenness, he proceeded to write the following epitaph:

> *John Adam lies here, of the Parish of Southwell,*
> *A carrier who carried his can to his mouth well,*
> *He carried so much, and he carried so fast,*
> *He could carry no more so was carried at last.*
> *For the liquor he drank, being too much for one,*
> *He could not carry off, so it is now carry on.*

Burgage Manor on Burgage Green was rented by Byron's mother whilst he was at Cambridge, and it was from here that he spent his vacations from 1804 to 1806. He made some friends in the town, who in turn encouraged him to write verses, which were later printed at Newark and entitled *Hours of Idleness*. It is not commonly known that he carved his name on the roof of the tower of Southwell Minster, but unfortunately this has long since been removed.

Many people refer to Southwell Minster as one of England's most beautiful buildings. About 1110 the Archbishop of York began the Minster that we see, after he had released the people of Notts from the annual pilgrimage to York on condition that they came to the church of St Mary of Southwell. Before the middle of the 13th century the small Norman choir had been replaced by the choir we see, a superb example of the Early English style at its best. The vestibule and the exquisite chapter house to which it leads were built between 1290 and 1300, and the richest stone screen in all England was set up 30 years later. The 15th century gave windows to the aisles, and the great west window, whose virtue is that it throws light into the nave.

We come to the Minster through one of its old gateways, its Norman arch under a stepped gable with a mediaeval niche.

As we walk between the churchyard lawns, the fine west front is before us, standing as it stood in the 12th century except for the great window, and the square broached spires (the pepper-pots) with which the twin towers were crowned last century. The fifth storey of one of these high towers is enriched with Norman interlaced arcading, while that of its companion has a series of pointed arches. The west doorway is splendid with zigzag ornament, which also adorns many of the windows and the stringcourse running round the Norman part of the church. On both sides of the west doors is beautiful old ironwork in scrolls.

A stately square tower rises from the middle of a cross. The Norman two-storeyed north porch (a charming feature of the exterior) has a barrel roof looking down on arcaded walls and a recessed doorway with seven orders of ornament. It frames a 600-year-old traceried door.

194

We should enter by the west doorway, for here the grandeur of the Norman nave bursts upon us. Sturdy round columns with carved capitals with strength enough to last forever support the moulded arches. Over them runs a stringcourse like the edge of a saw. Then comes the triforium, with wide arches on short shafts, and above these the smaller arches of the clerestory passage, which is lighted by the small round windows seen outside.

Very solid and impressive is this great nave, leading to the four colossal arches bearing up the central tower. They are carved with exceptionally bold cable moulding, and the capitals on which the eastern arch rests are among the earliest Norman work here, their dainty carving showing the Annunciation, the Nativity, the Entry into Jerusalem, Our Lord washing Peter's feet, and the Last Supper (portrayed with a gap at the table). For forty years these capitals were hidden by the organ; now only part of the organ is on the stone screen, and the carvings are revealed.

The north and south arches of the crossing open to transepts as old as the nave. The nave has a 19th century barrel roof, but the aisles have their original Norman vaulting. The undercutting of the capitals and the ornament in the mouldings are striking features of the lovely vaulted 13th century choir, which has a triforium and a clerestory. We come to the choir through a pair of charming iron gates in the middle bay of the stone screen; a gift in memory of a mother, they were made by a blacksmith of Brant Broughton.

The screen itself is a miracle in stone. It has looked as we see it for about 600 years, and is marvellous for its fine sculpture even in this place where the artist's chisel has produced what John Ruskin called the gem of English architecture.

Enthroned high up in this wonderful screen sits the Madonna, a beautiful figure with an angel beckoning her. On each side of the doorway are three stone stalls; one of them, carved at the back in about 200 diaper squares, was Cardinal Wolsey's seat when he lived at the bishop's palace after his fall. Along the top of the screen runs a row of carved heads, and over the stalls are exquisite canopies elaborate with foliage and finials, and heads hanging from the cusps. Everywhere on this screen we see the genius of the mediaeval artist at his best. Altogether there are 289 figures, an immense number when we consider the little space into which they are crowded.

To those who wonder at the quaint and curious things we sometimes find in our cathedrals, the Southwell screen is a wondrous picture book, for it is easy to gather from it something of the mediaeval craftsman's mind. It was not just a joke that he made plants grow out of a mouth, or chiselled ugly people; his strange grotesques were not just passing fancy. In those days before books this was the way of teaching; these things were the people's library, their picture gallery, their Bible. An ugly man was a bad man, the man with his tongue out was a gossip. Those who will interest themselves in these things will find these ancient sculptures full of good philosophy, with virtues and vices personified. We find here the head of a woman who seems to be in terror, and looking across we find the reason why, for there is a man like a brute. On one of the brackets is David playing the harp; on another is Saul falling on his sword in his tent; small as it all is, the pain in Saul's face is clearly seen. There is an exquisite suggestion of an angel listening, with the forefinger held up in a way familiar to us all.

We can see at a glance, looking across the choir to the sanctuary, that the beautiful seats for the priests must have sprung from the same mind and been done by the same hands as the screen. The five seats in the sedilia (the sixth has gone) are superbly canopied, but the canopies have been broken and were restored at the beginning of the 19th century. They seem no worse for it, but remain one of the most captivating achievements of craftsmanship in the country. The seats are divided by slender columns round which cluster the tiniest human figures tucked away among the foliage. There are about 75 of them, and about half are the originals. Groups of figures run along the top; a group showing the Flight into Egypt has a very fine head of Joseph carved in the middle of the 14th century. The tiny cusps have gems of sculpture hanging from them, and the roofs of the canopies are vaulted and bossed.

An admirable place is Southwell to those who believe the best days of the world have not yet been, that all the best work has not been done, for here, in this choir so full of beauty, the work of modern times is worthy of the old. Where this 14th century stone is wonderful, the 19th century woodwork is wonderful too. It is as if the man who set these seats in this great choir was moved by the spirit of beauty about him. It was Charles Henry Simpson who carved this marvellous range of oak stalls in the last years of the 19th century.

In these oak choir stalls is every kind of conception that comes to a carver who studies Nature in her infinite variety. There are many kinds of nuts and berries, mistletoe, honeysuckle, bulrushes, sunflowers, catkins, and lilies of the valley. There are thistles, clover, buttercups, and wild roses. There is a holly tree which would prick us if we touched it. There is bracken with leaves too delicate to touch. There is an arm-rest with primroses and butterflies, and ears of wheat with mice playing among them. There are birds in a fig tree, a serpent in an apple tree, a lizard in an oak tree, and two pigs eating acorns that have fallen. There are bats and fishes and toadstools, and peas in a pod, and we think the artist must have been very fond of music, for he has put among all this foliage something of the music of the countryside, a fiddle and a harp, a bird singing by its nest, and a lark at Heaven's gate.

Much of the carving runs right through the oak, and everywhere it has the variety of the garden and the fields. The pulpit matches the stalls in teak; it is very fine, with a Madonna and Child in the centre panel under the canopy.

We are prepared in this shrine for a noble revelation of our English architecture, and we come with great expectations to this famous chapter house. We are not disappointed. We come into it through the vaulted vestibule, charming in itself, opening off the north choir aisle by a lovely doorway carved all round with leaves. It has a dignity of its own, as if it knew where it is leading us. We see in the wealth of carving on its arcaded walls a remarkable sculpture of a lay priest pulling the hair of a regular priest, a lady with a brooch, a quaint creature like a baboon, a blackbird pecking berries, and the face of a man who seems to be winking.

So we come to what is probably the most beautiful doorway in any cathedral in England, divided by a single clustered shaft, with

o

exquisite carvings of leaves and flowers. It is a noble entrance to a place beyond compare, of which it has been said that it is among chapter houses as the rose among flowers. The doorway is recessed with a series of pillars, and the capitals of three on the right are carved from a single stone with oak and mulberry leaves and butter-cups. The maple leaves round the doorway spring from one wyvern's tail and run into another. The chapter house inside is built like York's, an octagon without a central column. It has 36 seats, with triangular canopies over them, and the carving of these canopies is one of the stone wonders of the world. We do not know who did them, but among the figures is one of a monk who may, we like to think, have been the artist himself, for his natural hair curls under his cap. Why is he so real? Perhaps it may be that he is the lifelike artist who gave this place immortal fame in art. To him all things were real, and all work was life.

There are corbels where they never could be seen; but long before Longfellow said so this disciple knew that the gods see everywhere, and the corbels nobody sees are as fine as all the rest. The crafts-man made a slip in his calculations, not finishing in line at the door, but he covered it up with a beautiful leaf. Over the doorway he put the head of a smiling man, and a dog to keep him company, looking down on all who come and go. Just inside the doorway he carved the head of a girl, with hair that might have belonged to the 20th century girl we saw standing beside it.

This unknown genius of Southwell copied his work from Nature; he took it from the fields hereabouts, and it is always true. His foliage may be tightly massed, but the stems are always there. His heads have plant symbols of the spirit of good and evil issuing from their mouths. He has a bird carrying its young from the poisonous ivy. He has two dogs with a hare run to earth, carved among ivy leaves, and we remember the gamekeeper's explanation that the hare seeks the ivy when it is about to die. He has a marvel-lous carving of acorn-cups from which the nuts have fallen, to be eaten by the pigs hidden below, a fancy the carver of the choir stalls was to copy nearly 600 years later. He has what has been called a May Queen, a woman with hawthorn leaves springing from her head like wings. He has monks with jester's caps, fabulous beasts, and on the top of a shaft from which the vaulting springs he has a goat eating ivy (he knew that it is harmless to them) and a herdsman blowing his horn.

The chapter house is built of stone quarried hereabouts, the stone which crumbled in our Houses of Parliament after only a hundred years. Here it is hard (with all this intricacy of carving) after six centuries, and from the canopied seats to the vaulted roof its condition is remarkable. It is flooded with light through its transparent windows, in which are set about a hundred pieces of 13th, 14th, and 15th century glass.

The east window of the choir is made up of two tiers of lancets, and has glass of remarkable interest in the lower tier, showing the Baptism of Christ, the Raising of Lazarus, the Triumphal Entry into Jerusalem, and the Mocking and Scourging. The windows are bold and aglow with colour, and some of the figures are supposed to be of historic characters, Martin Luther among them. The great interest of this Flemish glass is that it is from a church destroyed in Paris during the French Revolution. It found its way into a pawnshop and came to Southwell a few years after Waterloo. It is thought these windows may have been seen by Marie Antoinette on her way to execution.

There is a great window in the south choir aisle made into a mosaic with a thousand fragments of 13th century glass. The best of the modern windows is one by Christopher Whall, showing in glowing colours the Crucifixion and the Vision of St John. Some of the vivid glass in the aisles is interesting for its quaint scenes, one showing the Temptation of Our Lord, with Satan's eyes gleaming and a cloven hoof peeping from his robe. Another has Paulinus (who Christianised this part of the Trent Valley), holding a model of this Minster, which some say he founded. The bright red and blue glass in two round clerestory windows of the south transept was made by two boys, who took it into Norwood Park to burn in the colour.

Much of the impressiveness of this stately Minster comes from the fact that it is not encumbered with memorials. The monument which draws all eyes to it is the lovely alabaster tomb of Archbishop Sandys. He lies with two angels at his head and two at his feet, and in a panel his wife kneels with a perfectly charming group of eight children behind her. The tomb dates from c. 1588. In the south choir aisle lies the oldest stone figure here, a 12th century priest. A very holy place has been given to Bishop Riddings, 43rd headmaster of Winchester and first Bishop of Southwell. He kneels at prayer, magnificent in bronze, stretching out his hands. Of the second bishop, his successor Dr Hoskyns, there is a bronze showing him in his robes, and his kindly face comes to life as the bronze turns on a spindle at the touch of a finger.

The splendid brass eagle lectern in the choir once belonged to the monks at Newstead and was found in the lake there early last century. It was bought by a watchmaker at Nottingham who, on taking it to pieces, found in the pedestal a bundle of documents. These documents are today among the collections at Newstead. The new high altar dates from 1933.

Those who come to be surprised at Southwell and stay to love it will find themselves sitting perhaps on an old bench in the south transept. Men have sat on it for 500 years, and it seems to us the right place to sit and draw a last inspiration from the Stones of Southwell. These benches were once used for a court, and it was such seats that gave rise to the legal phrase "sitting on the bench". As we sit here we see, a yard or two away, the old stone seats by the transept walls built in the days before benches for those who could not stand in the church; it was such seats as these which gave rise to the saying that the weakest go to the wall.

But it is not only of such things that we are thinking: we are remembering that as we sit on this old bench and look along the transepts we are in the presence of Roman and Saxon and Norman, for we lift a little trap-door below our feet and look at a tesselated pavement that has been here 1700 years; the Romans made it. We look along the north transept to a doorway at the corner and there is a tympanum with David (now headless) fighting a lion and Michael slaying a dragon; the Saxons made it. We look up into the great central tower, with stupendous arches impressive enough to endure forever; the Normans made them. We look through the 14th century screen and see the marvellous carving of the oak stalls done as it were the other day; a 19th century craftsman made them. It may be doubted if we can sit in any other English cathedral with so much work spanning 17 centuries about us.

In 1956 the millenary of the Charter was celebrated and in connection with this great event, Southwell was honoured by the visit on June 9, 1956 of HRH Princess Margaret.

In the neighbourhood of Southwell is Easthorpe, where in 1805 a Mrs Elizabeth Brailsford decided to try her hand at raising an apple tree from seed. She placed two apple pips in a plant pot, and when they germinated she transplanted them into her garden. One took root. Mrs Brailsford's son-in-law, Mr Matthew Bramley, succeeded her as owner of the property, and a Mr Henry Merryweather, who recognised the virtues of this wonderful fruit, sought permission from Mr Bramley to take grafts. The request was granted on one condition, that the apple was called Bramley Seedling. Mr Merryweather raised a stock in his nursery; he planted an orchard, much of which still exists, and in 1876 he submitted specimen fruit to the Royal Horticultural Society, who granted an award and later a first class certificate.

Stanford-on-Soar. It is the farthest south of Notts. Near the church a small hump-back bridge which once spanned the stream stands among weedy shallows. It saw the passing of the ancient manor house by the church, and the building of a great house by Robert Raynes in the time of Charles I, on what was then a barren hill over a mile away. The present hall is on the same site, but the bare hill has changed, for a tree-lined road brings us to a park with glorious elms and limes and lovely grounds, now known as Stanford Hall. It was once the home of Sir Julian Cahn, who after purchasing it, spent £100,000 on transforming it to his liking. It had one of the most attractive private swimming pools in the country, with underwater lighting and an illuminated waterfall. In the grounds there were putting greens, a nine-hole golf course, a private hatchery to keep the lake well stocked with trout, and then to complete this extravaganza he built, at a cost of £73,000, one of the finest intimate theatres in the world. When Sir Julian died the hall was sold, and it is now a residential college of the Co-operative Society.

There are blocks of Mount Sorrel granite in the base of the splendid 15th century tower of the church, which is dedicated to St John the Baptist. The oldest part of the church is the 13th century arcade opening to the south aisle which was widened two centuries later. The north arcade is 14th century, and the fine clerestory was built about 1500. The chancel is made new, and the modern porch is on old foundations. Old relics are a piscina, a stone altar with five crosses, part of a coffin stone and a fragment of 13th century moulding in the vestry wall, and small original figures of angels at the ends of the tiebeams in the nave.

On the chancel floor is the fine 14th century brass portrait of a priest in robes, holding a chalice; it is one of only two ecclesiastical brasses in the county, and may represent Adam de Rothley. On an alabaster floorstone are the charmingly natural engraved figures of two Illyngworths of the 15th century, their faces rather worn.

In a recess in the wall of the north aisle, which he may have founded, lies the strange figure of a 14th century civilian with short hair and beard, high cheek bones, tightly closed lips, and a very long neck. He wears a closely-buttoned gown, has a sword, a dagger, and a pouch, and holds a heart in his folded hands.

It was Thomas Lewes, a London alderman who bought the manor from the Raynes family, and the raised vault of this family and the Dashwoods (whom they married) spoils the south aisle. Among their memorials is an inscription to Samuel Vere Dashwood, rector for 49 years of last century; and a charming little monument of 1911 to Elizabeth Dashwood has the head of a woman with two children standing out in white marble on a blue ground.

Stanton-on-the-Wolds lies south-east from Nottingham. Its cottages and farms are clustered on the windswept Wolds, and the tiny church is almost lost in trees. From the golf links by the churchyard there is a fine view of the Trent Valley.

The church of All Saints has only a nave and chancel under one roof, with a bellcote, but the nave has traces of Norman work in its walls, and the round bowl of a Norman font is cemented to the floor. A mediaeval lancet lights the west wall, the shapely little east window is 600 years old, and one with dainty tracery under its square head is only a little younger. The old piscina and aumbry are here, and the tiny 14th century doorway in the porch has a modern door covered with the lovely scrolls of two hinges.

Stapleford lies some six miles south-west of Nottingham.

The parish church of St Helen dates from about 1240–50 and is in the Early English style.

Attractive outside, the church has a tower and spire from the three mediaeval centuries. The nave arcades are 14th century, the north a little older than the south. From about 1300 come the doorway letting us in (sheltered by an 18th century porch), some windows in the south aisle, and the east window of the chancel with its beautiful example of early tracery, formed by the simple inter-section of the mullions. The font of this time has an unusual domed metal cover of about 1660. An oak carving of the Last Supper is foreign work, and was once the reredos. Two of the bells are believed to be 16th century.

For some generations the Teverys of Long Eaton were lords of Stapleford. Engraved on a floorstone are the portraits of Robert Tevery of 1571 in armour and his wife in Elizabethan dress. Gervase Tevery and his wife are lying on a massive monument; and kneeling on the floor are charming figures of three daughters and an only son, all four battered through having been moved about since they were placed here 300 years ago.

Next to the church is the memorial chapel built in 1925 in memory of those who lost their lives in the First World War.

Some years ago Stapleford's greatest treasure was moved from its place in the street and set up in the churchyard. It is the famous cross, which has stood while England has seen the rise of all its royal dynasties. It was here when the Saxons worshipped in a little church of wattle and timber, and perhaps before there was a church at all. This tapering shaft of a Saxon cross, ten feet high and perhaps

1200 years old, is adorned with a mass of crude and worn interlacing work, and has on one side what is believed to be the symbol of St Luke, a horned figure with wings, treading on a serpent.

A most interesting feature of Stapleford is the Hemlock Stone, a natural phenomenon 30 feet high, rising from a green mound. It is a great mass of red sandstone rock which has resisted the action of rain and frost longer than man can tell, and its strange shape makes a curious landmark. For thousands of years nothing has disturbed this solitary sentinel, which is about 70 feet round, and is said to weigh over 200 tons. It can best be seen from Coventry Lane.

It was here at Stapleford on July 21, 1875 that Arthur Mee, author of this series of books, was born. He received his education at the village school, and entered journalism in Nottingham at the age of 16. Five years later he went to London at the invitation of Sir George Newnes. Among his best-known works are the *King's England*, the *Children's Encyclopaedia*, and the *Children's Newspaper* (which has now ceased publication). Mr Mee was known to have refused a title on more than one occasion. He died in 1943.

Staunton. Hiding in a charming corner where the county meets Leicestershire and Lincolnshire is quiet Staunton, with a fine setting in the English scene and a fine place in our literature. A flagged path embowered in trees leads to the great house and the church, in delightful company, one rich in memories of the family who have been lords of the manor from the Conquest, the other with a goodly array of their memorials.

The long two-storeyed house, still the home of a Staunton and still partly 16th century, stands in a park with a lake at the foot of the sloping lawn where we hear the murmur of the River Devon and the little Winter Beck. Legend says that after staying here Scott made Staunton the Willingham of his *Heart of Midlothian*, describing it as "one of those beautiful scenes which are so often found in Merrie England".

A humble bell-rope and a beautiful golden key with a peacock under a crown keep alive the long association of the Stauntons with Belvoir Castle seven miles away. It began when the Norman lords

Southwell Minster

The nave of Southwell Minster

The door to the chapter house at Southwell

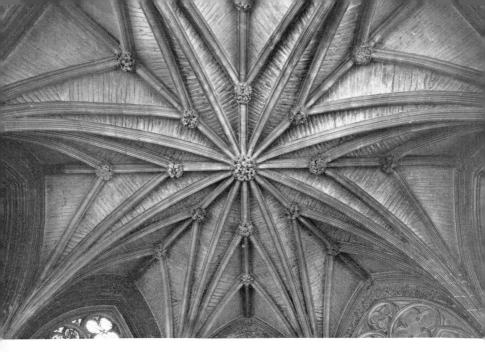

SOUTHWELL (*above*) The roof of the chapter house
(*below*) A detail of the sedilia

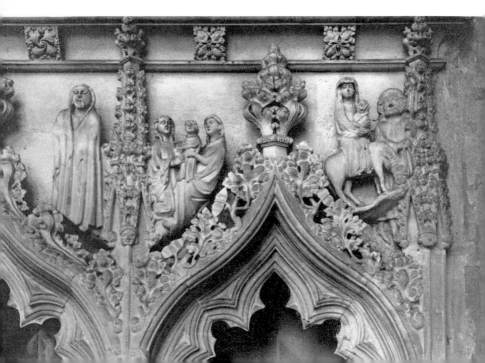

of Belvoir granted the manor of Staunton to an ancestor, on the tenure of Castle Guard which made him responsible for the castle's defence. The high tower at Belvoir is known as Staunton Tower, and when a sovereign visits the castle the golden key of the tower is presented by the head of the family. Now and then the Stauntons give a bell-rope to Bottesford church in memory of the days when its bells gave warning of approaching danger to the castle.

They have shared proudly in the story of our land. William was summoned to the military muster at Nottingham in 1297, Hervey was Chancellor of the Exchequer and Chief Justice in the 14th century. At the time of the Civil War William Staunton was the head of his house, and when Charles raised his standard at Nottingham he attended the king and followed him to battle. Staunton Hall was looted by the Roundheads, and their bullet holes are still in the fine old door.

The beautiful church of St Mary where many of them lie was made partly new last century, but the high tower, the lofty arcades, the aisle windows, and the charming north doorway are all from the close of the 14th century. The oldest relic is the fine Norman bowl of the font, enriched with interlaced arcading, its modern base set on a step which is part of a 15th century gravestone. There is an Elizabethan table, and an old almsbox made from the stump of a tree. The chief treasure of all is a beautiful oak chancel screen, with an inscription asking prayers for the soul of Simon Yates, who erected it in 1519.

The oldest of the monuments are two battered figures, one cross-legged and wearing fine chain mail, the other headless and almost legless: they may be the son and grandson of the founder of the house. An inscription to William de Staunton (of about 1250) is on a tapering stone which must have been an earlier memorial, for the arcading on its thick edge is about 1100.

At Staunton Grange there is a dovecote dating back to the 17th century with 1100 nesting places.

Stokeham is one of the smaller villages, but it has a fine view over 14 miles of pleasant countryside to Lincoln's towers.

The tiny church of St Peter has a Norman tub font.

There are two 13th century lancets, and the 15th century east window has the head of a man on its hood, smiling as if content that his church is so kindly restored. The pretty piscina is 14th century, there are old rafters left in the roof, an oak chest may be 700 years old, and in the churchyard is a stone coffin.

Strelley lies some 5 miles north-west of Nottingham beyond the housing estates of Broxtowe and Bilborough. The way up to the church and hall (marked by a sign "No Through Road") is lined by a wealth of trees. From Norman days to Charles II there was an unbroken line of Strelleys in this place which gave them a name and a home.

Strelley Hall was rebuilt in 1789 by Thomas Webb Edge, an ancestor of the present owner, Miss Edge. He employed Thomas Gardner, of Uttoxeter, as architect and builder of the new house. The original house and property was owned by the Strelley family and later passed into the Edge family. Walter Edge, a member of a junior branch of the Edges of Horton in Staffordshire, settled in Nottingham early in the 17th century and practised as a lawyer; his son Ralph, also a lawyer, was a well-known figure in Nottingham. He was Town Clerk and twice Mayor of Nottingham, and owned Strelley in 1651.

In the peaceful churchyard, where a fine old yew overhangs the road, is Sir Sampson's 14th century church of All Saints. It has remains of the earlier one in the wall of the south aisle, and a tower belonging to all three mediaeval centuries.

The clerestory is about 1500, and of the old glass shields and medallions some are 14th century and some Flemish work of 300 and 400 years ago. The font is 14th century.

A great possession is the almost perfect 15th century chancel screen, with beautiful vaulting. The Jacobean pulpit with a lovely canopy has some older tracery, and two old misericords in the chancel are quaintly carved with a bishop holding up a cross and a crouching grotesque with limbs branching into foliage.

On a beautiful tomb in the middle of the chancel, enriched with

14 angels holding shields, lies Sir Sampson, a knight in armour holding the hand of his lovely lady who wears a richly jewelled headdress; Sir Sampson's head rests on the crest of a strangled Saracen's head. Of the floorstones to others of the family round the tomb two have traces of figures, and one has a fine engraved portrait of a knight. Two are to brothers and their wives: Sir Robert Strelley who fought at Agincourt, and John of 1421. Another stone has fine brass portraits of Sir Robert Strelley of 1487 and his wife Isabel, sister of Cardinal Kemp.

On a traceried tomb with a handsome canopy adorned with figures in niches and angels lie the alabaster figures of John de Strelley of 1501 and his wife Sanchia Willoughby. John is a knight with his head on the family crest, and sitting on the back of the lion at his feet are two weepers.

Sturton-le-Steeple lies in the line of the old Roman road from Lincoln to Doncaster.

The church of St Peter and Paul is dominated by a splendid tower. With a lovely crown of battlements and 12 pinnacles, 9 windows, and a lofty arch, the tower is 600 years old in its lower half, and the upper storeys are 15th century. It is almost the only part of the church which escaped a fire at the beginning of this century; the rest has been reconstructed on the old lines with much of the old material.

The chancel is said to have been the original Norman church, and with the Norman masonry in its north wall is a Norman window now open to the vestry. The north and south doorways are Norman, and so is the bowl of the font, which came from the vanished church of West Burton; it is charmingly set on a flight of steps in the tower. An old piscina is restored, and the chancel screen is part of the beautiful modern woodwork here.

The oldest of the monuments is the stone figure of a woman in a wimple and a long gown, her hands at prayer. Though she has lain here 700 years her features are still clear. She was Lady Olive, and is believed to be one of the Thornhaughs who built the nave at the end of Norman days. They lived at Fenton half a mile away, but only the laundry and a few stone ornaments are left of their old home.

For a time Fenton belonged to a family who bore its name, and it is believed that Edward Fenton, the Elizabethan seaman, was born here. One of the bravest and most skilful of naval heroes, he accompanied Martin Frobisher in the voyage of discovery of the North-West Passage, and was pilot in the Admiral's ship in the fight that led to the defeat of the Armada.

Standing erect under a pillared canopy against the tower wall is the figure of Dame Frances Earle, blackened by fire, with a wrap over her head and draped round her. She was the mother of one of the Thornhaughs, and died about 1699 when 80 years old. Their most interesting memorial is a floorstone with arms inlaid with coloured marbles, marking the resting-place of Sir Francis Thornhaugh, the great Parliamentarian and friend of Colonel Hutchinson, whose wife wrote an account of his brave death at the Battle of Preston.

Sutton Bonington is two villages made into one. It is situated some 10 miles south of Nottingham, and its approach is made past the School of Agriculture. This school came into being in its present form in 1947 with the transfer to the University College of Nottingham of the buildings and land at Sutton Bonington held by the former Midland Agricultural College.

The village rests on a slope of the Soar Valley looking across the river into Leicestershire. The church with tower and lofty spire is that of St Michael. The south arcade is 13th century, the north arcade and much of the aisles are 14th, and the clerestory is 15th. There are stone seats round some of the pillars. The most interesting possession is the 600-year-old font carved with quatrefoils, its unusual feature being three projecting brackets, level with the rim. The oldest relic is part of a 12th century coffin stone in the outside wall near the modern porch.

St Anne's Church at Sutton has no tower, and nestles high on the hillside with an ancient bell swinging in the gable. What is left of the old church (after much restoration last century) is 14th century, the time of the nave arcade, the piscina in the chancel, and the font. In a recess in the chancel lies a knight in 15th century armour, a giant seven feet long with his feet on a lion; he was called Old Lion Grey. His identity is uncertain, though his collar of suns and roses assures us that he was a Yorkist.

The glory of this little church is its lovingly tended garden of roses, lawn, and trees, where we look over the village to the hills of Charnwood Forest.

Sutton-cum-Lound is 3½ miles north of East Retford.

Its church of St Bartholomew stands with limes and sycamores above the village. Its 15th century tower, with eight pinnacles and a lofty arch, has two bells which have been ringing since before the Armada. The stone-roofed porch and the rest of the walls are all embattled, and are adorned with pinnacles and a gallery of sculptured heads. Some are cunningly fashioned at the foot of the pinnacles.

The old doorway through which we enter has the original folding door with its old plate and ring. Over the doorway is a round arch which seems to be Norman. A beautiful 14th century arcade divides the nave from the aisle, and a similar arcade is between the chancel and its chapel. The lofty Norman chancel arch has been rebuilt, three lovely sedilia and a piscina are mediaeval, and a fine founder's recess has a feathered arch with pinnacles and a finial.

Three poppyheads of 23 old bench-ends are carved with an eagle, a happy-looking angel, and the trim head of a lady the villagers call the Queen of Sheba. The handsome bands of vine carving in two old benches in the chancel belonged to the old chancel screen, and remains of a 15th century screen are in the modern screen of the chancel chapel. An old pillar almsbox has three locks, an oak chest is 17th century, and another chest is shaped from a solid block of oak, its small cavity covered by a heavily iron-banded lid which is secured by an iron bar on the front of the chest. At the ends of the hammerbeams of the modern roofs of the nave and chancel are stone heads, most of them crowned.

Sutton-in-Ashfield is situated some 3 miles south-west from Mansfield, and is 12 miles north of Nottingham. Its main industry is coal mining, but a large part of the population is also engaged in the manufacture of hosiery, plastics, and light engineering.

It was Edward the Confessor's village before the Conquest, and Saxon names survive in its roads; but its story is far older than Saxon, for a silver coin of Caius Claudius Pulcher 93 BC was found in a garden in the town.

Four centuries ago this village saw a tragic figure pass through its streets a few days before he was to die. He was the fallen Wolsey, who spent the night at Kirkby Hardwick a mile from here when journeying slowly to Leicester. He may have seen the manor house not far from the church, for its oldest part comes from the early 16th century.

Here came George Whitefield to preach, and here was born, in 1812, that amazing Spencer Timothy Hall, who could plough and reap, stack and thresh and winnow, make a stocking and a shoe, write a book and print and bind it, and cure all sorts of ills. Perhaps the most astonishing Jack of All Trades of his day, he is buried at Blackpool, but he is still known as the Sherwood Forester, and will long be remembered here.

A long avenue of limes leads us from the road to the churchyard, the wrought iron gates of which were added in 1948 as a memorial to those who died in the Second World War. Within this church-yard is an ancient yew said to be 700 years old, with a trunk slender for its years and shorn of half its spreading branches. In its shade are 18th century stones of the Brandreth family, relatives of the Jeremiah Brandreth who was executed as leader of the pitiful Pentrich Rebellion (in which Shelley interested himself) during the general unrest after Waterloo. A stone by the path leading to the porch is in memory of Ann Burton, who, if she did nothing worth recording in her life, achieved something remarkable at the end by dying on the 30th of February in 1836. It is one of several records we have found of days that never were.

The church is of light-coloured local stone, and has some interesting old remains in spite of severe restoration. Built by the Suttons in the 12th century, it was given by them to Thurgarton Priory, and John de Sutton in the 14th century left money to build the tower and spire. An ancient floorstone in the chancel, engraved with a great bow and arrow, is said to have had an inscription to one of the Suttons. Another interesting relic of the family was found when the sexton was digging a grave in 1870. It was a tiny 14th century metal seal with a ring for hanging it round the neck, carved on one side with a fleur-de-lys and on the other with a monk and an acolyte sitting with open books. Above the monk was a squirrel cracking nuts.

The nave arcades come from the close of Norman days, and the chancel arch is half a century later. A lovely 13th century fragment is at the east of the north arcade, its three shafts crowned by a capital with three heads. The round bowl of a Norman font has been rescued from the vicarage garden. The top of a small shaft piscina, with scroll ornament, is a century older than Magna Carta.

Sutton-on-Trent lies 7 miles north of Newark on the A1. At one end of the village the lovely old church of All Saints adds beauty to the road; at the other stands a derelict windmill. A turn of the road near the church leads by a wayside stream to pretty gardens, one delightful with a rockery, old-world pump, and well.

The church came into Domesday Book, and its 13th century tower with a 15th century top still stands on its Saxon foundations, though it lost a spire a century ago. Deep battlements, with gargoyles below them, enhance the beauty of a remarkably fine 15th century clerestory, and faces adorn the windows all round the church.

A handsome addition is the early 16th century Mering Chapel, which may have been brought here from Mering across the river. Pinnacles enrich its buttresses and rise from its parapet, which is carved with flowers, shields, faces, and gargoyles; one gargoyle shows two lizard-like creatures coiling round a head. A beautiful roof looks down on the rich work inside, where great windows with fragments of rich old glass fill it with light. The walls are enriched with arcading, shields, and brackets, and the lovely piscina is one of three in the church. Two arches between the chapel and the chancel rest on a beautifully carved pillar, and under one of them is a great tomb, perhaps of Sir William Mering. Dividing the chapel from the aisle is a rare oak screen of about 1510, with delicate carving of tracery, bands of quatrefoils, and trailing flowers. Its loft, seven feet wide and almost like a gallery, overhangs both sides. It is a pity so fine a screen has been spoiled for the sake of the organ.

The sides of the chancel arch are late 12th century, but the arch and the nave arcades are a hundred years later. The bowl of the font may be 17th century on a mediaeval stem: its pyramid cover and the altar are Jacobean. Among the poppyheads of 15 old stall-ends are birds, bearded faces, a grinning face, and two women smiling at each other.

Lovely for its 14th century stonework and for its modern glass is the east window of the north aisle, shining with figures of St George, St Gabriel, the Madonna, and St Ursula. Except for some old fragments, it is the only coloured glass in the church.

Syerston lies close to the Fosse Way, but its few farms and cottages are untroubled by the stir of heavy traffic.

The church of All Saints is surprisingly pleasing inside, with walls aslant, traceried windows, and timbered roof. Except for its battlements the tiny tower is 13th century, and one of its two bells is older than the Reformation. The buttresses on each side of the church are as old as the tower, the entrance to the porch and the doorway into the church are 14th century. The chancel, made partly new, has its old piscina, a wooden arch on richly carved stone corbels, and a neat modern screen. The glass of the east window, glowing in rich colour with a scene of the Crucifixion, is to George Henry Fillingham, in whose memory the church was restored in 1896.

The treasure of the church is an exquisite little oak pulpit of 1636, its eight sides, backboard, and canopy all a mass of carved panels. The font, on a traceried shaft, is 600 years old.

The hall dates from 1795 and there is also a dovecote dating from 1801.

Thoresby House

West Stockwith Church

The monument of the forester with the horn in Skegby Church

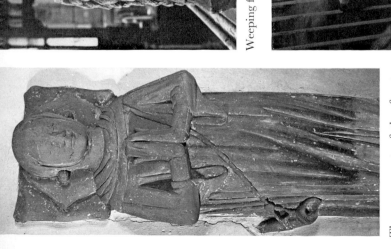

Weeping figures at the foot of the monument to John de Strelley in Strelley Church

Effigy of a knight in

The A46 divides the village from R.A.F. Syerston, which was opened in 1940. It is now a training station, and in 1964 was given the freedom of Newark.

Teversal crowns a green hilltop looking out to Hardwick Hall. It is a charming oasis, with the old church, the rectory, and the manor house old and new, its harmony of gables and mullioned windows as background to fine lawn and flowers.

The interior of St Catherine's Church is heavy with the aura of history. The organ nestles in the corner of a minstrels' gallery which looks down on dark brown, almost black, oak-boxed Jacobean pews. On the right of the church there is a pew once used by the lords and squires of Teversal Manor, and behind this are the tombs of the Molyneux family who once owned the manor and held the living of the church. Round the walls of the church are the hatchments of the Molyneux and several other families.

Two of the tower walls project into the western bays of the nave arcades. The south arcade is Norman, leading to an aisle which was widened in the 15th century. The 13th century north arcade, with two great corbel heads like masks, and capitals enriched with nail-head, opens to a narrow aisle with 14th century windows. A bracket in this aisle and the chancel arch are 13th century.

The Normans made the plain font. Fragments of ancient carved stones are in the outside walls and in the floor of the porch. In the south aisle wall is a tiny coffin stone with a cross, and above its east window is a stone with 1684, the initials I.M., and the cross of the arms of Molyneux which we see on the gate of the manor house. The nave roof has 15th century timbers and bosses, and quaint wooden figures at the ends of the beams. The altar table is Jacobean, and the chest is decrepit with its very long life.

A list of rectors since 1280 hangs inside the church. The first was Thomas Barry, who was appointed by Henry Pierrepont. The Molyneux family became responsible for the living in 1609, and retained it until 1828, when it passed, as did the manor, to the Earl of Carnarvon's family. In 1935 the living passed to Cambridge University.

P

In a crypt below the church lie the remains of members of the Molyneux family.

Thoresby Park, formed in 1683 by the Duke of Kingston, is the most richly wooded of the ducal estates. Bounding it on the south is Bilhagh (entered by the quaint gates crowned by two stone deer), with its ancient oaks from mediaeval days, and the glorious Ollerton beeches, which form a forest cathedral unsurpassed. It may be doubted if there is in England a more impressive natural nave than this. On the west of Bilhagh are the Birklands, renowned for their slender silver birches.

The splendid house stands near the lake of about 65 acres, and a road running east through the park from Budby passes nearby. It was built about 1870, near the site of a brick mansion which followed an older house burned down in 1745. It was in the older house that Lady Mary Montagu passed her girlhood years with her father.

The chief rooms of the house we see have decorated ceilings and floors and panelling of oak, walnut, or maple. There are fine carved mantelpieces in white marble, and the library chimneypiece shows a scene in Sherwood Forest. It is the home of Countess Manvers.

Thorney. In this quiet little place, delightful with orchards and glorious trees, the traveller will find a few ruins of an ancient church, and a modern successor of a remarkable kind. The old remains are two arches and pillars of a mediaeval arcade, a 15th century window and the top of another, and fragments of carved stones, set up in the churchyard which is screened from the hall by mighty elms and limes and beeches.

The church of St Helen was built in Norman style in the middle of last century, and is an unusual sight with its mass of carving inside and out, its huge blocks of stone needing the mellowing touch of time. We may imagine that the builders sought to make it a pictorial encyclopedia of church ornamentation in Norman England.

The arresting west front of the church faces the road, and is full of detail. The doorway has pillars all differently carved, a round arch with every manner of moulding and figure in cable, ropework, dragons, heads of humans and animals; and a hood with zigzag lines and wheels ending in crowned heads. Above the doorway are three lancets with pillars at their sides, and over them is a wheel window. A stringcourse with rings and chip carving ends at each side in a great projecting dragon's head with a curled tongue. There are 17 of these dragons round the church.

Crowning this remarkable west wall is a bell turret with two bells swinging in a round-headed arch with more carving, and below the turret are six grotesque corbel heads, part of a gallery of over a hundred which encircle the building and adorn the elaborate little turret between the nave and chancel.

Lofty hammerbeam roofs with carved beams and stone corbels of winged angels and heads of human folk look down on the spacious interior of the nave and chancel, dimly lit by narrow windows. The rich carving continues in the chancel arch, on the sedilia and piscina, and on the priest's doorway. The stone lectern and the pulpit, entered by a flight of steps from the chancel, are a study in themselves, the pulpit showing Bible scenes, the heads of the Twelve Disciples in tiny medallions, and the symbols of the Four Evangelists. The fine modern font is elaborate with arcading and a band of scroll work; and, as if not to be outdone by the new, the battered Norman tub font is here with its intricate arcading and lattice, fragments of knotwork mixed with foliage and quaint figures, and a plaited band round the rim of the bowl.

Over a mile away is Wigsley, with a small Methodist chapel.

Thoroton is known as the village which gave its name to the ancestors of Robert Thoroton, the county's historian. Everybody loves it for its rustic charm of green-bordered road, its round 14th century dovecote, wide views of serene countryside, and the old church in company with a white house and red-roofed barns.

The church of St Helen has an exquisite tower, and its graceful spire (with three tiers of dormer windows) have been a landmark for nearly 600 years. A stair turret projects from the tower; buttresses climb to the lovely parapet of open quatrefoils on a corbel table of great heads, with gargoyles at the corners; a niche on the west side, over 12 feet high, has sculptured figures at the sides of its elaborate canopy. The chancel is made new and the porch is modern, but the nave has a Norman arcade and a 14th century one. The plain round font is Norman. Older still is a charming little Saxon window which allows the dawn to steal into the vestry like a finger of light. Deeply splayed inside and out, it is less than two feet long and four or five inches wide. Built into the outside wall it is one of the stones of the vanished Norman chancel arch.

Thorpe is a secluded little village down a winding narrow road off the Fosse Way (A46) near to Newark.

Standing beyond the rectory lawn at a bend of the road is the church of St Lawrence. It was rebuilt in 1873 except for the low 13th century buttressed tower with a pyramid top. The font is a curious combination of an old step, a 14th century shaft, and a small bowl which may have been a Norman stoup; its domed cover is 17th century. Three other relics are a pillar piscina, a piscina niche, and Jacobean coffin stool. Nearly six centuries ago Sir William de Thorpe was fighting at Crecy, and was one of the company who saw Calais surrendered to their king; here in the church lies the battered stone figure of his widow, wearing a wimple, her feet resting on a dog, her arms broken.

One of the treasures of the altar is a silver cup given by Henry Druell as a thankoffering for his safe return from London in 1665, when the plague was raging.

Thrumpton occupies a position some seven miles south of Nottingham and is close to the Leicestershire border. Its fame is mainly in its Hall which is surrounded by 200 acres of parkland.

Without a doubt its most famous association has been with Byron, even though the poet himself was not linked with Thrumpton.

For some 600 years it was owned by a family named Putrell (later corrupted to Powdrill), who remained at Thrumpton Hall until they were attained for their part in the gunpowder plot in 1605. It was the Powdrills who concealed Father Garnett, one of the conspirators, in what is referred to as the priest's hole, which lies at the foot of a secret staircase built in the thickness of a chimney breast.

Later, when the Pigots gained possession of Thrumpton in 1607, they virtually rebuilt the house, but they incorporated much of the Powdrill house in the new building. Pigot married a woman of the St Andrew family, and used most of her wealth to improve the interior of Thrumpton Hall. Outstanding examples are the grand staircase and the panelling and carving of the salon. When Pigot died, his widow, who had been rich when she came to Thrumpton, was now so poor that she had to place the hall in pawn. And so it passed to a John Emerton of the Middle Temple. The Emertons and their successors, the Wescombes, have established two singular records; the first is for long life, and the other is that with but a single exception, they have been bachelors or childless. Emerton was followed by his nephew, and he by his son. This was John Wescombe, who died at the age of 87. Thrumpton passed to his nephew who did much to restore the house. He never married, and the three daughters of his brother, William, a clergyman, inherited his property. Lucy, who was 21 in 1844, married the 8th Lord Byron, and after his death married a Vicar of Thrumpton, the Rev. Philip Douglas. Her sister, Mary Jane, married another Byron, and her son took Thrumpton over when his aunt died in 1912 at the age of 88. For twenty-eight years Lord Byron was Vicar of Thrumpton, and when he died in 1949 at the age of 88 he was succeeded by the present owner, Mr George Fitzroy Seymour.

The gardens which surround Thrumpton Hall are divided by a ha-ha of the same mellow brick as the house. Before alterations carried out by Mr Emerton Wescombe early in the 19th century the approach to the house was through the fine stone-pillared gates at the top of the Broad Walk, and by means of a drive which led from them across the present lawn into a forecourt, which is now laid out as a formal garden. To the north of the house and separated from it by a stone balustrade and grass bank is a sheet of ornamental water.

One of the first larch trees to be planted in England grows in this garden and it has been the custom to plant cedar trees to commemorate historic occasions. The earliest was to mark the jubilee of King George III, and the latest to commemorate the coronation of Queen Elizabeth II. There is also an oak tree grown from an acorn of the Byron Oak at Newstead.

A little way from the Hall is the church of All Saints, which dates back to the mid-13th century. The church was restored in 1872 at the expense of Lady Byron, when the chancel was entirely rebuilt and its mural monuments transferred to the dim light of the base of the Early English tower. The nave windows are square-headed of the late 14th century Notts type, and to that decorative period most of the existing old masonry is assigned. The windows in general are filled with modern stained glass, largely presented by Dr Massey of Nottingham in memory of his father and sister, but Lady Byron has presented others, among them an ornamental screen of wrought iron. There is also a monument to Gervase Pigot.

Thurgarton nestles at the foot of low hills two miles from the Trent, and through it runs a stream spanned by many little bridges.

The way to the church is up a steep winding lane past pretty cottages. The church is dedicated to St Peter, and the lovely 13th century fragments of the old priory church were restored last century when the chancel and north aisle were built. For over 700 years its one remaining tower has stood at the north-west corner, crowned with 15th century battlements. A rare gem is the deep west doorway of the nave. It is one of the loveliest 13th century doorways in all England.

In the Domesday Book Thurgarton appeared as the fee of Walter d'Eyncourt, who was connected by marriage with William the Conqueror, it being one of his 34 manors in Nottinghamshire. Walter's heir, Ralph (his second son), was the founder of Thurgarton Priory. Like all the Augustinian houses in Notts, except Worksop, Thurgarton lost its prior during the Black Death of 1349. Twice it supplied priors to Newstead, William de Thurgarton in 1324 and Robert Cutwolf in 1424, but in spite of the wealth acquired as gifts accumulated Thurgarton did not become as important or as well-known as its sister house. It was not a royal foundation like Newstead, and it did not stand near a main road, and probably had fewer visitors except those bound for Southwell on ecclesiastical business.

Thurgarton Manor House, built in 1777, now occupies the site of the Priory buildings. It is now the headquarters of Boots Veterinary Research Department. Archeological finds in the area include the foundations of a sixteenth century house in 1947, remains of a Roman villa and also a stone coffin in 1951. In 1953 a second coffin and remains of an earlier building were found. One of these coffins is outside the entrance to the church, while the other can be seen close to the pulpit in the church.

Tollerton is some 4½ miles south-east of Nottingham, and its airport close by was opened by Sir Sefton Brancker on June 19, 1930. Nottingham Airport is leased to Truman Aviation Limited by the City Council, and it is from here that the city businessman can hire a plane to fulfil an engagement on the continent and travel in comfort. The weekend flier is also catered for by the Sherwood Flying Club, who operate from this airfield.

The village's two important buildings are the church, dedicated to St Peter, and the manor house, now St Hugh's College. The church, rebuilt, dates from 1812, but there are traces of 13th century work, namely the nave arcades and the blocked east window of the north aisle. St Hugh's College, once known as Roclaveston Manor, was for many years a Congregational College. On October 6, 1948 it was opened by Cardinal Griffin as St Hugh's Junior Seminary for the Catholic diocese of Nottingham.

Treswell is 5 miles south-east of Retford, and Lincoln Cathedral which is 15 miles away, can be seen from here on a clear day.

Its simple little church of St John the Baptist, with warm buff tints in the grey stone walls, is in a churchyard with fine trees (horse-chestnuts, limes, and firs) bounded on one side by the little Lee Beck, and on another by the rector's garden.

The lofty tower is 15th century. From the 14th come the doorway within the pretty rebuilt porch and the fine little chancel with beautiful tracery in its big windows. Built into an outside wall is about two-thirds of a fine Norman coffin stone, with stem and cross-head carved in relief. The north arcade is 15th century, its end arches, like the tower arch, resting on embattled corbels. The massive font is 500 years old and is carved with flowers in quatrefoils. The villagers take communion from a silver chalice of Elizabeth's day.

Trowell lies between Ilkeston and Nottingham just inside the Notts border. Collieries and ironworks are in its near view, but from the crown of the hill and the top of the church tower is a fine panorama of the Erewash Valley, and richly wooded hills with Charnwood Forest on the horizon. In the 15th century tower are the works of the old clock which used to tell the time in the biggest open market place in England, the great space in front of the Council House at Nottingham.

In the church of St Helen the clerestory is as old as the tower, and the nave arcades are 14th century. From the close of that century come the buttresses, the stone-roofed porch, the square-headed windows, and the beautiful font with quatrefoils and an embattled edge. The 13th century chancel has its old sedilia and piscina, a narrow arch reaching nearly to the roof, and a modern east window with angels looking down on Mary, Our Lord enthroned, and St Helena by a great cross. It is one of only two coloured windows, both showing fine figures in jewelled raiment; the Crucifixion is in memory of a rector's son who did not come back.

A wall monument to William Hacker (who has been sleeping here since 1668) recalls a family famous in the county; his cousin led Charles I to the scaffold. In the farmhouse facing the church is part of the old home of the Hackers of Trowell, and it was here that the last of this line, Sir John, broke his neck by falling downstairs in 1735. He lies in the church.

In 1951 Trowell became Britain's Festival Village. It was chosen from among 1,600 villages to appear in the Festival of Britain souvenir programme as a representative English rural community, because of the "ambition and courage" of its Festival scheme, and the fact that it lies within a few miles of the exact centre of England. Another reason was its unusual name.

Tuxford is a small market town some 6¾ miles south of East Retford. On July 8, 1218 King Henry III signed a Charter which allowed John de Lexinton and his heirs in perpetuity to hold in Tuxford a weekly market on Mondays and a fair annually on the Eve and Day of the Finding of the Holy Cross (May 2 and 3). Tuxford celebrated its 750 years of the granting of this Charter with a week of special events which began on May 5, and ended on May 12, 1968.

The oldest school, the Reed Grammar School, opened in 1669 and closed in 1916, and is now a public library. On the wall outside is a plaque to commemorate the Charter.

On the opposite side of the road stands the church of St Nicholas, which looks even older than its years, for the soft Tuxford sandstone is badly weathered. A few feet of herringbone masonry in the west wall of the south aisle takes its story back perhaps to Saxon days, but the church is chiefly mediaeval. The tower and spire are 14th century except for an older window and doorway, and the spire, which has four dormers halfway up, has the singular appearance of being broached though it rises within a parapet. It is an interesting example of the passing of the broach with the coming of the parapet.

The 15th century south porch and a doorway a century older bring us to a nave crowned by a fine clerestory, its windows only a little shorter than the similar ones in the aisles: it was built in 1475 by Sir John Stanhope, whose arms are on the battlement. The nave arcades are 14th century, except for the 13th century pillars on the north side and the half-pillars on the south. The chancel was made new in the closing years of the 15th century, but its arch, part of its north arcade, and its piscina, are 700 years old. There is fine 15th century tracery in the modern chancel screen; the nave roof has some timbering and bosses of that time; and on the ends of the roof beams are ten painted angels resting on stone heads. The 17th century font has a fine pyramid cover and a suspended canopy, both richly carved, the canopy having the inscription "Francis Turner made this 1673".

The east end of the south aisle was the chantry of St Lawrence, and in its east window we see him in old black and yellow glass, holding his grid. On the wall below is a quaint stone sculpture of about 1400, showing the saint lying on the grid under a rich canopy, and figures of three men rather battered, one with the bellows having lost his head. The old piscina is still here, and resting on a bracket carved with a bearded face is part of a draped figure. Built into the wall of the modern north porch is a gravestone showing the head and shoulders of a priest recessed in a quatrefoil, a chalice below his praying hands.

The north chancel chapel was widened in the 18th century to be a burial-place for the Whites, lords of Tuxford for many generations. The alabaster figures of Sir John White of 1625 and his wife lie on a tomb, their heads resting on tasselled cushions, both without hands or feet but wearing beautiful ruffs. Sir John, with a pointed beard, is in armour; his lady's mantle and gown have exquisite borders, and she has a fine chain round her shoulders. Charles Lawrence White, mortally wounded in 1814 at Bayonne, has a white wall monument with a carving of his grave and those of three brother officers.

One of two ancient figures in the chapel is a cross-legged knight with a broken sword, his feet on a battered beast; the other is a slender woman in alabaster, wearing a long gown adorned with roses, her feet on two small dogs; one is biting the other's ears and the other his companion's paw. The modern pulpit is richly carved with a border of vines, and figures of St Agnes, St Anne, and Our Lord on the Cross.

Tythby or **Tithby** is a pleasant neighbour of Bingham with neat houses huddled close about the parish church of Holy Trinity.

Its queer tower is fairly modern except for the buttresses, and it wears a pyramid cap. From the 14th century come the nave arcades, the priest's doorway, the lovely ironwork on an old chest, and the font (on which the date 1662 tells of its restoration after being cast out by the Puritans). There are two old roofs, an old piscina, and an old poppyhead seat. Among the odd things here are a row of hat pegs on the chancel wall, an eight-sided pillar boarded round, a brick pillar climbing through the gallery from the floor to support a tiebeam, and a strange assortment of chairs and pews.

There is a 15th century inscription to Thomas Chaworth, one of the family who were lords of Tithby for many generations and built the first Wiverton Hall close by. In the churchyard is a cross to Lina Chaworth-Musters, who died at the hall in 1912.

Under a tomb in the churchyard lie Tithby's Darby and Joan. They were John Marriot and his wife Mary, who both lived to be 94, John dying in 1866 and Mary following him the year after.

He first deceased her, she a little tried
To live without him, liked it not, and died.

The small altar to the right as one enters the church is in memory of Mary Agnes Craig and dated January, 1960.

Underwood, 2 miles south-east of Codnor, occupies a lofty position commanding extensive, but not beautiful, views of Derbyshire.

The church of St Michael and All Angels was built in 1888–89 in the Gothic style, consisting of a chancel, nave of four bays, aisles and south porch, and massive tower.

Upton lies a short distance from Southwell and is approached by a steep hill. At the corner of a lane stands an attractive thatched post office, and it is down this lane that we get a glimpse of the church of St Peter. From the churchyard there are fine views, and Lincoln Cathedral can be seen on a clear day. Elms and great chestnuts surround this splendid 15th century tower. Buttressed to the top, it is crowned with eight pinnacles clustered round a central one, known as the Nine Disciples. Up in the tower is a priest's room with a fireplace, and holes in the walls where doves nested in olden days. It is one of the very few tower dovecotes still left in our churches.

Mediaeval windows fill the church with light. The nave arcade with clustered pillars, the rebuilt chancel arch, and the small arch between the aisle and the shallow transept, are all 13th century. The transept has a tiny peephole, and has been restored in memory of ten men who died for peace. The 14th century font has been brought back from the churchyard. By the pulpit are fragments of two earthen jars which were used in olden times as amplifiers of sound, the first loudspeakers. The greatest possession here is a lovely chest over six feet long, adorned with iron bands and stars with tiny roses and trefoils; it may be 13th century.

Here was born one of a great host of 19th century men who made their way from small beginnings and built up our knowledge of the world. He was James Tennant, who began work at a shop dealing in minerals and shells, and grew up to be Professor of Mineralogy at King's College. He was one of a family of 12, his father an officer of the excise; his mother belonged to a yeoman family living in Upton for two centuries. Young Tennant was able to hear Michael Faraday's lectures at the Royal Institution, and Faraday became his friend. He was one of the first experts to confirm the genuineness of the first diamonds found in South Africa, and he was in charge of the cutting of the Koh-i-nor for Queen Victoria's crown.

Walesby lies 4 miles west of Tuxford and close to Ollerton. It is proud of its fine little church of St Edmund with its 15th century tower, and of the glorious trees in the churchyard; two splendid beeches bring us to the door (though one is now only half of its old self), two others are in a majestic row of limes, and there are ancient yews.

Its oldest possessions are a plain Norman doorway and the fine Norman bowl of the font; over the doorway is a modern porch with fragments of 13th century arcading in its walls, used now as a vestry. The north doorway, with part of an ancient coffin stone for a step, opens to an interior filled with light by charming mediaeval windows. The nave arcade comes from the close of the 13th century, its short arches on tall pillars.

The restored piscina in the 14th century chancel has a strange old head supporting the projecting drain, the face all awry, and resting on the hands of two arms coming from the wall. Over the piscina a small crowned head is wearing away, and on an old bracket in the aisle lies a stone corbel carved with a face. The 17th century pulpit has panels carved with thistles and leaves, and eight oak benches 400 years old have set the pattern for the new ones.

In 1938 through the generosity of Col N. G. Pearson and a grant from the National Fitness Council, the Nottingham Scout Association were given 160 acres of heath and woodland at Walesby as a permanent camping site.

Walkeringham is 4 miles north-west of Gainsborough and a mile from the Trent.

The church of St Mary Magdalene has nothing older than its thirteenth century nave arcades, the pillars resting on fine square bases made eight-sided at the top. From the 15th century come the tower, the clerestory, and most of the windows, and two arches in the north wall of the chancel. These arches rest on a 13th century pillar, and on their hood are three quaint little heads. An old face peeps unexpectedly from the wall of the north aisle.

Much old timber remains in the roofs; there are three old benches, a Jacobean table, and an elm chest with its original ironwork (over 400 years old) and a new lid. The altar rails are very beautiful with trailing vine and grapes and ears of wheat hanging from the rail, and four splendid poppyheads carved with foliage and partridges among growing corn. We found the vicar and the sexton working here like two mediaeval craftsmen, adapting the 400-year-old screen to let more light into the chancel; using the upper part to enclose the vestry (where there is other old screenwork), and embodying the 17th century pulpit with the base.

On an elaborate monument kneel Francis Williamson and his wife, he in rich attire, and she in a full-skirted gown and flowing headdress of Stuart days. Three sons kneel below, and a rhyming epitaph bids us use this monument as a mirror in which to see ourselves:

Then thoughts and cares for long life save,
And be undressing for the grave.

Wallingwells. Its great days are gone, and with them the glory of the big house and the beauty of the fine park. A modern house turned into flats, it has stones in some of its walls which come from Norman days, for in it were built materials from Ralph de Cheurol-court's nunnery of the reign of Stephen.

Buried near the house are several stone coffins and in one opened about 100 years ago was found the body of Dame Margery Dourant, the second prioress. Her body was in perfect condition, and with her were a pair of shoes and a silver chalice.

Warsop is divided into two parts, Market Warsop and Church Warsop, with the River Meden dividing them. This mining town on the border of the Dukeries was mostly open forest as late as the 18th century. It is situated five miles from Mansfield on the Mansfield to Worksop road.

Looking down to its busy neighbour, Church Warsop is delightful with the old church of St Peter and St Paul standing high above the road.

Old yews grow about the church, which came into Domesday Book and still has much old work to show. Except for its 14th century top storey, the tower is chiefly Norman, with an original buttress, a small Norman window with a Maltese cross cut on one side, and a fine Norman arch with cable moulding on the capitals. The priest's doorway, and a blocked doorway in the north aisle, are also Norman. From the 15th century come the lofty entrance to the porch and the north arcade of the nave. The doorway letting us in, the south arcade with stone seats round two clustered pillars, and the lovely sedilia and piscina, are from the end of the 13th century. The chancel arch of this time was raised three feet in the 15th century by placing short shafts on the old capitals; and the clerestory comes from the end of the same century.

The east window glows richly with the Crucifixion and the Ascension, in memory of Sir Richard Fitzherbert of 1906, rector and lord of the manor. Some 15th century beams are left in the roofs of the nave and chancel. The chancel roof is enriched with six gilded angels, and bosses with flowers, an angel with a shield, and a lion;

two bosses in the nave have a woman's head and a grotesque with hands in its mouth.

An effective addition of over 400 years ago is the vestry on the south side of the chancel, but its outer entrance and its pinnacles are modern work. It has two quaint gargoyles, and three small windows with old glass made up from fragments found in the chest, among the oldest fragments being a 13th century head of a woman saint. A 14th century head with a beard and a curious brimmed hat reminds us of the merchant in the Canterbury Tales who wore a "Flandrith bever hat".

Other memorials include those to the Wyld family, who built the Manor House here. The oak reredos is modern, and has rich tracery and canopied figures of Peter and Paul.

For more than 20 years the church rested in a cradle of wood and steel against the possibility of subsidence through mining in the vicinity. This cradle has now been removed, and the church restored to its former beauty.

Watnall is really two hamlets, Watnall Chaworth and Watnall Cantilupe, and is situated near to Greasley. Watnall Hall, once the home of the Rollestons, was demolished in 1962, and as the village is without a church there is little left to attract the historian. A meteorological office has been in operation here since 1941, and serves a wide area including that of Nottingham.

Wellow lies in a charming setting under Wellow Park. At one of its lovely spots a wooded lane comes from Rufford to Wellow Dam, a placid pool in a wayside common; another delightful lane has splendid views of Sherwood Forest as it climbs to the edge of the park, bringing us to a field with the moated site of a fortified house that belonged to a lord of the manor in the 13th century.

On the village green stands a maypole, which was put up in April, 1966 to replace the old one which was blown down in a gale. The pole is 66 feet high.

The much-restored little church has a sturdy 14th century tower with a corbel table under 15th century battlements and pinnacles.

The nave arcade is about 1300, and one of its corbels is like the head of a monkey. Several windows are mediaeval, and a lancet comes from the close of the 12th century. Under the tower is a font bowl at which Norman children were baptised, now used no more. The modern stone pulpit has a figure of St Swithin, and it is to this Saint that the church is dedicated. The clock face on the tower of the church was made and erected by local craftsmen to commemorate the Coronation of Queen Elizabeth II in 1953.

The original ducking stool is still at Wellow Dam, and near the Methodist chapel there is another stone, all that remains of the village stocks.

West Bridgford is situated on the south bank of the River Trent. The earliest known reference to it is contained in the Anglo-Saxon Chronicle which records that in 924 Edward the Elder, who had recently conquered the Danes and was erecting forts throughout his kingdom, ordered a bridge to be built across the Trent, and a burgh (defensible place) to be constructed on the south side of the river.

The parish church of St Giles was largely rebuilt at the end of the 19th century, but incorporates part of the ancient church. The 15th century tower (with earlier masonry in its base) still stands at the west end of the old nave, and into the old porch have been built two 14th century windows from a vanished wall. Here still is the 14th century arcade, and in the old chancel (now a chapel) are lovely canopied sedilia with quaint tracery. The old aisle has its double piscina and the 13th century lancet; the font is 600 years old.

Within a 14th century recess belonging to the old chancel and now in the new, lies the sadly battered figure of a mail-clad knight with crossed legs. Known as the Stone Man of West Bridgford, he has found a peaceful resting-place after a strange adventure, for until 1893 he had been standing a long time on duty as a boundary stone in a field near the spot where Melton Road and Loughborough Road meet. We cannot be sure who he is, but he is over 600 years old, and may be Sir Robert Luteril, a lord of the manor.

Welbeck Abbey

Wollaton Hall

The gatehouse of Worksop Priory

Worksop Priory from the south

Outside in the churchyard is an interesting selection of engraved slate headstones.

Just inside West Bridgford after crossing Trent Bridge there are two sports grounds. The first is the home of Notts County Cricket Club, and the scene of many Test Matches, while a short distance away is Nottingham Forest Football Club Ground.

About 150 years ago West Bridgford was a village with about 235 people. Today it is an urban district with a population of 28,000.

West Drayton is a cluster of farms and cottages and a tiny church off the A1 road. A footbridge from the churchyard and a field path towards the hamlet of Rockley brings us to a delightful spot where the River Maun goes racing by the white walls of the old mill house, now a charming dwelling.

We enter the simple church of St Paul by the Norman doorway, the shafts on each side supporting an arch carved with zigzag under a scalloped hood. Near it is an old stoup. A Norman coffin stone, carved with a cross and a sword, lies outside below the west window; the fragment of another of the same time is built into the wall inside. The only old windows are the east and west, both 15th century, with pleasing modern glass.

West Leake is a small village on a little hill with a stream winding from the Wolds to the Soar.

The church of St Helen is approached through a lychgate, which opens into a churchyard with many fine trees. Among the monuments of the church is that of a lady of the 13th century, who is to be seen in a canopied recess in the chancel, while that of a man of a century later is in a recess of the transept. Another mediaeval civilian, wearing a belted gown, lies in a richly canopied recess in the aisle. There is nothing older here than the small Norman doorway, now built-up, and some 12th and 13th century coffin stones. The chancel and the long nave arcade are 14th century, though the aisle itself is made new. Two stout oak benches are at least 400 years old.

Weston is mentioned in the Domesday Book where it is spelt Westone. The name is thought to come from West Tun meaning West Farm.

The church of All Saints is approached by an avenue of fine old yew trees. In the churchyard is part of the shaft of an old cross with a sundial on top.

Two stages of the tower are 13th century, the top storey and the spire coming from the 14th. A scowling face is among the corbels on the 14th century nave arcades; another (round which the pulpit is fitted) shows a face baring its teeth, as if at the parson. At the base of a corbel supporting the 600-year-old chancel arch is a queer little figure which seems to have the body of a snake with the bearded face of a man.

Except for old fragments, the only coloured glass in the mediaeval windows is of dainty formal pattern in the east. The chancel has its old sedilia, and the south aisle a piscina. A worn stoup is near the door, and a fine chest is 500 years old. We measured a stout old ladder to the belfry at 67 inches round.

There is fine old carving of tracery and elaborate arcading in the modern chancel seats and the screening of the vestry. Thirteen bench-ends of the 15th century have tracery and roses in quatrefoils; there is a Jacobean altar table, the nave roof is 1768, and fine floral bosses adorn that of the chancel. The tub font was here when Gilbert de Archis gave the church to the monks of Blyth in the 12th century.

A moated manor house once stood at the northern end of the village, but all traces of it have now gone.

West Stockwith is like a quayside where the Chesterfield Canal comes into the Trent, which is a tidal river here and is joined by the Idle. Its neighbouring village, East Stockwith, which is in Lincolnshire, can be seen across the water. The approach from Misterton is over a steep and narrow hump-backed bridge.

Its church of St Mary was built in 1722 by the executors of William Huntingdon. It has a marble monument with his lifesize figure in a half-reclining attitude, showing him holding a drawing of a sailing ship. The inscription describes him as a ship's carpenter, and tells of the charities he left to this village where he worked.

Whatton-in-the-Vale is a quiet little village just off the main road near to Bingham.

The church is dedicated to St John of Beverley. Restorations carried out in 1870 included the rebuilding of the chancel and of the central tower with its sturdy spire. A transept was destroyed, and the Norman arch once on the south side of the tower is now on the north, hidden by the organ but seen outside. From about 1300 come the north porch, the inner doorway, and the nave arcades. The double piscina is mediaeval, and the font is 17th century.

The stained glass window at the east end of the south aisle (showing Saints Peter, John, and Our Lord) is by Burne-Jones, executed by Morris and Company and the other windows contain glass by leading, if somewhat less well-known, 19th century glass painters.

Part of the church was once used as a school, and the splendid monument of Sir Hugh de Newmarch of about 1400, defaced with innumerable names and initials, bear sample evidence of that time. He lies on a tomb with 20 shields, an alabaster knight in chain mail and SS collar, one leg missing and one half of the other foot left to rest on a lion. His worn belt must once have been fine, for one of the medallions has carving as fresh as the day it was done, and has on it a kind of butterfly with wings spread out like fans, and a quaint and vivid face. It is a little gem worth finding.

In a restored recess of the north aisle lies the stone figure of Robert de Whatton, who was vicar here from 1304; his hands are at prayer, and he wears the simple dress of a canon of Welbeck Abbey. Sir Richard de Whatton of 1322, with his legs crossed and wearing chain mail, lies on a splendid stone tomb with shields.

Very fine is an alabaster floorstone with the engraved portrait of a man with flowing hair, wearing a long gown with a purse. It is the most stirring of all Whatton's possessions, for it is the portrait of Thomas Cranmer of 1501, who doubtless brought his famous son to worship in this church before he grew up to be Archbishop of Canterbury and to die for his faith. Born at Aslockton close by, the

Archbishop is said to have loved to listen to Whatton's tuneful bells.

Other old relics are a richly carved founder's recess with ball-flowers, battered now and without a tenant; and the head of the old village cross which was found last century in a cottage wall at Aslockton. It is elaborately carved with figures of Peter and Paul, St James with two others, and Our Lord with Mary and John.

Widmerpool is in the heart of the Wolds and amid some of the loveliest woodland scenery in the county. The church of St Peter and St Paul is hidden from the village by numerous trees, and the approach to it is down a lane passing over a small bridge where the lane divides, one route going to the Hall and the other to the church. The latter dates from the late 1880's while the tower is 14th century. Although the interior is lit by electricity, there are attached to each pillar wonderfully worked wrought iron lamp holders with oil lamps. The lectern too has some lovely wrought iron work, while the candelabra of the same fine workmanship once suspended from the ceiling has now been placed on the floor by the pulpit as it was considered unsafe. In a dimly lit corner at the rear of the church is a monument to Harriet Annie Robertson, wife of Major George Coke Robertson who owned the hall close by. A few feet away is a 14th century font. In the churchyard are the graves of two unknown soldiers slain at Willoughby Field in the closing years of the Civil War. This church is delightfully set amid tall cedar trees whose branches reach up towards the sky.

Widmerpool Hall, a short distance away, is a mid-Victorian Gothic country house, which was bought by the Automobile Association in 1950 and opened the following year as a patrol school.

Wilford is some two miles south of Nottingham's city centre, and lies by the River Trent. It is approached by the Wilford Toll Bridge, and the power station stands on the opposite bank of the river.

The church of St Wilfrid is mainly mediaeval. The low tower and the fine chancel are 15th century; from the close of the 14th come the porch, the nave arcades, and the chancel arch, and most of the south aisle, which has a piscina of 1300 and four floorstones of the 12th and 13th centuries. The old stairway still climbs to the loft and the roof. There is beautiful modern craftsmanship in the handsome chancel screen, the screen of the tower and the vestry, and the benches with traceried ends. A fine Kempe window has twelve minstrel angels, and a vivid window with the Wise Men is in memory of Kirke White. His medallion portrait is on a wall.

It was here at Wilford, along with Clifton, that the poet Henry Kirke White found inspiration for much of his work. Born in Nottingham in 1785 on the site now occupied by the Council House, he came with his books to stay in the village while preparing for the university, and lodged in a cottage with a garden reaching down to the river. There he would dream as he looked out on a scene which was Wilford's great joy, a never-to-be-forgotten landscape of swift-flowing river, meadowland carpeted with crocuses in spring, and Nottingham with its castle silhouetted against the sky. Eventually, thanks to the patronage of the Rev Charles Simeon, he went to St John's College, Cambridge. By the end of the first term he was pronounced the first man of the year. However, overwork brought on a complete breakdown of his health, and he died in college on October 19, 1806. He was buried in Cambridge but the graveyard was done away with in 1860, and it was later learned that his remains had been cremated and the ashes sent to the house where he was born. The ashes were scattered in Wilford Churchyard in April, 1950. It was his wish to be buried here, for he once wrote the following lines about it:

> *Here I would I wish to sleep. This is the spot*
> *Which I have long marked out to lay my bones in.*
> *Tired out and wearied with the riotous world,*
> *Beneath this yew would I be sepulchred.*

Willoughby-on-the-Wolds is situated near the border with Leicestershire. It gave its name to a great family 700 years ago, and some of them lie here in the fine old church of St Mary and All Saints. A part of their old home remains in the farmhouse and cottage near the church. The first of them was Ralph Bugge, a rich

Nottingham merchant who bought land here in the 13th century; his son changed his name to Willoughby. In the next century they were in possession of Wollaton, and had begun a long association with that village which ended only in 1924, when the splendid house they built in Elizabeth I's reign became one of Nottingham's great possessions.

Their splendid monuments are in the 14th century chapel of the church, which has nothing older than the 12th century nave arcades. A hundred years later are the tower and spire, the chancel (with modern windows), and its arch. The clerestory is about 1500. The font, the fine piscina, and part of a stone altar, are mediaeval, and a 20th century screen is a thankoffering for peace.

The stone figures of Sir Richard de Willoughby (a cross-legged knight of 1325) and his wife represent the parents of another Sir Richard—a famous Lord Chief Justice, who lies on his alabaster tomb in his robes of office, with a sword and a roll in his hand. It was his marriage that brought Wollaton to the family. The alabaster figure of his son Richard lies between the chapel and the aisle, on a tomb enriched with heraldic shields. On a splendid tomb with sculptured figures in 18 niches lies Sir Hugh Willoughby of 1448, wearing richly decorated armour and a wreathed helmet. With him is one of his wives in a long gown, a cape tied with a tasselled cord, and a mitred headdress. There are also two ancient stone figures of women in wimples.

A small brass in the floor of the north aisle marks the resting-place of Michael Stanhope of Shelford, who was slain "in Willough-by Field in 1648, being a soldier for King Charles the First". This was the last struggle of the Civil War in Notts, when the Royalists under Sir Philip Monckton were routed by Colonel Rossiter. Tradition says the skirmish took place in a field near the church, and that the villagers climbed the church tower to watch the fray; it is more probable that the site was nearer the Fosse Way, which passes by the village after entering the county at Six Hills, where Notts points a finger into Leicestershire. On this famous road, near Willoughby, is the site of one of the five Roman stations in Notts, Vernometum.

A graveyard near Broughton Lodge was excavated in 1964, and it soon became apparent that the Roman-British settlement Vernemetum, one of four townships between the two great urban centres of Ratae and Lindum (Leicester and Lincoln) could not be far away. Roman pottery in large quantities was discovered, dating from the 3rd and 4th century Roman–British occupation. In June, 1968 the skeleton of an Anglo-Saxon dating back to about 500 AD was unearthed.

Winkburn. One of the county's hidden villages, lying in the valley of the tiny River Wink, it has a few houses and farms, an ancient church by the great house, and wonderful trees.

Winkburn Hall, once the home of the Burnells, is now in a state of disrepair.

The church of St John of Jerusalem can now be seen to better advantage since the collapse of a wall of one of the outbuildings of the estate.

The oldest part of the church is the tower, which is for the most part Norman; the belfry windows are adorned with zigzag and cable moulding, and the Norman archway to the nave is carved all round with heavy zigzag. In an ancient frame of carving with a small figure of a saint, on an outside wall of the tower, is a later stone telling of restoration in the 17th century. One of its three bells of 1633 was lent to Southwell Minster when the bells there were being recast.

A lofty Norman doorway, carved all round with beak-heads, opens to the interior, which is quaint with 17th century furnishing, box-pews, spiral altar rails, a small altar table, a commonplace screen, and a charming three-decker pulpit with a canopy. There is a Jacobean chest, and a decrepit one much older. The font is 17th century. There is bright glass in memory of the Burnells who, after the Dissolution, followed the Knights Hospitallers as lords of the manor.

Engraved on his tomb are the arms and portrait of William Burnell of 1570, his features worn away; he was auditor to Henry VIII, and brother of Edward Burnell whose fine monument is in Sibthorpe church. William Burnell of 1609 kneels in his wall monument, a lifesize figure in armour, holding a long metal sword; the inscription tells of the marriages he made for his four daughters.

After nine generations at Winkburn, the male line came to an end when Darcy Burnell died in 1774. His initials are on the great lead cistern by the porch, and his elaborate monument has lifesize figures of a bowed woman and an angel holding a plaque with his portrait.

Winthorpe lies between the Fosse Way and the Trent, 1½ miles north-east of Newark. Here the little River Fleet dives underground by the inn at the side of the green.

During the Civil War Winthorpe was one of a chain of villages held by Parliament during the last siege of Newark, and in the Second World War it saw much activity when an airfield was built close by.

The church of All Saints dates from 1886–87, and has a tower and spire 105 feet high. An elaborately carved stone reredos has figures in niches.

Woodborough. The approach to Woodborough from Nottingham's Mapperley Plains is made down Bank Hill. Here roads meet by bright gardens and a stream goes on its way to the Dover Beck. Woodborough was once a busy centre of the old stocking knitters, and it was to one of these that a son was born in 1769. He was George Brown, and although brought up in the trade he had a thirst for learning, which took him to the village school and ended in fifty years of ministry, preaching the gospel from house to house. When he fell ill at Worcester they brought him to Woodborough, where he died in 1833.

It was the home of some of the Strelleys from the time of Edward III to Elizabeth I's day, and it is to Richard Strelley that Woodborough owes its crowning glory, the splendid 14th century chancel of the church. While his father was rebuilding Strelley Church, Richard erected this stately chancel with fine windows, gabled buttresses with grotesque heads on each side, and beautiful sedilia and piscina. Modern days have enriched his 14th century work with a fine gallery of glass, and with fine woodwork.

The great east window (which Richard adorned with heads of his king and queen) has in it the Crucifixion, Paulinus, and St Swithin. In others we see the Madonna between saints, Apostles and Nativity scenes with fine horses and camels and rich gifts, David with his harp, Dorothea with apples, Columba with a church, Chad with Lichfield Cathedral, Hugo with a model of Lincoln, and Cecilia with an organ.

The hand of a clever craftsman is seen in the poppyhead stalls, their shallow canopies carved with quatrefoils in tracery, and in the reading desks with symbols of the Evangelists; the craftsman was Mansfield Parkyns, who, after a life of great adventure, came to live at Woodborough Hall. He spent two years on the work with the help of two joiners, doing all the designing and most of the carving himself. It was a labour of love in memory of his wife, and it proved to be a memorial to himself, for we read that these choir stalls, the last work of his life, were designed, carved, and given on Christmas Eve, 1893 by Mansfield Parkyns. He died on January 12, 1894, aged 70. He carved the screen across the tower arch, and designed the pulpit. He sleeps outside the church he helped to enrich.

Except for a few fragments, the rest of the church has nothing of the glory of the chancel. The nave and aisles are later in the 14th century, and the tower is perhaps 16th. Three massive old tie-beams support a mass of timbering in the fine steep roof of the nave, there are fragments of glass 600 years old, and there is a Jacobean altar table given as a thankoffering for the end of the Civil War. Older than all the rest are two 12th century coffin stones, a beautiful Norman doorway with shafts and three orders of moulding, and the Norman font (like part of a round pillar) adorned with bands of zigzag. Two old gable crosses are restored.

The parish church of St Swithin's has a custom that survives to this day. Each year on Shrove Tuesday a bell is rung from the parish church to tell housewives when to mix the batter for the day's special dish—pancakes. This was first done in former days when it was the duty of the village's oldest apprentice to ring the bell. Before that time the bell was probably rung to summon the people to church to be shriven. Just when this all began seems a little obscure, but it was revived in 1921 by the then vicar, the Rev Miles Atkinson.

Worksop is often referred to as the Gateway to the Dukeries, and is the second largest non-County Borough in England. Its attractions are a noble church with grand Norman remains, and the charming Gatehouse of a lost priory. Worksop is situated on the River Ryton, with the Chesterfield Canal passing through.

The Priory Gatehouse is perhaps the town's most precious possession, and dates from the 14th century.

Adorned with gables and buttresses and saints in canopied niches, it was guest-house as well as gatehouse, and has a big upper room with a fine window. The gateway itself has three fine arches, and its original black and white roof with moulded beams. It was probably built by Thomas, Lord Furnival; and towards the end of the century the monks added the charming porch to serve as a shrine for pilgrims, giving it a doorway on each side, a lovely window, a stairway to the upper room, and a very beautiful vaulted roof of delicate tracery, still in splendid condition.

As we stand under the gateway, one of the outer arches frames a charming view of a tall tapering cross on a flight of seven steps. It is restored with a new head, and was brought here from opposite the church gates, where in olden days Radford Fair was held round it; during the Commonwealth banns of marriage were published from the steps. The other end arch frames a delightful picture of the church, with its twin western towers about 90 feet high.

The story of the priory church of St Mary and St Cuthbert goes back to early in the 12th century, when Sir William de Lovetot invited the Black Canons to found a monastery, granting them the small Norman church already here. The monks set to work to build a larger church, which consisted at first of a chancel, transepts, and one bay of the nave, round a central tower. By about 1160 the rest of the nave was completed and given for the use of the parish, but at the Dissolution Thomas Cromwell and his master Henry VIII destroyed the monastic part of what had become a noble church, leaving the nave, its aisles, and the two west towers.

So it has stood for centuries, a magnificent fragment of a great building which is being given back in our own day some of its lost glory. The grand Norman nave is 140 feet long and 60 wide, opening to aisles with stone vaulted roofs. Above the ten bays on each side is a handsome triforium and a clerestory of round-headed windows. The arches of the arcades and of the triforium are rich in ornament as clean-cut as if carved yesterday. The eastern bay of each arcade is different from the rest, for these two, with a fragment of the south transept, are the remains of the earliest work of the monks.

The big south porch (its beauty enhanced by the noble avenue of limes leading to it), has a stone-vaulted roof and a trefoiled niche in its east wall, and shelters a lovely doorway with a round arch on six shafts. It frames a beautiful door which is one of the precious things of the church, for, though patched here and there, it is the original door made of yew wood from Sherwood Forest late in the 12th or early in the 13th century. Its mass of exquisite ironwork, richly wrought in sweeping scrolls, is claimed to be the earliest example of its kind in England.

The deep west doorway, with shafts and zigzag ornament, has a lovely modern door with ironwork to match the old. A smaller doorway with a similar modern door opens to the north vestry, which had a beautiful vaulted roof, and was originally the parlour where the monks received their guests. Joining this north-west end of the church are slight remains of the priory cloisters. The north-west tower is about a hundred years older than its companion, and was raised when the other was built, both being finished in the 15th century. After the destructive work of Thomas Cromwell the ruins became a quarry of hewn and carved stone, from which houses, a farmhouse, and a watermill were built. The mill and some of the buildings were demolished in 1932, and the stones of the old Priory were used again in restoring the central crossing and the north transept. The south transept was rebuilt as a thanksgiving for the end of the First World War, and the beautiful lady chapel, with charming lancet windows is a memorial for a second time, for in addition to the many names on the oak panelling of those that died, there is an inscription cut in stone telling that the chapel was founded in the 13th century in memory of a Lord Furnival and of the Crusades in which he fell. His body was brought home by his brother and buried here. The architect of the restoration of the church and the gatehouse was Sir Harold Brakspear, his plans being carried on after his death by his son.

Lady Joan Furnival of 1395 lies in the nave, a battered alabaster figure wearing a lovely netted headdress, and a mantle over her long gown. Her husband, Sir Thomas Neville of 1406 (brother of the famous Ralph Neville, Earl of Westmorland), is one of the two battered knights lying on each side of the altar, both with legs missing below the knees. The other knight is a 14th century Furnival.

The south aisle has a 700-year-old piscina, the modern font has lovely foliage and medallions of the Four Evangelists, and the modern iron screenwork in the eastern bays of the arcades is delicately wrought with flowers. The chapel has an Elizabethan altar table, an oil painting of the Madonna and Child is by Domenichino, and the painting of the Holy Family is by Perugino.

In a glass case let into the wall near the vestry door is a skull, perhaps of one of the Sherwood Forest archers, *still penetrated with the tip of an arrow which carried death in its flight*. It was found near the porch last century, a grim and intimate touch with the life of the Forest in those far-off days. Big wooden figures of the Madonna and St Cuthbert are of interest for being the work of one of the congregation, who also carved the three figures of the Rood.

The custom of an old tenure is still observed at Worksop when a sovereign is crowned. The lord of the manor has to find a right-hand glove, and supports the king's right hand holding the sceptre.

About a mile out of town on the Mansfield road is Worksop Manor, dating from the 16th century and once the home of the Earls of Shrewsbury. It was consumed by fire in 1761 and replaced by the present Palladian building.

Wysall is a charming village on the edge of the Wolds about nine miles south-east of Nottingham. The church is dedicated to the Holy Trinity, and on entering we see the lovely font with a round bowl on five shafts which dates from the 13th century, and from its close comes most of the tower, with an earlier arch resting on foliage corbels, and a 15th century window; its small spire is 600 years old. The belfry is reached by a wonderful old ladder with a handrail and candle spike. The nave arcade, and the aisle with a fine east window, are 14th century. From the end of the 14th comes the chancel, and the clerestory is 100 years younger.

The 15th century screen has small holes in two panels which were used as peepholes to the altar. The oak pulpit of about 1400, perhaps the oldest in the county, has come into its own again after having been displaced by one of stone. Three sturdy oak benches are over 400 years old; there is an old chest, and two old misericord seats are carved with quaint faces. Very impressive is the old timbering of the chancel roof.

The dainty brass candelabra in the chancel was given "for the use of Psalm singers of Wysall church in 1773". A painted wood panel is a memorial to George Widmerpole of 1689, and on an alabaster tomb lie the splendid figures of Hugh Armstrong and his wife Mary Sacheverell, both wearing ruffs.

On the same wall as the entrance to the church is a small glass case in which the old lock and key from the main door of the church has been preserved.

APPENDIX

Places of interest open to the public

(* Indicates property in the care of the Ministry of Public
Building and Works)
(† Indicates National Trust Property)

It is advisable for intending visitors to check times of opening as these occasionally vary.

Linby: Newstead Abbey.
Mattersey: *Mattersey Priory.
Nottingham: Thrumpton Hall.
　　　　Wollaton Hall.
　　　　Worksop Priory Gatehouse.
Ollerton: Thoresby Hall.
Nr. **Worksop:** † Clumber Park.

NOTTINGHAMSHIRE TOWNS AND VILLAGES

In this key to our map of Nottinghamshire are all the towns and villages treated in this book. If a place is not on the map by name, its square is given here, so that the way to it is easily found, each square being five miles.